AF270320

The Meaning of It All

The Meaning of It All

The Meaning of It All

Ultimate Meaning, Everyday Meaning, Cosmic Meaning, Death, and Time

RIVKA WEINBERG

OXFORD
UNIVERSITY PRESS

Oxford University Press is a department of the University of Oxford.
It furthers the University's objective of excellence in research, scholarship,
and education by publishing worldwide. Oxford is a registered trade mark of
Oxford University Press in the UK and in certain other countries.

Published in the United States of America by Oxford University Press
198 Madison Avenue, New York, NY 10016, United States of America.

Library of Congress Control Number: 2025040575

ISBN 978–0–19–775802–1

DOI: 10.1093/oso/9780197758021.001.0001

Printed by Integrated Books International, United States of America

The manufacturer's authorized representative in the EU for product safety is
Oxford University Press España S.A. of Parque Empresarial San Fernando de Henares,
Avenida de Castilla, 2 – 28830 Madrid (www.oup.es/en or product.safety@oup.com).
OUP España S.A. also acts as importer into Spain of products made by the manufacturer.

To anyone who has ever been told to cheer up

Contents

Acknowledgments

I have benefited beyond measure from many rounds of discussions, comments, critique, encouragement, and feedback on the ideas in this book from the endlessly generous Yuval Avnur, David Boonin, Paul Hurley, Iddo Landau, Dion Scott-Kakures, and Saul Smilansky.

For very helpful comments and discussions on various parts of this book, I thank: David Benatar, Jeanine Diller-Murphy, Dale Dorsey, Johann Frick, Martin Glazier, Daniel Groll, Rom Gruman, Joseph Gruman, Zev Gruman, Moshe Halbertal, Chris Heathwood, Masahiro Marioka, Bohdi Melnitzer, Thaddeus Metz, Alastair Norcross, Sharon Street, Samuel Scheffler, David Velleman, Susan Wolf, and Fiona Woolard.

Thanks as well to audiences at Rocky Mountain Ethics Congress, University of Colorado (2018, 2021, 2022, 2023, and 2024); University of Haifa (2019); 2nd and 4th International Conferences on Philosophy and Meaning in Life (Waseda University, 2019, and University of Pretoria, 2022); Brooklyn Public Philosopher's Series (2019); Festschrift for David Velleman, New York University (2022); Conference on the Value of Human Life, Hebrew University (2023); University of Kansas (2023); and the Eastern APA (2023). Thanks to *The Journal of Controversial Ideas* and to *The Philosopher* for permission to use previously published work. And, finally, thanks to Lucy Randall at Oxford University Press, for invaluable editing and for steering this book from inception to publication.

Being a meaning freak is a burden to others, and one that friends are not designed to carry. To carry that weight, you need philosopher friends, who have a high tolerance for that sort of thing, and family, to whom you come as you come. For tolerating at least some of that burden nearly all of the time, I thank my very dear philosopher friends Yuval Avnur, David Benatar, David Boonin, Paul Hurley, Jeanine Diller-Murphy, Iddo Landau, Dion Scott-Kakures, and Saul Smilansky. For tolerating it as it comes and when it comes, I thank my large and long-suffering family, especially my sisters Esther Posen and Miriam Perr, who have carried more than their fair share for more than half a century. Special thanks to my husband, Zev Gruman, and to my children, Rom (Rami) and Joseph (Joey) Gruman, for putting up with the freak, forgiving (I hope) some of it, and always, always, supporting my work.

Introduction

"What's the point?"

Almost every thinking person has had that thought, most more than once or twice. You can stock your life with meaningful work, people, activities, and art, and yet—as you marvel/laugh at the banana duct-taped to the wall in the museum, as you watch the waves on the beach with your adorable children, as you weed your garden, or practice your cello, or find the love of your life, you can still ask: what's the point of it all? Right in the middle of all of these meaningful, seemingly pointful, points of life. Granted, you're more likely to worry about the point of life when you are working too hard or when things are not going well. But you're also more likely to worry about the point of it all when things have gone extremely well—when you've finally reached that promotion, received an award, raised your children—exactly when it seems like that question should arise the least! Why is that?

It's because there are different kinds of meaning. When you practice your cello, appreciate art, or nurture your children, you are doing what I call "everyday" meaningful things, and experiencing Everyday Meaning. When you wonder about the point of leading and living a life at all, you are questioning your life's Ultimate Meaning. When you have accomplished a meaningful milestone in your everyday life, sometimes the problem of Ultimate Meaning seeps in, making you wonder about the meaning of all of your efforts at running your life, since achieving some meaningful success or fulfillment in part of your life can naturally make you think about the meaning of the whole enterprise.

Clearly, when thinking about meaning, it helps to be specific about which meaning of meaning you mean. Unfortunately, few terms are as ill defined, vaguely explained, poorly understood, and sloppily discussed as the term "meaning." (I know! How can this be?) No wonder it's been so difficult to make progress in this crucial area of thought and human endeavor. We don't even know what we are talking about. But now, we will. I will set out the different kinds of meaning, and the different characteristics that meaning can have within each kind. Then we will be able to get a clearer picture of what kinds of meaning there are, and what kinds of meaning might be available to us.

I'll take an expansive approach to the meaning of meaning and consider everything it might mean, but not in a muddle. Let's separate out the meanings of meaning. There are three kinds of meaning and six characteristics or aspects of meaning that can apply within a kind. The kinds of meaning are Ultimate Meaning, Everyday Meaning, and Cosmic Meaning. The characteristics of meaning are value, significance, impact, explanation, purpose, and point. Here's a little chart, to illustrate:

	EVERYDAY	COSMIC	ULTIMATE
Value			
Significance			
Impact			
Explanation			
Purpose			
Point			

Value refers to *worth*; **significance** refers to how much something *matters*; **impact** refers to *effects*; **explanation** refers to *coherence* or making *sense*; **purpose** refers to the *reason something is done*; and **point** refers to the *valued end* of why you are doing something. For example: when you nurture your children, it is valuable because of all the values involved, i.e., what is worthy in that activity, the love, intimacy, joy, etc. It is significant because your children and their well-being matter to you, to society, to them, etc. It is impactful because being nurtured affects a person's current and future well-being. It has the characteristic of explanation because it makes sense to nurture your children—it is coherent with the overall way you wish to live, it is consistent with their needs and your aims, etc. It is purposeful because you are doing it for a reason and it has a point because the nurturing is aimed at or grounded by the valued ends of love, caring, and the children themselves. We can acknowledge some overlap in the characteristics of meaning, but it is helpful to recognize each of them because they still are not exactly the same thing; e.g., significance will affect value because how much something matters affects its worth, and impact will affect significance because how impactful something is affects how much it matters, but each characteristic of meaning is still an aspect of meaning in its own right.

Nurturing your children is something you might do that has Everyday Meaning. **Everyday Meaning** refers to the *value* and *significance* in our everyday lives, including values like truth, morality, beauty, and love, and the significance of engagement with them. It includes the *purpose* (the reason for which something is done) and *point* (the justifying valued end) of much of our meaningful, everyday lives, which aim at these valued ends. It includes the *impact* we have on ourselves, on others, and on the world around us, as well as the *explanation* of some of our meaningful activities and pursuits. **Cosmic Meaning** refers to our meaningful role in the cosmos: to the *significance* and *value* of our cosmic niche, to the *explanation* of our role in the cosmos, our *impact* on the cosmos, and the *purposes* or *point* of the cosmos and our place in it. **Ultimate Meaning** refers to the point of leading and living a life *at all*. Why bother with the project, effort, or enterprise of life? What's the valued end of doing the whole thing? Ultimate meaning is the end-regarding justifying reason, the valued end, or the point of leading and living a life. (Thus, unlike Everyday Meaning and Cosmic Meaning, which may have any or all of the six characteristics of meaning, Ultimate Meaning includes only one characteristic: point.)

I will begin by addressing Ultimate Meaning (Chapter 1). What is the point of leading a life? That is the question of Ultimate Meaning. One way to think about the difference between Ultimate Meaning and Everyday Meaning is to note the difference in the questions, "Why pave the road?" or "Why be a chef?" and the questions, "Why live?" or "Why lead your life at all?" When we look at these different questions about the point of an activity, we may note, to our relief, that it is not very difficult to find points or valued ends to our efforts within a life; e.g., the point of paving the road is to make it safer and easier on the butts for the people you value— your valued ends—who drive on that road. The point of being a chef is to express your culinary creativity and provide people with nourishment. You, your culinary art, and the well-being of the people you feed are the valued ends which make your cooking an activity that is not pointless. But it is harder, and, as I will demonstrate, flat out impossible, to find a point or a valued end to living life at all because points are valued ends and valued ends lie separate from the acts and enterprises for which they provide a point. Since your life includes all of your valued ends, the effort of leading and living it has no external or separate value to serve as the point for that effort. Leading and living one's life is a special sort of effort because it includes all of your other ends and values so *that* effort or enterprise—the meta-project of leading and living a life—has nowhere outside of itself to reach for a point, leaving it pointless. This is very sad because, since we live our lives and structure our leading-a-human-life agential efforts both in parts and as a whole, it is fitting to be sad to recognize that leading and living a life is pointless. Ultimate Meaning is metaphysically impossible, and that is a very sad truth.

However, Everyday Meaning (Chapter 2) is indeed possible for us—thank goodness!—and comes in a wide variety of activities and pursuits, all involving valued ends. Those valued ends are not merely subjective, i.e., not dependent on personal perspective, because a person can be mistaken about meaning and value. For example, if Jonas Salk, developer of the polio vaccine, thought his medical career was meaningless, he would be mistaken. His medical career was valuable, and had significant impact on many people. He successfully worked for the valuable purpose of improving health and quality of life for humanity. In contrast, if someone thinks that counting the number of her eye blinks per day makes for a meaningful way to spend her days, she is wrong and can be said to be wasting her life. We will therefore see that subjectivists about meaning are wrong. Since Everyday Meaning is objective, we can aim at it and miss. There is thus an achievement aspect to meaning. Because meaning is somewhat aspirational and achievable, wasting opportunities for meaning is contrary to meaning, and failure, which is inevitable if you aim appropriately high, generally undermines meaning. (This is one of several unavoidable meaning quandaries.)

But what about Cosmic Meaning (Chapter 3)? Isn't that the grandest and most important kind of meaning? Short answer: Not by a long shot. Recall that Cosmic Meaning refers to our role in the cosmos. That role may be natural, supernatural, theistic, or atheistic. However, even assuming all the miracles in the world, we will see that Cosmic Meaning is unlikely to amount to much, especially in the ways in which it is supposed to be uniquely powerful, i.e., by supposedly providing us with cosmic purpose (finally, a *reason* for why we are here), and Ultimate Meaning. Since Ultimate Meaning is metaphysically impossible, nothing can give us that, not even god. As for cosmic purpose, communing with god or basking blissfully in the glory of god in the afterlife can seem like a meaningful cosmic purpose until we try to seriously picture it. Once we do, the problems proliferate. Bliss per se may be desirable, but a positive emotional state, by itself, does not seem particularly meaningful. (Consider: in this life, is simply feeling good among our most meaningful experiences?) Communing with god in the afterlife seems to have more potential for meaning because it involves a way of relating, not just a positive emotional state. However, it puts us in a largely receiving role which is not really a purpose worthy of our potential (among other problems). Same goes for returning to from whence we came by merging with the divine or becoming one with the universe—that's what all this hullabaloo is about? Just to find our way back and reintegrate into where we started from? Hardly an inspiring reason to go through the whole thing.

Many argue that cosmic value—value based on our role in the cosmos or value from a cosmic perspective—provides us with Cosmic Meaning due to its perfect nature, its everlasting duration, its ability to makes sense of some value dilemmas, and its providing us with value from a cosmic perspective. Here, too, I will show that these Cosmic Meaning prospects turn out to be similarly disappointing, even cosmic justice, which, as it turns out, is neither as simple nor as satisfying as one might hope. We will see that Cosmic Meaning, while not impossible, is not very consequential on any of the characteristics of meaning.

You might think that a supernatural or theistic cosmic order offers us the promise of an afterlife, which at least solves some of the meaning problems posed by death. Death (Chapter 4) has been widely argued both to give life meaning and to undercut life's meaning. Death is argued to give life meaning by lending our lives stages, a shape, and the coherence of a narrative, with a beginning, middle, and end. It's argued to undercut life's meaning by annihilating us, limiting the impact and significance of our efforts, and eventually wiping all vestiges of our lives away. However, in fact, it is time, and not death, that is both necessary for meaning yet undermining of meaning. Time gives shape to our lives by allowing for sequence, which allows for a narrative that makes some kind of sense (the explanation characteristic of meaning). Without time, it's hard to imagine a life that makes sense and has a meaningful trajectory. It's hard to imagine life at all. A timeless life sounds more like a dream, where the rules of reality don't apply and we have no way to predict what comes next or how to have real effects. Not exactly the setting for efforts, activities, or projects that are aimed at or grounded by value, have impact and significance, and are purposeful or have a point. Time is needed for meaning. Similarly, it is time and not death that is necessary for the risk, reward, dynamism, and forward motion connected with meaningful activity. Without death, so long as we live in time, risk, reward, and forward motion would remain in our lives, giving it meaningful structure. Without death, starting a relationship, a pursuit, or a project would still include risk, reward, dynamism, and causality. These ventures could succeed or fail, result in fulfillment or disappointment, etc. Without death, we would still have resource limitations and we would still be vulnerable to all outcomes and effects short of death. Both risk and reward would remain meaningful without death and perhaps become even more significant since their effects would last a lot longer and thereby have a deeper and more meaningful impact. Time is the background condition for meaning. Yet time also erodes meaning. If we lived forever, we would live to see what time does to our accomplishments, commitments, and efforts: everything eventually wears away. That would be painful to watch (over and over and over again). And, if we lived forever, we would likely have a hard time maintaining the psychological memory and continuity that provide the scaffolding for our sense of personal identity. Eventually, time itself might annihilate us. For meaning, death is a red herring. It's not the problem (or the solution). Time is the problem (and the solution).

Time (Chapter 5) provides for the dynamism that allows for meaning, yet time also gives rise to the erosion process by which a lot of meaning drains out. It's a conundrum—what I call the time-meaning conundrum. We want the meaning, but we don't want it to crumble. Yet it seems that time gives us both: it provides us with opportunity for meaningful engagement, but it also wears away a good deal of our meaningful achievements, commitments, and projects. We must face the fact that time is necessary for meaning yet time erodes meaning.

What can we do about the time-meaning conundrum? Some argue that living in the present will reduce the agony of time's erosions. However, this is the opposite of what might enhance or increase meaning because meaning borrows from the past and looks toward the future: your grandfather's watch is significant to you because of its history; the college fund you contribute to for your children is significant to you because of its intended future. You might right a past wrong and work for a more just future, all efforts which are meaningful because of the past, the present, and the future. Thus, living in the moment, its sloganesque popularity notwithstanding, will decrease meaning. We will examine some other recommendations and ideas about how to live a life subject to the erosions of time while escaping the time-meaning conundrum. None can work. We cannot escape the time-meaning conundrum. However, we can tease out some insights from failed attempts to escape time's wounds and thereby make progress toward coping with things as they are. That will involve, as I will explain, engaging with Everyday Meaning, paying attention, and accepting suffering. A meaningful life is one lived in the fullness of time—appropriately appreciating the past, present, and future—accepting suffering, acknowledging our tragic losses and limitations, and making the most of Everyday Meaning (L'chaim?).[1]

---

[1] Note on names: Names in the text that are not otherwise identified by profession or famously obvious are names of philosophers.

Suggestions for How to Read This Book

Through a veil of tears. With some coffee and chocolate, to make it feel somehow tolerable. Like life, this book begins with a wail and ends in bittersweet resignation, with some heartache, hope, despair, inspiration, and consolation along the way. If you're mostly interested in death and time in relation to meaning, you can skip the Everyday Meaning and Cosmic Meaning chapters. (In fact, you can probably read any of the chapters that interest you on their own.) But you have only one measly life to lead. Why not see what kind of meaning you can squeeze out of it? If you care enough about meaning to start the book, have courage and a little patience, and read it straight through. You can have some fortifying alcohol while you do it. (It'll pair well with the coffee.) Get through the first ten to fifteen pages where some important concepts and clarifications are set out and then the rest will come easy—you'll slide into the vortex of illumination and desperation, with some beautiful, wistful, flickering lights at the end of the tunnel.

1

ULTIMATE MEANING

We Don't Have It, We Can't Get It, and We Should Be Very, Very Sad

Ultimate Meaning

First, the bad news. Life is pointless. I don't say that flippantly or glibly. I mean it and I will show it. The "meaning" of life can refer to several different things, including value, explanation, impact, significance, purpose, or point. One cause of some confusion in the literature on the meaning of life is that which meaning of "meaning" is being used is often unspecified, even when the various meanings of the term are acknowledged. In this chapter,[1] I'll focus on "point" or "pointlessness," as I take that to capture the essence of the problem of the meaning of life: it's pointless. Not necessarily the things we do or projects we pursue within a life, but the effort or enterprise of having lived your entire life—what I call its "Ultimate Meaning": the point of leading and living a human life at *all*.

Just as the meaning of life is sometimes discussed without sufficiently specifying which meaning of "meaning" is in play, having a "point" is often invoked without sufficient explanation.[2] What

---

[1] Many arguments in this chapter appeared in Rivka Weinberg, "Ultimate Meaning: We Don't Have It, We Can't Get It, and We Should Be Very, Very, Sad," *Journal of Controversial Ideas* 1 (2021): 4–24.

[2] David Wiggins doesn't define what it means for something to have a point, but he comes closer than most to getting at its meaning by speaking of points, ends, and values in close enough proximity as to suggest an important relationship between the terms. (See Wiggins, "Truth, Invention, and the Meaning of Life," *Proceedings of the British Academy* 62 [1976]: 331–378.)

exactly does it mean for something to have a point? A point is a valued end;[3] an enterprise or effort has a point, or is purposeful, if we have justified reason to do it because of its valued end.[4] Thus, the builder drives the nail into the wood to build a hut for a point, an end of value. What ties point to value is the end-regarding reason you build the hut: you build the hut because you value the shelter provided by the hut. (And you value the shelter because you value yourself. We can continue to ask about value until we arrive at something that has intrinsic value.) In your hut-building enterprise, the shelter (or the person enjoying it) is your valued end, or the point of all that building.[5] Points have "value commitments"[6] and involve valued ends. If an enterprise is directed toward or grounded by[7] an end, then the end is being valued; it's the *point* of the enterprise. This doesn't entail that seemingly process-oriented pursuits are pointless and not directed toward or grounded by any valued ends. For example, if we value the process of running or having coffee with friends, it may seem like there are no external ends involved, yet we don't find those pursuits pointless. But, even in those cases, the reason we don't find the pursuits pointless is that they do in fact involve valued ends, namely, the exhilarating feeling of running or the joy of intimacy with friends. And those valued ends, although reached throughout the time engaged in the pursuit, still lie separate from the pursuit itself. I will belabor this claim of externality of values to acts for a bit (sorry—a bit of technical

---

[3] I think value is objective (see Chapter 2), but for this discussion, I use what I take to be the weaker, and thus more inclusive standard of value—whatever is valued—because I mean to show that Ultimate Meaning is impossible for us even if we use the more inclusive standard of value.

[4] See Michael Ruse, *On Purpose*, Princeton University Press, 2018.

[5] See Ruse, *On Purpose*, p. 11

[6] See Ruse, *On Purpose*, p. 99.

[7] Purposeful pursuits need not be "aimed" at an end. They can be grounded by an end of value, e.g., keeping a promise, which may be grounded by rather than aimed at the value of persons as valued ends. But *projects*, *efforts*, or *enterprises* tend to be more goal oriented, *aimed* at ends.

tedium before the fun stuff) because it's important to the argument and is often disputed or misunderstood.

Values Are External to Acts and Efforts

Some activities are aimed at a final end (*telic*); some are not aimed at a final end (*atelic*). *Telic* pursuits, such as building a house, are aimed at a final end—at completion. *Atelic* pursuits, such as taking a walk for pleasure, are not aimed at completion or a final state.[8] Both kinds of pursuits can have a point, but, still, in both cases their points are values that lie outside the pursuits themselves. Activities such as playing with your children, having coffee with friends, or going for a stroll are not aimed at completion, but they're not point-less because they're grounded by or aimed at *external values* of love, intimacy, joy, etc. If you take a walk to the grocery to get some milk, the walk is aimed at an end; if you walk to enjoy a pleasant stroll, the walk is not aimed at getting anywhere. But the point of either effort, be it the walk for milk or the stroll for pleasure, still lies in a value external to walking itself: the point lies, respectively, in the person enjoying the milk or the sheer joy of ambling about, both of which are external to the actual *telic* or *atelic* walking itself.

You might think that you value, say, playing with your children, for its own sake, but the play itself is not the valued end—it's not the act of stacking blocks that is itself the point of stacking them. We want to know: *why* stack blocks? What is our valued end here? The reason we might value stacking blocks with our children is that we value our children, we value the love between us, we value the joy of play, we cherish the intimacy, the knowledge of each other, etc., and those values—the children, the intimacy, the knowledge, the joy— are the points or the valued ends of playing with our children, and they're separate from the actual playing. The valued end isn't the

---

[8] See Kieran Setiya, "The Midlife Crisis," *Philosopher's Imprint* 14 (2014): 1–18, 12–14.

playing (that's often pretty dull). It's external to the playing, even if it is attained while playing. The point isn't the running; it's the exhilaration derived from it, etc. Things that may be *intrinsically* valuable, such as happiness, beauty, or truth, can serve as valued ends for the effort or enterprise of pursuing happiness, making something beautiful, or acquiring knowledge, but they're *external* to the pursuing, making, appreciating, or acquiring them and that's why they can serve as the point of doing those things or engaging in those efforts. Projects, efforts, and enterprises consist of things we do or pursue, not values. Thus they may be grounded by or aimed at intrinsic values, but they remain separate from the valued ends that provide a point to engaging in those pursuits, efforts, projects, or enterprises.[9]

The Point (i.e., External Valued End) of Efforts, Pursuits, Enterprises, etc.

When you're hungry, the point of eating is to enjoy the taste of food and become sated because satiety, you, and enjoyment are valued ends; when you're nice to grandma, the point of your niceness is that grandma and her feelings are valued ends to you. Lots of pursuits, efforts, and projects aren't pointless because they are

---

[9] Some argue that when we *run joyfully* or *play intimately*, we're doing different things that have different values inextricable from the act itself and the attitudes we bring to it, such that the value is part of the act itself. (See Michael-John Turp, Brylea Hollinshead, and Stephen Rowe, "Don't Worry, Be Happy: The Gettability of Ultimate Meaning," *Journal of Controversial Ideas* 2 [2022]: 9–37, 10–11.) But this mischaracterizes the relationship between acts and values. Value, however particularized, still lies outside of the act itself. The value may be realized while doing the act, but that doesn't mash the value right into the act itself. The act is the act (stacking blocks, smiling, eye contact); the value (intimacy, love) is the external aim or ground of the act. If the block stacking is intimate, then you have a reason to do it; you've succeeded in your aims, and then it's not pointless. It feels different: it feels intimate rather than intolerably dreary (if you're lucky!). It's pointful rather than pointless because it is aimed at or grounded by a valued end, but that valued end is still external to the act. (See Weinberg, "Replies to Critics," *Journal of Controversial Ideas* 2 [2022].)

directed toward valued ends. That's the good news. Being nice to grandma is somewhat safe from the perils of pointlessness, at least in my view. So is having coffee with friends, reading a book, getting out of bed, and quite possibly most of the things we do. The only little problem is that the effort or enterprise of leading your entire life is pointless.

Enterprises or projects are distinguished from isolated acts or merely existing in states, such as being alive or being asleep, by the sustained, coordinated effort we put forth in a somewhat unified or systematic way, directed toward valued ends. When we consider the enterprise of living a human life, what's the point of it? Within our lives, we may have lots of pointful things to do, from isolated acts to grand projects that can span a good deal of our lives. Many pursuits are pointful *within* a life, grounded by or aiming at valued ends within the life, but what is the point of leading a life at all? As we lead our lives, which takes lots of effort, and involves, as Thomas Nagel puts it, "decades of intense concern,"[10] what is our justified valued end? Why live?

Why We Can't Get It

We can't possibly have a point to leading a life because valued ends are external to the efforts toward which they are directed. Efforts, projects, and enterprises need valued ends as reasons to justify doing them in order for them to be purposeful, or to have a point. Of pursuits, efforts, or enterprises, we can always ask, "Why do x?" "Why engage in y?" Valued ends give us answers in the form of justifying reasons of valued ends, and lie separate from the pursuits or projects. Learning is purposeful because truth is a valued end, building because shelter is a valued end, keeping promises because trust and people are valued ends. A pursuit, effort, or enterprise is

---

[10] Thomas Nagel, "The Absurd," *Journal of Philosophy* 68 (1971): 716–727, 720.

not a reason. It needs a reason, a valued end outside of itself, in order for it to have a point. When we question the point of an effort or enterprise, the question is aimed at its end—it is not itself the end; the end is external to it or separate from it. But your life encompasses your entire life and all that you value in it.

The values in your life, e.g., truth, justice, love, etc., may be what you use to guide you in the building and shaping of your life, just as, say, the values of symmetry, beauty, and durability may be the values you use to guide you in the building of a hut. Those values help you understand what makes something a good hut or a good life, and may help you understand how to go about building a good hut or constructing a good life. But they don't tell you why you're doing it in the first place; they don't give you the end-regarding justifying reason, the valued end, or the point of building a hut or leading a life. The point of building a hut, like all points, will lie outside the hut, as we have noted. But there's nothing external to your life to serve as the point of leading and living it because your life includes your whole damn life. Human life includes its entirety—actions, values, hopes and dreams, detritus—leaving nowhere for us to reach for a valued end to serve as a point for leading and living it.

You might think that when you do things that affect other people and impact future generations, you're aiming at values outside of your life.[11] After all, these acts touch other lives, including lives not yet begun, and may seem to give you a way to aim your life at an external point of value. If only it were that easy! Alas, although effects of, say, justice realized in the world, may be external to you and have an impact that extends beyond your lifetime, that doesn't change the location of the value of justice and your activities aiming at it *within* the effort, project, or enterprise of leading and living your life. The fact that the effects of justice are external to you doesn't entail that, as you lead your life, working toward justice is something

---

[11] See Turp et al., "Don't Worry, Be Happy," and Weinberg, "Replies to Critics."

you do *outside* the enterprise of leading your life. How can that be? Where are you doing this pursuit of justice? In which project does it have such an important place? In your side-life-job that's not part of the enterprise of leading your life? That cannot be the case because you have but one life to lead. Everything you pursue and everything you value are part of the life you lead, part of the meta-effort or meta-project of leading and running your life. You care about justice and you care about other people. So these other-regarding values figure prominently *in* the meta-effort or meta-project of running your life. (In other words, because your valued ends are valuable to you, you include them in the meta-project of running your life.)[12] You do your everyday valuable and meaningful things, like protesting or filing lawsuits, and those activities aim at justice, which is a non-selfish, other-regarding value outside the act of protest but still *inside* the meta-project or effort of running your life.

The project or enterprise of leading and living your life includes your relations with the world—that's why you bother with all those other pesky people—and, in pursuing those relations, you may appeal to or aim at interpersonal values or values that are not self-centered, values that are important *in* the meta-effort or meta-project of leading your life. But that won't give you an external end-regarding reason, a valued end, for the meta-project of running your life, which is an effort, enterprise, or project of its own. That separate enterprise of leading and living a life, that you put so much effort into, has nowhere to reach for a point. To illustrate:

If you masturbate, you're doing something alone, probably for the valued end of pleasure. If you have sex with someone else, you're doing something relational, maybe for the valued ends of love, intimacy, and also pleasure (if you're lucky!). But in both cases you are still doing something well within the confines of living your life and the meta-project, effort, or enterprise of running or leading it. Expanding further out relationally—participating in

---

[12] See Turp et al., "Don't Worry, Be Happy," and Weinberg, "Replies to Critics."

an orgy, say—will not change this. You could even will your busy penis to science for the enlightenment of future generations and the betterment of posterity, which would be other-regarding, not self-centered, and have effects beyond your lifetime, but it would still be something you did and a value you aimed at as part of or within the effort or enterprise of running your life. And that's how it all gets sucked in, so to speak. No matter what you do or aim at, it's all internal to the meta-project, effort, or enterprise of running or leading your life, leaving *that* project, effort, or enterprise with nowhere to reach for a valued end, or point.

Because your life includes your entire life, and all the meaningful pursuits within it, there's nothing external to it to serve as a valued end toward which the effort of leading it is directed (or by which it is grounded). This doesn't mean that your life is worthless or insignificant or not valuable in other ways. It just means that it's pointless.

In his famous paper, "The Absurd," Nagel notes that we can justify acts within a life even if we cannot justify carrying on an entire life:

> Chains of justification come repeatedly to an end within life, and whether the process as a whole can be justified has no bearing on the finality of these endpoints. No further justification is needed to make it reasonable to take aspirin for a headache, attend an exhibit of the work of a painter one admires, or stop a child from putting his hand on a hot stove. No larger context or further purpose is needed to prevent these acts from being pointless.[13]

He then goes a step further, arguing that just as we ask why we should take the aspirin, we can ask why we should care about our own suffering. He takes this to show that ultimate justification is impossible, and vaguely unnecessary:

---

[13] Nagel, "The Absurd," p. 717.

We can ask not only why we should take aspirin, but why we should take trouble over our own comfort at all. The fact that we shall take the aspirin without waiting for an answer to this last question does not show that it is an unreal question. We shall also continue to believe, there is a floor under us without waiting for an answer to the other question. In both cases it is this unsupported natural confidence that generates skeptical doubts; so it cannot be used to settle them.[14]

But here we can distinguish between value skepticism and the problem of life's pointlessness. Taking the aspirin doesn't seem pointless because it's directed toward valued ends, namely, ourselves and therefore our feelings. We can question why we value not suffering but, usually, we find good reasons for this valuing. When questioning why bother taking the aspirin, Nagel is gesturing at a form of value skepticism. But you don't need to be a value skeptic to worry about the valued end of the enterprise of life. Value skepticism and the problem of life's pointlessness are separate problems. (Although value skepticism entails life's pointlessness because if we have no values we can't have valued ends, one need not endorse value skepticism in order to think that life is pointless.) Taking an aspirin is directed toward a valued end and therefore isn't pointless. The same can't be said about leading our lives, not because we are value skeptics but because we cannot have an end outside of life to serve as a valued end for leading and living it. So the problem of life's pointlessness does not "suggest thereby that all reasons that come to an end are incomplete."[15] It just suggests, correctly, that all reasons that fail to arrive at a valued end are not reasons that can provide us with a point for an effort or enterprise.

It's helpful to distinguish between what I call Everyday Meaning from Ultimate Meaning. Everyday Meaning refers to the value and

<hr>

[14] Nagel, "The Absurd," p. 724.
[15] Nagel, "The Absurd," p. 718.

significance in our everyday lives, including values such as beauty, love, and truth, and the significance of doing things that engage with them. It includes the purpose (i.e., the reason for which something is done) and point (i.e., justifying valued end) of much of our meaningful, everyday lives, which aim at and reflect these valued ends. It includes the impact we have on others and on the world around us, as well as the explanation of some of our meaningful activities and pursuits. Ultimate Meaning refers to the point of leading a life *at all*. Why bother with the project, effort, or enterprise of life? What is the valued end of running a human life? Ultimate Meaning is the end-regarding justifying reason, the valued end, or the point of leading a life at all. Distinguishing between Everyday Meaning and Ultimate Meaning makes sense of feeling that life is pointless while still caring very much about everyday matters such as your stubbed toe or your child's first words. It makes sense of finding life pointless yet still caring deeply about other people, your work, and the health of our planet. These sorts of sets of views, which can seem paradoxical, are not all that uncommon, and become understandable once we distinguish between Everyday Meaning and Ultimate Meaning.[16]

In his later work, Nagel seems to characterize the problem of Ultimate Meaning differently, and more in line with distinguishing Ultimate Meaning from Everyday Meaning, saying: "The problem is that although there are justifications and explanations for most of the things, big and small, that we do within life, none of these explanations explain the point of your life as a whole."[17] But he maintains the characterization of the problem of Ultimate Meaning as a regression of justification: x gets its meaning from y,

---

[16] It's also important to distinguish between Ultimate Meaning and *Cosmic* Meaning, which is the focus of Chapter 3. Ultimate Meaning refers to the point of living a life at all, and that point need not be cosmic.

[17] Nagel, *What Does It All Mean? A Very Short Introduction to Philosophy*, Oxford University Press, 1987, p. 95.

y gets its meaning from *z*, and then we have the problem of no ultimate answer to questions of meaning.[18] And he maintains, again, that ultimate justification is both impossible and vaguely unnecessary, saying: "What kind of answer would bring all of our 'Why?' questions to a stop, once and for all? And if they can stop there, why couldn't they have stopped earlier?"[19] He further claims that the problem of Ultimate Meaning comes from taking an "outside" perspective, explaining, "Looking at it from the outside, it wouldn't matter if you had never existed."[20]

But the problem of Ultimate Meaning is not merely a result of the possibility that all justification might be regress-prone (whether or not that's true), as we can see by the contrast cases of Everyday Meaning, where we do find points—valued ends— to things we do and projects we undertake. And it doesn't originate from taking a step outside your life to take a peek at it from that "outside" perspective either. Instead, the problem of Ultimate Meaning—its metaphysical impossibility—results from the nature of points (i.e., that they are separate from the activities, pursuits, projects, and efforts toward which they're aimed) and the nature of a human life (i.e., that it includes its entirety, including your Everyday Meaningful activities and values). We can see that problem from right here, from right inside our lives and the effort we put into running them.

For Nagel, when we take a step back and look at human life from an external perspective, we can't find a point to it. And he's right to think that points involve *something* external, but that externality is not a *perspectival* one. We can see the pointlessness of living and leading a human life from inside that very effort or enterprise because it is the effort or enterprise itself that demands a point, a

---

[18] Nagel, *What Does It All Mean?*, pp. 96–98.
[19] Nagel, *What Does It All Mean?*, p. 98.
[20] Nagel, *What Does It All Mean?*, p. 95.

justified valued end. The externality that shows us that life is point-less is the externality of *values* to pursuits, efforts, enterprises, and projects. It is because values lie outside of or external to the efforts or enterprises for which they can serve as a point, and because the effort or enterprise of living and leading a human life includes all of human values[21] and our everyday engagement with those values, that we come to realize that living and leading a human life is point-less. It has nowhere outside of its effort or enterprise to reach for a point or valued end for that effort or enterprise.

We cannot find a valued end for leading a life, or for life itself, and life itself can't be that end since it's the *enterprise*; it needs a valued end in order to have a point. Life itself is a biological state, not a reason at all, and isn't a reason for living any more than jump is a reason for jumping or a hut is a reason for building.[22] It's the joy of jumping or the shelter of the hut that can provide a valued end, a point, for the effort, project, or enterprise. We can have many valued ends within our lives, and they may provide points for many of our efforts *within* our lives, but they can't provide a point *to* or *for* leading our lives at all. Our lives may be full, even meaning*ful*, overflowing with purposeful projects and enterprises, but living life itself isn't one of them. It can't be. There is nothing that lies sep-arate from it to serve as its valued end. This may not seem so bad. If our lives are full of meaningful efforts, projects, and pursuits, who cares about the container in which all this great purposeful, pointful stuff sits? If your life is meaning*ful*, why worry about the meaning *of* it?

---

[21] By "human values," I mean what people value (see note 3).

[22] Intrinsic value is that which is valuable in itself or for its own sake. We might test for intrinsic value by analyzing whether there is another value on which the value of the thing in question depends. That may be why intrinsic value tends to be abstract, e.g., beauty, freedom, or truth. Freedom, beauty, and truth are abstract and arguably intrinsic values which can serve as valued ends for the act or enterprise of ensuring freedom, making something beautiful, or acquiring knowledge. Life is not a good candidate for intrinsic value because it's an empirical, biological *state*, not a value, let alone an abstract value, and (unsurprisingly) its value can be reasonably questioned (is life worth living?).

Why Care?

If all I show is that leading a life is pointless but most of what we do in our lives may not be pointless, that may not seem particularly significant. We may note that many things *in* life are purposeful and have plenty of value, making life itself a container, of sorts, for valued ends but not the kind of thing that is itself directed toward a valued end. I think that this often incompletely articulated problem of the meaning *of* life can lead to a switch from thinking about the meaning *of* life to thinking about meaning *in* life and, indeed, much recent philosophical talk about life and meaning has made that switch.[23] The shift in talk of meaning *of* life to meaning *in* life has been at least partially motivated by the sense that it's confused or futile to ask about the meaning of life. However, in fact, it's not confused to ask about the meaning of life, once we specify that we are asking about the point of life and that by point we mean valued end. And it's not futile to ask whether leading and living a human life can have a point; it's just sad because the answer is, unfortunately, no. Life is pointless. Perhaps the shift in focus from meaning of life to meaning in life constitutes a tacit acknowledgment that it is the projects and pursuits within a life that can be pointless or purposeful, meaningful or meaningless. The project or effort of living and leading a human life—living at all—can only be pointless.

But, while it's important to think about meaning *in* life, it is also important to think about the meaning *of* life because we lead one entire life as an effort or enterprise of its own. In the course of our lives, we can think about *how* to live, and hopefully arrive at answers grounded by values, perhaps enabling us to live more meaningfully. Aristotle can direct us regarding the constitutive ends of a good life, and how to live well.[24] Kant can tell us about the

---

[23] See Susan Wolf, *Meaning in Life and Why It Matters*, Princeton University Press, 2010; Iddo Landau, *Finding Meaning in an Imperfect World*, Oxford University Press, 2017; and Thaddeus Metz, *Meaning in Life*, Oxford University Press, 2014.

[24] See Aristotle, *Nicomachean Ethics* (c. 350 BC), Terence Irwin, trans., Hackett Publishing Company, 1999.

fundamental values of valuing oneself and others as ends in themselves that structure a good life.[25] But those are answers to how best to live. It still makes sense to wonder, why live at all? What is the valued end for *that* enterprise? We put great effort into it, into the running of our lives as an effort or enterprise of its own and, just as with our other efforts, it makes sense for us to want to see that effort as going somewhere and having a point.

Anyone who dreams and plans for the future, who thinks about how the past fits into their present and future, who thinks about the shape of their life, their reasons for living, the legacy they hope to leave—in other words, anyone who lives a human agential life—is *leading* a life—running a life—which is an effort, project, or enterprise of its own. You need not view your life as one project with a defined goal to be subject to the pointlessness problem of Ultimate Meaning. The problem of Ultimate Meaning applies to lives that are not led as projects, but still led as efforts. So, maybe you don't consider your life a project you construct and lead but you still put effort into shaping your life as a whole: you get married, or don't; you choose a hard job or go for the one that lands in your lap, or the only one you can get; you pursue hobbies or you laze around when you can; you raise children or chickens, or become a loner, etc. You have ideals and values. You don't just thoughtlessly do "whatever" all the time. We each put effort into leading our lives overall, as one life we lead. Some argue that our lives are a story we tell ourselves; we have a narrative identity, we want our lives to make sense as a *whole*.[26] But why are we writing a story? Why bother? Why all that effort? We're not merely alive, like a bacterium or even a rat; we *lead* lives, we run our lives as a sustained effort or enterprise,

---

[25] See Immanuel Kant, *Groundwork for the Metaphysics of Morals* (1785), Allen Wood, Ed. and trans., Yale University Press, 2002.

[26] See David Velleman, "The Self as Narrator," John Christman and Joel Anderson, Eds., *Autonomy and the Challenges to Liberalism*, Cambridge University Press, 2005, pp. 56–73; and Johan Brännmark, "Leading Lives: On Happiness and Narrative Meaning," *Philosophical Papers* 32 (2003): 321–343.

often attempting to fit its pieces together into a purposeful whole.[27] Not entirely, of course. We may live for the moment sometimes, doing "whatever," but a life led that way all the time would likely seem fragmentary, incoherent—not only pointless, but centerless, agentless; not a truly human life.[28]

Agency, authorship, and the leading of your life is a human feature that can come in degrees and variations. And for those who hardly care about the overall shape, structure, and purpose of their lives, noting life's pointlessness will perhaps be less devastating. (So they may be merely sad, rather than very, very sad at our realization about life's pointlessness.) But this lesser devastation comes at the cost of reduced agency and coherence, which makes those less devastated lives, in a melodramatic but probably still accurate sense, less human and no less pointless. Another way of putting this point is that the tragedy of the human condition is perhaps less tragic if you're less human. Still, we are all human, and we all, to some degree, put effort into running our lives as an enterprise, effort, or project of its own.[29]

We run our lives not only in parts but also as a project, effort, or enterprise of its own. As discussed, enterprises or projects are distinguished from isolated acts or merely existing in states, such as being alive or being asleep, by the sustained, coordinated effort we put forth in a somewhat unified or systematic way, directed toward

---

[27] See Brännmark, "Leading Lives."

[28] Agency is not something every person has all the time. We aren't very agential as babies or when in a coma. Some people have severe cognitive disabilities that limit their agency. Are their lives pointless? Well, all lives are! But I'm also saying something else: I'm saying that a life of diminished agency is usually less meaningful because Everyday Meaning is harder to achieve without agency (see Chapter 2). My point here is that a full human life includes being an agent, and agents *lead* lives.

[29] Galen Strawson famously argues against this commonsense view of how we lead our lives, claiming to be "completely uninterested in the answer to the question, 'What have I made of my life?' I'm living it . . . what I care about, insofar as I care about myself and my life, is how I am now" (*Things That Bother Me: Death, Freedom, the Self, Etc.*, New York Review Books, 2018, p. 83). This seems way too extreme a claim to me and denies too much about the human experience of setting goals, trying to live by ideals, reflecting on the kind of life you would like to lead, and, yes, putting forth some effort into leading a life. Strawson is wrong about this.

valued ends. Which valued ends can serve this role for leading a life? Not just the projects and efforts within it but the project and effort of leading the entire it?

If the answer to that question is nothing, then it makes sense to be saddened to realize that. It makes sense to be disappointed that there's no valued end to leading a life at all because, just as we justify our efforts and enterprises within our lives by the valued ends toward which they are directed and would be disappointed to discover that there were no such valued ends, we have the same sorts of reasons to want the leading of the entirety of our lives, the effort or enterprise of *it*, to be directed toward a valued end. When we discover that this cannot be the case, we have reason to regret this fact; reason to be sad and wish things were different, even though they couldn't possibly be different.

Thinking of your life as a somewhat purposeful enterprise run by you as an agent is one of the things that makes running out of dental floss worth it. Lots of boring, effortful, annoying things, such as keeping yourself in the floss, take up lots of our efforts between the otherwise purposeful pursuits within our lives. Why do we keep on keeping on? Yes, we have Everyday Meaning, and that is no small thing. It enables us to lead a meaningful life. But it doesn't negate noticing that there's this other kind of meaning—Ultimate Meaning—which we have reason to want, and it is a sad aspect of the human condition that we can't have it. There is no contradiction between appreciating Everyday Meaning and wondering, still, why are we bothering to lead a life at all?

You might think that if our lives are suffused with Everyday Meaning, that has to be enough. What's missing?[30] If my conception of a flourishing life includes appreciating art, baking fluffy-as-clouds cakes, being a good friend, and working as a compassionate

---

[30] I discuss the relative importance of Everyday and Ultimate Meaning in "Between Sisyphus's Rock and a Warm and Fuzzy Place: Procreative Ethics and the Meaning of Life," *The Oxford Handbook of Meaning in Life*, Landau, Ed., 2022, chapter 19.

insurance adjuster, what sense does it make to ask me what the point of living this sort of life is? The point is the Everyday Meaning, the living of this meaningful life. And that's not entirely illegitimate: our everyday activities can be pointful in the everyday sense. And thank goodness for that because, without Everyday Meaning, everyday life might well be unbearable. But you're not just appreciating art, baking cakes, being a good friend, and compassionately doing your productive and worthwhile job. You're also putting effort and agency into the meta-project, which is the running of your life; conducting the enterprise of living; *leading* a life. That is an effort or enterprise of its own and not simply the aggregate of your other efforts. So, to the question, how else do we live our lives but in this Everyday sense? In the Ultimate sense, I'd say. It makes sense for us to want that effort, project, and enterprise to have a point of its own. (Aspiration: to every effort, enterprise, project, or job, a point.) What is missing, despite Everyday Meaning, is a point for the leading and living of our lives as an overall effort of its own. What is missing is Ultimate Meaning. We live our lives in both the everyday and ultimate sense, and it is therefore reasonable for us to want both kinds of efforts to be pointful rather than pointless. That doesn't mean that when we realize we lack Ultimate Meaning we should kill ourselves[31] or despair of Everyday Meaning. It just means that, just as we accept other sad things we can't change, we recognize a particularly sad aspect of the human condition, which is that we cannot have Ultimate Meaning.

As rational agents, we're inclined toward striving, toward conducting projects or enterprises that are grounded by or aimed at valued ends, and toward leading our entire lives in that way too since that too is an effort or enterprise of its own. Although almost everyone puts effort into running their lives as an effort

---

[31] There can be many reasons to continue living rather than commit suicide, including curiosity about life and events, fear of death, loyalty to family and friends, commitments we have made, and Everyday Meaning.

or enterprise of its own, not everyone does so with the same degree of effort aimed at achieving some kind of overall coherence and purpose. Those of us for whom life is more of an effort than a joy are more likely to find Ultimate Meaning especially important because we put a great deal of effort into leading our less than blissful lives and, without a point to it all, that effort can feel like a slog: draining, exhausting, even alienating (because the connection between the effort and the point is missing). Those to whom life seems effortless (anyone?) or those who happily treat life like it's the journey rather than the destination that matters are likely somewhat less bothered by a lack of Ultimate Meaning than those of us who find an arduous, perilous, and difficult journey to nowhere distressingly pointless. Some, perhaps the laziest and happy-go-luckiest among us, may even feel relieved to discover that there's no Ultimate Meaning because that can remove the onus of pursuing it, leaving one more carefree to enjoy the pleasures of everyday life. Thus, we can recognize some reasonable variation in how much Ultimate Meaning matters to us relative to Everyday Meaning, but Ultimate Meaning still matters quite a bit. The fact that we can have Everyday Meaning, while crucial to the meaningfulness of our everyday lives, doesn't somehow solve the problem of the lack of Ultimate Meaning. It makes sense for us to want both.

Having pointful pursuits within our lives is surely better than not. Probably *much* better, and plausibly better relative to the value of our valued ends. The rat pressing the right lever for tastier bits of food has pointful activity, but tasty bits are not as valuable an end for our efforts as is, say, living morally or composing beautifully. Still, not having any valued end for the entire enterprise of leading and living a human life makes life a kind of tragic enterprise, even in the face of Everyday Meaning. We've gone from exalted, noble strivers, creators and shapers of the enterprise of life (not merely the projects within life) to mere *containers* of value: from purposeful constructors of our life stories, with agential unity and worthwhile ends that provide us with reason to live at all, to *cups*. Sad!

Thus, regardless of the value we can enjoy within our lives, discovering that leading life itself, each of our lives themselves, is pointless should make us sad because it is a fitting response to the facts—i.e., what is the case: that life is pointless—and to our values, i.e., what we have reason to care about: that leading a life should have a point in its entirety, that there's a point to the hard, wearying, unified, and agential enterprise of leading a human life at all.

Attempts at a Solution to Life's Pointlessness

Over the millennia that humans have been working so hard and long at leading their lives, I am not the first to notice that life is pointless. Many solutions have been offered, though they are not always easy to follow because different meanings for the problem of meaning of or in life may be used at different points in the discussion.[32] But I've specified the problem I'm addressing as the lack of a valued end to the enterprise of life. That can help us analyze solutions that seem to be directed toward that problem (whether they're explicitly formulated that way or not). I'll address the solutions that go most directly to the problem of the overall pointlessness of the enterprise of leading a life at all. None of them work as solutions, though all are quite fascinating and valuable in other ways, including as a coping mechanism, good advice for living a good and perhaps even meaning*ful* life, a hazy hope, or a compelling way of thinking about the problem.

---

[32] Robert Nozick's discussion of the meaning of life is notable in this regard. It is a wide-ranging and fascinating discussion in which the term "meaning" is used very broadly, to mean nearly all the possible meanings of "meaning," at various points in the lengthy discussion (*Philosophical Explanations*, Harvard University Press, 1981, chapter 6).

Overview

Many philosophers who address the problem of the meaning of life recommend hard work toward a valuable, yet likely unattainable, end of value which extends in some way beyond the individual.[33] It's unclear why the work has to be hard, but it seems plausible to think that if it's too easy it won't be fully engaging or psychologically fulfilling. Of course, if we're looking for a point to life, the ends that ground it must be valuable, so it's clear why the end must be of value. But why must it reach beyond the individual? And why must it be unattainable?

I suspect that the "beyond" recommendation is a way of getting closer to addressing the problem of pointlessness: the reason the goal, end, or grounding value has to be somehow "beyond" the individual is that a point is a valued end, and an end is separate from the effort or enterprise. Thus, for something to serve as a point for leading a life, it has to be in some way separate from or external to it. And, since we can't do, ground by, or aim at anything truly external to our lives because our lives encompass their entirety, the best philosophers can do with this problem is to recommend getting your value as far away from your own little life as possible. Hence, the nearly ubiquitous connection made between meaning and an end beyond yourself: help others, pursue justice, live for god or the afterlife, etc.

Yet, while it's valuable to alleviate suffering or help the downtrodden, we may still wonder about the point of the entire enterprise of these suffering and ameliorating lives, even as we acknowledge the value of helping others once we're all busy living and suffering. Within the lives, we can see the point of alleviating suffering. But

---

[33] See Brännmark, "Leading Lives," pp. 321–343; David Cooper, "Life and Meaning," *Ratio* 18 (2005): 125–137; Antti Kauppinen, "Meaningfulness and Time," *Philosophy and Phenomenological Research* 84 (2012): 345–377; Landau, *Finding Meaning in an Imperfect World*; Neil Levy, "Downshifting and Meaning in Life," *Ratio* 18 (2005): 176–189; Nozick, *Philosophical Explanations*; and Wolf, *Meaning in Life and Why It Matters.*

why do the whole thing? Why lead and live a human life? The suffering and the ameliorating of the suffering—the whole cycle seems pointless. Many projects that seem to extend beyond the self merely postpone the problem or widen the circle of pointlessness. Helping others or trying to improve the world for future generations can seem to give us a value outside of our lives, but, as noted earlier, doing for others or for future generations is still something we do and a value we aim at within the effort or enterprise of running our own lives. So this "go outside yourself" for Ultimate Meaning is advice that cannot work. The most it can do is widen or postpone the problem, putting off the reckoning. Imagine the world improved enough—then what? What's the point of the rest of your life? (At some point, things are good enough, no? Otherwise, we are just slaves to the unending labor of improvement, with each generation similarly, drearily, and pointlessly indentured to the next.)[34] Less selfish ends still occur within life and cannot provide a point for the enterprise of living it, as we can see by imagining justice achieved—then what? The world is sufficiently improved, then what? But the problem is not as stark or as in-your-face as it would be if your end was, say, to play solitaire every day, which is directed toward a valued end more clearly well within your sole, personal, everyday life.

Positing god or the afterlife as the point of life are common examples of widening and/or postponing the problem of pointlessness. What's the point of doing god's will or existing in the afterlife? Say we have a blissful afterlife. That can seem like the point of life: to achieve a blissful afterlife. But it really only postpones the question, as we can see by imagining life extending into some sort

---

[34] Samuel Scheffler persuasively argues that future generations provide current generations with meaning. If he's correct that we "borrow" meaning from the future by imagining our impact on future generations, that can be viewed as a means of postponing the reckoning if we take him to be referring to Ultimate Meaning. His argument is more persuasive when correctly understood as being about Everyday Meaning (see Scheffler, *Death and the Afterlife*, Oxford University Press, 2013).

of afterlife. Okay, you get there, you're happy, now what? What's the point of the rest of your life/afterlife? Once again, we will note that our lives include their entirety, including their possible afterlife portion, leaving no valued end to serve as a point for living, or afterliving, it. Adding an afterlife epilogue to a regular life just postpones the question by making your life last a lot longer and have this second supernatural chapter.

And why think that an unattainable end is better than an attainable one?[35] That can seem the opposite of what might make life less pointless because what's the point of aiming at something unreachable? It sounds frustrating, at best, and maddeningly pointless at worst. So why recommend that as a way of living a pointful life? The reason for this recommendation is revealed by noting what happens when an end is achieved—then what? If your end is to eat the five tomatoes on your plate and you eat them, what's the point of the rest of your life? You're left to notice that your life encompasses the tomatoes and thus eating those tomatoes cannot save your life from pointlessness. But if eating the tomatoes is a valuable end, then walking toward them may feel purposeful and you may not notice that all that walking hasn't made your life's entirety any less pointless until you reach the table, sit down, and eat them. Thus, the more unlikely it is that you will ever reach those tomatoes, the more likely it is that you will not be directly confronted with the fact that pursuing the valuable end of getting to them does not make your life any less pointless. But the fact remains. The same applies to loftier, more valuable, and more other-regarding ends. If your end is helping others or achieving justice, think about what would happen if those worthwhile ends were met. You would feel great

---

[35] The crisis of meaning that can be caused by attaining a goal is addressed by both Levy, "Downshifting and Meaning in Life"; Landau, *Finding Meaning in an Imperfect World*, pp. 145–162; and Julian Baggini, *What's It All About?: Philosophy and the Meaning of Life*, Oxford University Press, 2007, chapter 5. Elijah Milgram makes the point differently, arguing that aiming at a point for leading life as a whole—what he might call a "project life"—is doomed to failure and therefore a mistake (*Mill and the Meaning of Life*, Oxford University Press, 2019).

for a bit, and then wonder: now what? You would notice that the valued end of helping others or living in a just society occurs within your life, is encompassed by your life, and therefore cannot serve as a valued end for leading it.[36] It seems that the unattainability of the end serves to mask its ultimate failure to provide Ultimate Meaning rather than to actually provide Ultimate Meaning.

(Another problem with needing our valued ends to be unattainable in order for our lives to have a point is the contradiction it forces us into: we have to want what we claim not to want, e.g., we have to want injustice or suffering to persist so that we have something unattainable to fix or alleviate, but the injustice and the suffering are supposedly the things we are trying to eliminate because we don't want them.)

You might wonder about seemingly *inexhaustible* values we can aim at, such as, say, love. Perhaps unattainable is just the wrong term used for the kinds of values that can provide a point to living a life at all. Perhaps inexhaustible values can serve as sources of Ultimate Meaning, without leaving us at a "now what?" point. But I'm skeptical of the plausibility of inexhaustible values and therefore think it is no accident that philosophers have recommended unattainable goals instead. It seems that, for any value, we can reach a saturation point or an achievement point beyond which more of that value ceases to be valuable to us. Beyond a satisficing point of justice, living for it or continuing to pursue it would seem pointless and counterproductive; nitpicky, annoying, not valuable. Even love, if we had too much of it, might begin to feel smothering or, at some point, irritating, overwhelming, or just *too much*. (I can imagine ending a relationship for reasons of this sort.) There is even a documented phenomenon of seeing something so cute that you can't stand it and want to obliterate it.[37] I therefore think

---

[36] Baggini challenges the claim that helping others is the meaning of life by arguing that it implies that when everyone has been helped we will have nothing to live for, and is therefore a self-defeating view (*What's It All About?*, chapter 4).

[37] See John Hamilton, "When Cute Is Too Much, the Brain Can Get Aggressive," *National Public Radio, Morning Edition*, December 31, 2018.

unattainable is no misnomer for the recommendations in the literature that wrestles with a sense of life's pointlessness.

That's the general solutions picture: aim outside yourself and make sure you can't quite get there. Neither idea works. I'll turn now to specific attempts to solve the problem of life's pointlessness.

Leading Lives

Several philosophers have noted the importance that the narrative trajectory of a human life plays in leading a meaningful life. Antti Kauppinen contends that meaningfulness is a function of the structure of an agent's goal-directed activities, which satisfies the human agential pride of being the protagonist in pursuit of a valuable goal.[38] He concludes that "life is ideally meaningful when challenging efforts lead to lasting success,"[39] ideally beyond the individual herself. Kauppinen frames his discussion in terms of human good and exemplars of meaningful lives, and he defines meaningfulness as "appropriateness of feelings of fulfillment and admiration."[40] Within the context of his argument, he is certainly correct to note that ends are important components of meaningfulness and that, when thinking about human meaningfulness, the agential unity and narrative trajectory of human lives are crucial factors. They contribute to the meaningfulness of the narrative. But why write the story? What is the valued end for the writing or living of the entire life story, a story which encompasses its own end and cannot last beyond its last page, so to speak? What Kauppinen makes clear, however, is that, for people, meaningfulness demands a point. We want our projects and efforts to be directed toward

---

[38] See Kauppinen, "Meaningfulness and Time," p. 358.
[39] Kauppinen, "Meaningfulness and Time," p. 346.
[40] Kauppinen, "Meaningfulness and Time," p. 346.

valued ends, and want the leading of our lives to have a point, a valued end.

Both Neil Levy and Johan Brännmark focus on the fact that people lead lives as central to our pursuit of meaning, and they note as well both the importance of having ends, and the difficulty of finding an end that can provide a point for leading or living a life.

Brännmark argues for placing purposefulness at the center of accounts of human good because we don't merely live, we *lead* lives and, therefore, he says, a good human life involves purposive narrative meaning, or a point.[41] Since the valued end should ideally be of great value, we do better, he says, when pursuing grand goals, such as love, truth, and justice, which provide worthwhile ends for us, even though he concedes that there's no answer to the skeptic about "purposive meaning."[42] He notes that it's even worse if you become too absorbed with the singular pursuit of one of those ends of great value because you can lose individuality—your very narrative soul!—and become "like a cog, losing the rationale for this life being yours to lead."[43]

Here too we are getting closer to the problem: to the fact that people lead lives and want that enterprise to be going somewhere, to be directed toward something, to have a point, a valued end. But we still don't find any solution or facing up to the sadness of the impossibility of a solution. Sure, justice and truth are ends so abstract and difficult to achieve that, like tomatoes situated very far away, we may notice less that our life encompasses our efforts toward those valued ends, but encompass them it does nonetheless. Those ends can only provide purposes for projects or efforts *within* our lives, but they cannot provide a point *to* or *for* living our lives at all.

---

[41] Brännmark, "Leading Lives."

[42] Brännmark, "Leading Lives," p. 339.

[43] Brännmark, "Leading Lives," p. 340. Milgram uses the example of John Stuart Mill's "project life," as he calls it, to make a similar point about the self-defeating nature of lives lived as the singular pursuit of one end or goal (Milgram, *Mill and the Meaning of Life*).

The problem we face when we achieve an end only to notice that our lives encompass it and have themselves no valued end may be what motivates Levy to claim that meaningful lives are attained through hard work that we cannot imagine completing.[44] Because the pursuit of a meaningful end can seem to be rendered meaningless in its achievement (e.g., Sisyphus's rock stays on top of the mountain—then what?, Levy asks), in our pursuit of a valued end for life, "nothing will fail here like success."[45] Thus, he recommends pursuit of valued ends such as justice, art, or truth, toward which we can make incremental progress but never achieve or even be able to fully imagine achieving: "Since we cannot know what the final goal might be like, we cannot imagine completing our project, and therefore we cannot be shaken by the image of its completion,"[46] he explains. This may work to help us not realize that our lives are pointless but only by placing the tomatoes so far away that they are even out of the reach of our imagination, so to speak. This seems less like a satisfying solution and more like a method for being less compelled to face the problem. Our failure of imagination does not save our lives from pointlessness; it can only save us from effectively imagining or realizing that our lives are pointless. Yet pointless they remain.

The Mysterious, Ineffable "All"

As we noted, the externality of a valued end is often the implicit factor motivating discussions of meaning as connecting to something beyond the individual. David Cooper reasons that for x to be meaningful, it has to relate to meaningful y, which gets its meaning from meaningful p, etc. Therefore, living a human life itself must

---

[44] See Levy, "Downshifting and Meaning in Life."

[45] This is one of the most penetrating things anyone has ever said on this topic. Levy, "Downshifting and Meaning in Life," p. 182.

[46] Levy, "Downshifting and Meaning in Life," p. 185.

get its meaning from something beyond it: "human existence is meaningful only if it is 'answerable' to what is 'beyond human.'"[47] Otherwise, he says, we are struck by the possibility that our efforts are pointless. But what is the beyond human to which human existence is answerable to? Here Cooper concludes that the best we can do is to accept that the answer must be "mysterious, ineffable," the noumena that we can't see.[48]

Robert Nozick also articulates the problem of meaning as a problem of moving goal-posts, or a regress that we find ourselves in when seeking a point to life. Even when pursuing valued ends, he says that we can still ask what our lives amount to and whether the ends have any significance or meaning.[49] I've noted that when we ask what our lives amount to, we aren't necessarily being value skeptics—we aren't necessarily questioning whether, say, it is valuable to appreciate art or love our children. Instead, we may be noticing that these valued ends occur within our lives and don't provide us with a valued end to the enterprise of living and leading our lives at all. But Nozick sees a regress indicating a problem of limits. Whatever we do toward value within our lives, he says: ". . . we can still ask what it all amounts to. . . . We can distance ourselves from the life, see it as the particular things it was, notice its limits, and wonder whether really it has any meaning."[50] Thus, Nozick concludes:

> The problem of meaning is created by limits, by being just this, by being merely this. . . . However widely we connect and link, however far our web of meaningfulness extends, we can imagine drawing a boundary around all that, standing outside looking at the totality of it, and asking, "But what is that meaning of that, what does that mean?" . . . To see something's limits, to see it

[47] Cooper, "Life and Meaning," p. 126.
[48] See Cooper, "Life and Meaning," p. 132.
[49] Nozick, *Philosophical Explanations*, pp. 578–579.
[50] See Nozick, *Philosophical Explanations*, pp. 578–579.

as that limited particular thing or enterprise, is to question its meaning. . . . In imagination, we stand outside the thing and ask for the meaning of the totality.[51]

Since Nozick puts the problem of meaning in terms of limits, it follows that he sees the solution as somehow limitless. When seeking a point to our lives, Nozick recognizes that, "Once you come to feel your existence lacks purpose, there is little you can do."[52] That is correct! He should have stopped there, and let the tragic reality sink in. Instead, he invokes the Kabbalistic concept of *Ein Sof*, literally meaning "there is no end," or limitless, and metaphorically meaning pure god, the infinite, boundless,[53] to gesture toward Ultimate Meaning as perhaps somehow being *Ein Sof*, as that which needs no connection to anything else to have meaning. Because it's limitless, there is no place to stand separate from it and question its meaning, and it can therefore "stand as its own meaning."[54] This idea is reminiscent of some Kabbalistic[55] and Buddhist[56] views of life as ultimately aiming to merge into one infinity. And from within that infinity, there is no external standpoint from which to ask for justification, purpose, or point.[57]

---

[51] See Nozick, *Philosophical Explanations*, pp. 595–598. This way of putting the problem of meaning has some similarity to Nagel's articulation of the absurd as resulting from being able to transcend our limits in thought, to stand outside ourselves, and question the meaning of our lives (see Nagel, "The Absurd").

[52] See Nozick, *Philosophical Explanations*, p. 588.

[53] See Jewish Virtual Library, American-Israeli Cooperative Enterprise, 1998–2024, http://www.jewishvirtuallibrary.org/ein-sof; and Nozick, *Philosophical Explanations*, pp. 600–610.

[54] See Nozick, *Philosophical Explanations*, p. 604.

[55] See Daniel Chanan Matt, *The Essential Kabbalah: The Heart of Jewish Mysticism*, Castle Books, 1997.

[56] See Hiroshi Obayashi, Ed., *Death and the Afterlife: Perspectives of World Religions*, Praeger, 1991, Part III.

[57] Nagel also sometimes seems to wonder whether if there were a solution to the problem of Ultimate Meaning, it would have to work that way, as does Benatar, at times. In *What Does It All Mean?* Nagel considers: "Can there really be something which gives point to everything else by encompassing it, but which couldn't have, or need, any point itself? Something whose point can't be questioned from outside because there is no outside?" (Oxford University Press, 1987, p. 100). In *The Human Predicament*, David Benatar reasons somewhat similarly about temporal limitlessness, arguing that if we had

This is an intriguing conception of the problem of meaning or pointlessness, but I think it gets things exactly backward. The problem of pointlessness is not that we can stand outside the project and question its point—that's fine as long as we have an answer to that question, as we often do (as discussed): e.g., the point of eating is to eliminate the suffering of hunger, and enjoy the taste of food. We can stand outside these efforts and question the value of their ends by asking, "Who cares if you're hungry?" "Why care about suffering?" but we find answers fairly readily available: we value ourselves because we are rational, moral agents and/or because we have interests, and since others are similar in relevant ways, we value them and their feelings. If we don't care about anything, we are committed to extreme value skepticism, contradicted by the nearly universal values of avoiding suffering, and valuing many positive feelings. The problem of life's pointlessness is not that we're able to ask the question about valued ends. It's that we can't have an answer, because nothing lies separate from it to serve as its valued end. We may value avoiding suffering but the point of leading a life can't be to avoid suffering because why then bother with the whole thing? (And if we manage to avoid suffering, then what?) What is the point of bothering to lead a human life? What is the valued end to the project, enterprise, and very hard work of leading a human life? If we extend ourselves or connect ourselves to something limitless, infinite, or boundless, all we do is extend the space from which we cannot draw an *answer* (because our enterprise now occupies that space, indeed all space, and seeks a valued end to that whole, now hugely infinite, situation). But we don't make it impossible or nonsensical or beyond our imagination to ask the *question*. The question comes from inside the enterprise,

no temporal limits, then "the purposes internal to your life might well suffice" because there would be no limit to transcend (Oxford University Press, 2017, p. 56). However, as I show here, we arrive at the problem of Ultimate Meaning from the fact that we are engaging in an effort, project, or enterprise of living a life, and nothing lies outside of the enterprise of life to serve as a point for living it because your life includes its entirety. A less limited enterprise would make finding something external to it harder, not easier.

no matter how expansive it is. The question of a point arises from the fact that we are engaging in an enterprise, regardless of how limited or unlimited it may be. And our lives, be they limited or limitless, still include their entirety, leaving us no answer to the question about their valued end. If our lives or we ourselves were less limited, we would restrict the space from which we might be able to draw an answer to the question of the valued end of life's enterprise, but we would not thereby eliminate or answer the question.

Our lives remain pointless. And that fact remains sad.

Can we find something wrong with this view?

Objections

Everyday Meaning

You might think that Ultimate Meaning lies in providing us with the opportunity to achieve Everyday Meaning. After all, if we didn't lead our lives, we couldn't engage with Everyday Meaning. In this way, our overall effort at leading a life can be seen as a necessary condition for Everyday Meaning and, therefore, the point of leading and living our lives would be that this is necessary for attaining Everyday Meaning. However, while a necessary condition for Everyday Meaning might give our lives Everyday Meaning, it won't give leading our lives at all a *point*, because the values we aim at in our meaningful everyday pursuits cannot serve as points for leading our lives at all, and, therefore, serving as necessary conditions for those same values can't either.

Recall: if I work as a lawyer fighting for civil rights, the point of my efforts is justice, which is part of my Everyday Meaning. But justice cannot serve as the point of leading my life, even if we think of our overall efforts as necessary conditions for my Everyday Meaningful fight for justice, as I will notice by imagining justice achieved—then what? What is the point of the rest of my life? (Sisyphus's rock doesn't roll back down. And then? We are faced with the fact that getting it up isn't the point of Sisyphus's life since his life goes on, it contains the rock, wherever he gets it to stay, etc.) My life contains the justice in it and that's why justice cannot serve as a point for the all-encompassing effort of leading or running the enterprise of life; it cannot provide Ultimate Meaning.

Aha, you might say, but without the life you are working so hard to lead, you would have no container, so to speak, for the justice you value. Perhaps the point of life is to serve as a container for the points or valued ends of our everyday pursuits. I turn now to this possibility.

The Container Solution

Instead of seeing the enterprise of leading a life as a pointless container, as I alluded to earlier, you might think that the point of the effort of leading a life is to provide a container for all the valuable ends within a life, just as the point of any container is to hold the stuff in it. Containers aren't pointless—their point is to contain things. So why not be happy to realize that your life is a container for all the valuable things in it?

Because the point of a container is not simply to contain things because what is the point of containing things? The point of containers is to contain things in service of the point of other pursuits or projects. The point of a cup is to hold the coffee so that you can drink it. Without a container, the coffee is all over the place and very hard to drink. So the cup operates in service to your valued end of enjoying the taste and stimulating effects of coffee. Your sock drawer is similar: it contains your socks, thereby making it easier for you to find them and have a less chaotic life. The value of the sock drawer lies outside the drawer and its sock contents—it lies in you, the person outside the drawer whose life is improved by having a container for their socks. When we apply this container logic to life itself, we run into the same problem we had in the first place—that there's nothing outside of it or external to it to serve as an end of value. The purposeful ends are not within; not in the coffee cup or the drawer or the life-container.

If running your life is containment service, like a coffee cup or a sock drawer, what's the point of it? What's the point of containing coffee, socks, or truth? If we think that your life as a container of value has a point because the justice or truth in it are valuable and you couldn't have them without having a life to put them in, we can wonder, just as we did before, whether justice or truth can be the point of life. And we can then note, just as noted earlier, that they can't be, as we see when we imagine justice achieved or truth attained—then what? We are left, once again, to realize that since justice and truth occur within a life, are values within a life, they cannot serve as ends of value for the arduous enterprise or effort of running a life. We return to the fact that ends of value do not lie within. The container solution doesn't work.

It can seem like the answer because it can seem to take our point outside of our life activities, such that the point isn't, say, justice itself, which occurs within a life and so can't serve as the point of leading a life, but the *containment of justice*, which seems more like the enterprise of leading a life itself. But we then have to ask about the point of the containment of things and we are back to where we started from—to the coffee, the socks, and the justice, which are all valuable but still don't serve as the valued end, or the point, of containing them. The problem with thinking that life's point is being a container of value is that when we press against *which* values make that containment ultimately pointful, we find none are external to the enterprise of running a life, so none can serve as a valued end for that effort.

Seeking a Point to Life Is a Category Mistake

We might consider asking for the point of life, or being sad that there isn't one, to be a category mistake, akin to asking, "When is a potato?" or being sad that your baby has a name but not a number, or that your nose is neither odd nor even (even if it's both unusual and symmetrical). Potatoes don't have times, and noses aren't even or odd. What sense would it make to be sad about that? Seeking the "when" of a potato or the oddness or evenness of a nose is incoherent; potatoes and noses are not the kinds of things that have times or oddness/evenness. It is incoherent to demand that of them and nonsensical to bemoan the fact that your nonsensical demands cannot be met. When we ask what the point of life is and are sad to discover that life can't have a point, are we making a category mistake? Are we nonsensically bemoaning an incoherence?

I don't think so. Leading a human life is an effort or enterprise we all engage in, just as we engage in many other projects within our human lives. It can then come as a disappointing surprise to note that, unlike many other of our purposeful enterprises, leading life itself cannot have a point. Asking whether life is pointless is not incoherent—we understand the question and are capable of sensibly answering it; we just don't like the answer. It's more similar to a ninety-nine-year-old man being sad that he can no longer run a marathon in under two and a half hours than it is to a numberless baby. The fact that ninety-nine-year-old men are not the kinds of things that can run marathons in less than two and a half hours (at least not yet) doesn't make asking whether they can a nonsensical category mistake, nor does it make it a category mistake to bemoan the fact that they can't.

The Fallacy of Composition

You might object that seeking a point to living at all is an instance of the fallacy of composition, i.e., of attributing to the whole what is true of the parts. But, as we noted, life is an effort or enterprise that we engage in both in parts and as an effort or enterprise of its own. It therefore makes sense for us to want that effort or enterprise to have a point because it is the valued ends toward which our efforts are directed that serve to help us justify or makes sense of those efforts.

Agency?

When we speak of living a life—the effort or enterprise of running or leading our lives—you might wonder whether we may be referring to the act or effort of being an agent, which might aim at the end of value of agency or autonomy. Could the value of agency be the point of leading a life? I don't think so because the value of agency doesn't make just any exercise of it valuable or purposeful. The value of autonomy or agency doesn't confer value or a point to just anything you do autonomously or as an agent. Agency may be valued but it won't provide us with a valued end for living because it doesn't answer the question, which is: As an agent, why do *this*? Why lead and live a life?

Fun!

Because it's fun. Who cares if life is pointless? It's delightful! Well, maybe for you, and even maybier for you your whole life. Some people suffer nearly all the time and nearly all people suffer some of the time. I suppose some may find life so enjoyable that they don't care whether it's pointless. However, given how much people suffer in life, I find that view staggeringly insufficient. But, even if life were more similar to a pleasure trip, it would still be sad that it was a pointless pleasure trip because, as leaders of lives, it makes sense for us to want our work to be going somewhere, or directed toward something, rather than pointless, even if pleasurably so.

Meaning Superstars

What about people such as Martin Luther King Jr., Jonas Salk, or Beethoven? It seems ludicrous to say that their lives were pointless. The point of Martin Luther King Jr.'s life was to advance civil rights, the point of Jonas Salk's life was to prevent polio, the point of Beethoven's life was to create music so sublime that it still makes our hearts burst hundreds of years later. No? No.

When thinking about people of extraordinary achievement and heroism, I think we become starstruck and somewhat confused. These historical heroes are such superstars in other aspects of non-Ultimate Meaning, such as significance, impact, and values within a life (e.g., justice, knowledge, art, and benevolence) that we may be so overwhelmed by how meaningful their lives are in so many aspects of Everyday Meaning that we're reluctant to deny them *any* kind of meaning, even Ultimate Meaning. But even for the superstars, we can ask about the valued end of them conducting the enterprise of their lives. We may find it less pressing to have an answer to that question when they shine so brightly in other dimensions of meaning. But they still lack this one. Imagine if Jonas Salk or Nelson Mandela lived for hundreds or even thousands of years past their heroic accomplishments: we might then also imagine them wondering what is the point of leading and living their lives, overall. If we imagine our meaning heroes living centuries past their accomplishments, we can then see the question of Ultimate Meaning emerge more clearly, when not overshadowed by an exceptionally meaningful accomplishment within a life.

Live for Others

If leading your life can't have an overall point for yourself, maybe it can serve as a part of someone else's purpose, thereby allowing you a derivative purpose for your life. Living as a footstool for a great artist or living as an expression of god's creativity are examples of these kinds of derivate purposes or points you might think your life can have. Maybe god is intrinsically good and so are god's purposes, maybe the great artist's valuable art will be of higher quality because she had a great footstool to support her.

These do seem to be potential ways for your life to serve *a* purpose. The problem is it wouldn't be *your* purpose; it would be god's or the artist's. A shame for you to live as a mere means to other people's purposes. I don't think that counts as a point for you leading and living *your* life. You might as well be living someone else's life.

Moreover, note that these sorts of solutions are just variations on the "living beyond yourself" recommendation for meaningfulness that I noted earlier, when I said that positing god or the afterlife as the point of life are common examples of widening and/or postponing the problem of pointlessness. What's the point of doing god's will or existing in the afterlife? Less selfish ends still occur within life and cannot provide a point for the enterprise of living it, as we can see by imagining the great artist's masterpiece achieved—then what, my dear footstool? (We're just moving the tomatoes.)

It Doesn't Matter If Life Is Pointless

I've argued that life's pointlessness is sad for us. Not all agree. Nagel, for example, takes his conclusions about life's absurdity in stride. He says that ironic resignation is an appropriate response to life's absurdity and argues that no great angst is merited because if nothing matters, then it doesn't matter that nothing matters.[58] That is a confused conclusion. The view that if nothing matters then it doesn't matter that nothing matters is as facile as it sounds

---

[58] See Nagel, *The Absurd*, p. 727.

and is based on nothing more than an equivocation about the term "meaning." When we are sad to notice that nothing matters, we are sad that life doesn't have a *point*. Telling us that this tragic fact doesn't "matter" is telling us that this tragic fact is of no *significance*. But of course it is significant. How could finding out that life is pointless be considered insignificant? It devalues our striving, our agency, and the lives we work so hard to lead. If we don't equivocate between the "pointless" and "insignificant" characteristics of "meaning," we don't find ourselves in the Nagelian wonder-world where life is pointless but we have no reason to mind.

It's Futile or Pointless to Be Sad About Life's Pointlessness

Why be sad about life's pointlessness? Isn't that also pointless? You might think that lamenting life's pointlessness is futile, and itself pointless, like crying for the moon. If you can't do anything about it, why bemoan it? Uh, because it's sad. We may value truth regardless of its prudential or instrumental value in a particular instance. There is dignity in facing the facts, and humanity in responding with appropriate sadness to sad facts. Sad facts warrant sadness.[59] Sometimes, wishing for or lamenting the impossible is silly, like crying for the moon, or being sad that you're not a number. But, when the impossible would be great for us, and when its absence leaves us lacking something it makes sense for us to want (and even to work for), then it is fitting for us to be sad and disappointed.

John Shand says that "if life is pointless and everything we do without value, then there can be no more value in a life that faces up to that truth than in one that doesn't,"[60] and to argue otherwise

---

[59] See Nelson Cowan, "Life Is Pointless—Good Point . . . and How Do You Feel About That?," *Journal of Controversial Ideas* 2 (2022); and Weinberg, "Replies to Critics."

[60] See John Shand, "How to Live," *The Journal of the Royal Institute of Philosophy* 82 (2007): 347–348.

is to insist that although nothing has value, facing that truth does have value. But accepting that leading a life is pointless does not commit you to the view that *nothing* has value; it only commits you to the view that leading and living a life is not directed toward a valued end. That doesn't mean that nothing in life or anywhere else in the vast universe has no kind of value at all. It doesn't entail that truth has no value, or that discovering and acknowledging truth have no value.

Conclusion

I have argued that "point" is one of the characteristics of "meaning," and that a point is a valued end. I have also argued that our grand enterprise of leading a life, of living at all, cannot have one. This does not entail value skepticism, but it's still pretty sad, as value conclusions go. We can have valued ends within life, but the fact that leading a human life at all is pointless can cast a pall over the pursuits within it that seem otherwise valuable or purposeful. (Putting little meaning bits or even grand meaning chunks into our pointless life container is not what we thought or hoped we were doing with all of our efforts, is it?) Let us acknowledge what we are facing here: Running a life, conducting a life, living a life, is a tragic enterprise. One cannot help but strive and struggle and try to make something of it, of yourself; but, sadly, it is ultimately and invariably pointless.

2

EVERYDAY MEANING

Aim High, Aim True, Fail

Finished crying? All right, then. Let's consider what may make our lives "Everyday Meaningful." Recall that Everyday Meaning refers to the value in our everyday lives, e.g., beauty, love, freedom, and truth and the significance of doing things that engage with them. It includes the purpose, i.e., the reason for which something is done, and point, i.e., justifying valued end, of much of our meaningful, everyday lives, which aim at and reflect these valued ends. It also includes the impact we have on ourselves, others, and the world around us, as well as the explanation of some of our meaningful activities and pursuits.

This comprehensive account of Everyday Meaning allows us to explain what is meaningful about coherent efforts that have deep impact and significance but are not good because they are aimed at or grounded by values that are negative. They aren't meaningless, they matter a great deal, but their meaning is negative. Usually, when we talk about meaning, we're talking about positive meaning and here too, unless otherwise specified, when speaking of meaning, I refer to positive meaning. However, I contend that Everyday Meaning can be positive when the values or purposes the relevant efforts or pursuits involve are positive, and negative when they are negative.

Consistent with this reasoning, we will see that Everyday Meaning, including its value characteristic, is objective rather than subjective (i.e., not perspectival), and that meaning is somewhat aspirational, which means that we can aim at it and miss. There is thus an achievement aspect to Everyday Meaning (just an aspect because you can have Everyday Meaning by virtue of being a person, which is intrinsically valuable and significant, but doesn't involve "doing" or achieving anything).

Negative Meaning

A life full of Everyday Meaning need not be a good life. In fact, it can be the polar opposite of one. You can pursue valuable ends, act with coherence and purpose, and have deep, long-lasting impact and significance in the most abysmal of ways if the values toward which your efforts are aimed or by which they are grounded are bad, mistaken, or evil. Were Hitler's projects meaningless? That seems breathtakingly dismissive to say. Meaninglessness would be quite the step up for Hitler. If only his projects were meaningless! Instead, the points and purposes that Hitler pursued were coherent, had deep, devastating, and widespread impact, and were unfortunately uniquely and terribly significant. Negative meaning occurs when the significance, coherence, impact, purpose, and point of an effort, activity, or pursuit are negative or when the values involved in those efforts, activities, or pursuits are negative or contrary to what is valuable. Negative meaning can also occur when a failed positive effort or tragic event has deep negative impact and significance, as we will see shortly. Negative meaning is worse than no meaning.

Some describe what I call negative meaning as "anti-matter"[1] or "anti-meaning"[2] because the values involved in these kinds of pursuits work against positive value. This can make sense for theories of meaning that focus only on value as meaning but it

---

[1] See Metz, "Recent Work on the Meaning of Life," *Ethics* 112 (2002): 781–814.

[2] See Stephen M. Campbell and Sven Nyholm, "Anti-Meaning and Why It Matters," *Journal of the American Philosophical Association* 1 (2015): 694–711.

exposes their narrowness. "Anti-meaning" or "anti-matter" doesn't fully capture what I characterize as negative meaning because it doesn't pay enough attention to the explanation, significance, impact, purpose, and point characteristics of meaning. Being able to account for the meaningfulness of misguided or downright evil efforts such as Nazism or white supremacy while simultaneously accounting for their negative value further shows the advantage of a fully explicated theory of meaning in which all the kinds and characteristics of meaning are accounted for. It's more accurate to describe meaningful efforts that run contrary to positive values as negative meaning. Meaningful, but in a bad way. This implies some ability to distinguish positive from negative value. It invites the question: whose values?

Subjective or Objective Meaning?

As we have noted, it's not as if no one ever noticed that life is ultimately pointless; many live on long past that realization. Existentialist philosophers go beyond concluding that life is ultimately pointless, most concluding that life has no real or objective meaning at all.[3] Not even Everyday Meaning. After considering suicide as a potential response to what they take to be life's utter meaninglessness, some of the more modern Existentialists advise us to make our own meaning[4] by living in accordance with what we

---

[3] See Jean-Paul Sartre, *Existentialism Is a Humanism* (1946), Carol Macomber, trans., Yale University Press, 2007, pp. 20–24 and 37–40; Albert Camus, *The Myth of Sisyphus* (1942), Justin O'Brien, trans., Vintage/Penguin Random House, 2018, pp. 20–22; and Martin Heidegger, *Being and Time* (1927), John Macquarrie and Edward Robinson, trans., Martino Fine Books, 2019, pp. 1–25; among many others.

[4] Richard Taylor, arguably a modern Existentialist, claims that the transience of our achievements renders our efforts pointless and therefore meaningless, and that meaning is internal, coming from our own will to live as the beings we are ("The Meaning of Life," *Good and Evil*, Prometheus, 1970, pp. 19–28). It's not clear exactly what kind of meaning this is, how it works, or why we should find it meaningful. I recommend a different way of looking at the relationship between transience and meaning (see Chapters 4 and 5).

personally value.[5] Not the worst advice—if the world won't provide you with meaning, it can seem sensible to try to make your own meaning. But not the most satisfying advice either because making up your own meaning can feel fake: a comforting illusion at best, and a pathetic delusion if that's how you feel about comforting illusions. So the Existentialists proceed a step further, arguing that they're not telling us to just make stuff up. We should each make our own meaning authentically—authentic to the values of the individual, and resistant to insidious societal influence.[6] Again, sensible. If value is subjective, it makes sense to decide what *you* value and live in accordance with those values for Everyday Meaning. But that can still seem to smack of artifice, like made-up meaning with a layer of your own proclivities somewhere in there, partially obscuring or distracting you from how bogus it all is.

And, with a few muted protests here and there decades later,[7] that's mostly how things stood in philosophy, meaning-wise, for an embarrassingly long time. A philosophical scandal, really. It took more than half a century before a sustained and systematic stand about that somewhat depressing, incompletely explained, makeshift, "DIY" approach to meaning was set forth in Susan Wolf's seminal book, *Meaning in Life and Why It Matters*, wherein Wolf forcefully argues that meaning demands subjective engagement with *objective* value.[8] It's not enough to authentically feel that writing out *War and Peace* by hand over and over makes for

[5] See Sartre, *Existentialism Is a Humanism*, and Heidegger, *Being and Time* (the theme runs through the entirety of these works). See Camus, *The Myth of Sisyphus*, pp. 3–10 and 93–113. Kierkegaard and Tolstoy draw a different conclusion from life's apparent meaninglessness, contending that only god can make life meaningful. They urge a religious approach to the problem of meaning. See Søren Kierkegaard, *Fear and Trembling* (1843), Alastair Hannay, trans., Penguin Classics, 1986, pp. 41–56; and Leo Tolstoy, *A Confession* (1882), Alymer Maude, trans., Dover Publications, 2005, Section IV.

[6] See Camus, *The Myth of Sisyphus*; Sartre, *Existentialism Is a Humanism*; and Heidegger, *Being and Time*; among others.

[7] See W. D. Joske, "Philosophy and the Meaning of Life," *Australasian Journal of Philosophy* 52 (1974): 93–104; and Norman Dahl, "Morality and the Meaning of Life: Some First Thoughts," *Canadian Journal of Philosophy* 17 (1987): 1–22.

[8] Wolf, *Meaning in Life and Why It Matters*, p. 9.

a meaningful life.[9] Your subjective engagement, which Wolf thinks is a necessary component of living a meaningful life, must engage with objective value in order for your life to be meaningful.[10] Otherwise, you could think your life is meaningful, but, as you spend your days counting the blades of grass on your front lawn, your so-called meaning is illusory.[11] You're not engaging with real positive value. (I might add that you aren't having much of an impact, doing significant things, acting for reasonable purposes, or putting forth effort toward really valuable ends either.) You are wasting your life (more on that later).

Objective Meaning

But is there such a thing as objective value or is value inherently subjective? When meaning theorists deliberate about the objectivity of value, roughly speaking, they take something to be subjective when its truth depends on one's personal perspective rather than on a fact of the matter that is true or false regardless of point of view.[12] Whether broccoli tastes delicious is subjective, whether water boils on Earth at 212 degrees Fahrenheit is objective.

Of course, we aren't going to settle the debate over the objectivity or subjectivity of value here. Central, classic Western ethical theories argue for objective value,[13] and I think they do a pretty

---

[9] Wolf, *Meaning in Life and Why It Matters*, pp. 16 and 36.

[10] Wolf, *Meaning in Life and Why It Matters*, p. 20.

[11] See Aaron Smuts, "The Good Cause Account of the Meaning of Life," *Southern Journal of Philosophy* 51 (2013): 536–562, 537.

[12] There are several ways to parse the objective-subjective distinction. I use a simple distinction common to the debate among meaning theorists. Other characterizations include that objectivity refers to facts backed by good reasons (see Nagel, *The Last Word*, Oxford University Press, 2001, chapters 1 and 2), and internal vs. external reasons (see Bernard Williams, "Internal and External Reasons," *Rational Action: Studies in Philosophy and Social Science*, Ross Harrison, Ed., Cambridge University Press, 1979, pp. 17–28, and John McDowell, "Might There Be External Reasons?" *World, Mind, and Ethics*, J. E. J. Altham, Ed., Cambridge University Press, 1995, pp. 65–85).

[13] Aristotle argues for objective value based on human nature and well-being. (Though some may interpret Aristotelian value as "Good-for" value) (*Nicomachean*

good job (that's why they're classic!). And many contemporary philosophers persuasively argue that even if value is not immune from skeptical doubts, it is no more dubious or inherently subjective and suspect than any of our other supposedly objective beliefs, such as scientific truths.[14] Some contemporary philosophers challenge the objectivity of values,[15] but this is not a prevailing view. Other philosophers, both classic and contemporary, argue for objective value *relative* to an entity, good as "Good-for"[16]— objectively real, but true only in relation to a functional system; e.g., water is good for goldfish, or social connection is good for people. (As opposed to, "Water is good.") I think it's clear that "Good-for" value exists, and that is sufficient for robust Everyday Meaning.

Still, I can't help being a value objectivist. I find it impossible to imagine that we're wrong, transfixed by perspective, or merely culturally conditioned to hold certain widely accepted values; e.g., "it is wrong to torture a child for sport." I cannot imagine any conditions, any misconceptions, any anything that could make that statement incorrect. This doesn't prove value objectivism—as I mentioned, there is no shortage of solid arguments for that[17] (though they don't

Ethics, Book I, Sections 7 and 13); Kant argues for objective value based on rationality (*Groundwork for the Metaphysics of Morals*); and Mill argues for objective value based on empirically considering what people value for its own sake (*Utilitarianism*, 1861). Some classical philosophers disagree: See David Hume, *A Treatise of Human Nature*, 1739, Book 3, Section 1, and Friedrich Nietzsche, *Beyond Good and Evil* (1886), R. J. Hollingdale, trans., Penguin, 2003.

[14] See Nicholas Sturgeon, "Moral Explanations," *Morality, Reason, and Truth: New Essays on the Foundations of Ethics*, David Copp and David Zimmerman, Eds., Roman and Allenheld, 1985, pp. 49–78; Peter Railton, "Moral Realism," *The Philosophical Review* 95 (1986): 163–207; and Ronald Dworkin, *Justice For Hedgehogs*, Harvard University Press, 2011; among many others.

[15] See J. L. Mackie, *Ethics: Inventing Right and Wrong*, Penguin Books, 1977; and Gilbert Harman, *The Nature of Morality: An Introduction to Ethics*, Oxford University Press, 1977, Section I.

[16] See Aristotle, *Nicomachean Ethics*, Book I, Sections 7 and 13; Christine Korsgaard, "On Having A Good," *Philosophy* 89 (2014): 405–429; and Sharon Street, "Nothing 'Really' Matters, but That's Not What Matters," *Does Anything Really Matter? Essays on Parfit and Objectivity*, Peter Singer, Ed., Oxford University Press, 2017, pp. 122–149.

[17] See notes 13 and 14.

sway all the skeptics). Instead, it (partially) explains why I cannot help being a value objectivist (perhaps with some vague Cartesian cachet—or taint—as the case may be).[18] As such, I am an objectivist about value for Everyday Meaning as well, though, as I'll explain, "Good-for" accounts of value are sufficiently non-subjective to avoid the absurdity of having to say that the blades-of-grass counter is doing something meaningful.

There are various versions of objective value meaning theories, all motivated to some degree by the seemingly obvious fact that you can be exceedingly wrong about value and meaning: wrong to think it's valuable or meaningful to spend your days counting blades of grass, killing innocent people for fun, counting your breaths per day, etc.[19] Objective value meaning theorists have arguments of varying strengths, grounded by a variety of underlying objectivist ethical theories.[20]

Regarding objective value theories, take your pick! I say that not because they are all equally compelling (they're not),[21] but because

[18] Descartes searches for truth in part by considering that which cannot be called into doubt, and one of the ways he tests for the possibility of doubt is whether he can imagine conditions under which the belief in question is false. See Rene Descartes, *Meditations on First Philosophy* (1641), Donald A. Cress, trans., Hackett Publishing Company, 1993, Meditation I.

[19] It is this intuition that motivates much of Erik Wielenberg's rejection of meaning subjectivism (see Wielenberg, *Value and Virtue in a Godless Universe*, Cambridge University Press, 2005, pp. 22–25). Wielenberg assumes an Aristotelian account of value, for the most part.

[20] Metz argues that a human life is meaningful to the extent to which, while observing moral constraints, one uses reason in ways oriented toward the good, the true, and the beautiful (*Meaning in Life*, chapter 13). He seems to rely mostly on Kantian ethical theory. Ben Bramble argues that leaving the world better off for your existence suffices for meaning ("Consequentialism About Meaning in Life," *Utilitas* 27 [2015]: 445–459). Bramble's view is explicitly Consequentialist. Smuts argues that your life is meaningful insofar as you are responsible for goodness (Smuts, "The Good Cause Account"). Smuts relies on Consequentialist ethical theory.

[21] Regarding meaning, because most versions of Consequentialism reduce all intrinsic value to happiness or the like, its conception of objective value is reductive and can fail to capture other values (though Consequentialists may argue otherwise). See Elizabeth Anderson, *Value in Ethics and Economics*, Harvard University Press, 1993; Judith Jarvis Thomson, "The Right and the Good," *Journal of Philosophy* 94 (1997): 273–298; and Richard Yetter Chappell, "Deontic Pluralism and the Right Amount of Good," *The Oxford Handbook of Consequentialism*, Douglas W. Portmore, Ed., Oxford University Press, 2020, pp. 498–512.

there is widespread agreement among most ethical theorists, philosophers writing about meaning, and the overwhelming majority of humankind, regarding the value of, say, kindness, justice, knowledge, beauty, freedom, love, etc., and, conversely, the negative value of cruelty, injustice, oppression, willful ignorance, hate, etc. It is to this widely agreed-upon set of values that I appeal when I say that Everyday Meaning engages with objective value. (We may disagree as to what is beautiful, kind, or just, but we generally agree that beauty, kindness, and justice are not worthless or contemptible ideals. They are valuable.)

For all of these reasons—because I'm persuaded by classic and contemporary value objectivists, because I find it impossible to imagine that value is entirely subjective, and because I think it's self-evident that you can engage with exceedingly wrong values for meaning, even if you think they're the right values—I conclude that the value that Everyday Meaning engages with is objective value (though "Good-for" value is sufficient). For reliable Everyday Meaning, the values you engage with should be cognizant of and conform to the constraints of objectivity (either straight-up objectivity or "Good-for" objectivity). Otherwise, you could end up ludicrously counting blades of grass while thinking that you're engaged in a meaningful project rather than wasting your chance at one or gratuitously killing innocent people while thinking you're aiming at a valuable end. For Everyday Meaning, the purposes and points that ground your efforts or toward which your efforts are aimed should be tied to values that are indeed valuable.

I am also a meaning objectivist because efforts, projects, and pursuits can be objectively meaningful in terms of their impact, significance, and explanation. Either your efforts have an impact or they don't. Did your scientific discovery make a difference to future inquiry or not? Did your work stocking supermarket shelves make it easier for people to find the food they needed or not? Did your dancing bring you joy and enhance your dance partner's experience or not? Impact is not entirely perspectival. Same goes for significance and explanation, and for the same reasons. Your efforts, projects, and pursuits are either significant or they're not. They either make sense, have coherence and explanation, or they don't. I see no reason to think that the thinking makes it so—that your subjective view is the only thing that counts—regarding these characteristics of meaning. Impact on yourself and personal significance can be meaningful as well, though whether they're present or absent from your efforts, projects, and pursuits is an objective fact, just as your headache is subjectively experienced but you either have one or you don't. Thus, there is an objective aspect to this subjective part of an objectivist account of meaning.

Finally, being an objectivist about meaning makes sense of the common ways in which a person's existence or experiences may be deemed meaningful even if the meaning is not experienced or even known by that person. Objective meaning makes sense of the meaning created when parents grieving the death of their infant decide to establish a charitable foundation in their baby's memory, or when friends of a murdered woman form a neighborhood watch in her name, etc. In these sorts of cases, which aren't unusual, the stated motive is not only perhaps to give meaning to the grieving person but, also and more primarily, to confer meaning to the dead people: that the loved ones will not have died "in vain," for nothing; that they will not have had a meaningless existence or suffered a meaningless death, even though the meaning conferred by the organizations established in their names will not be subjectively experienced by them.

Objective-Subjective Meaning

Even if we assume that there is objective value, we may wonder whether engaging with objective value requires a subjective feeling of engagement in order to be meaningful. This is Wolf's view. Wolf maintains that we must assume that there is objective value in order for the concept of meaningfulness to "be fully intelligible"[22] because it's absurd to consider a life that revolves around loving your goldfish to be meaningful even if it feels that way to you.[23] But she further argues that without the feeling of subjective engagement (i.e., "subjective attraction";[24] you're "into it"), even a person doing things that engage with objective value will not have meaning.[25] For Wolf, meaning requires a feeling of subjective engagement with objective value.[26]

This is different from thinking that you must *believe* your engagement with objective value is valuable in order for it to be meaningful. You might think that belief that you're engaging with objective value is a prerequisite for the subjective feeling of engagement, but the two don't have to come together: the feeling and the belief are separable. You might believe your engagement with objective value to be meaningful without having the feeling of subjective engagement, and you might have a feeling of subjective engagement without the belief that you're engaging with objective value. Wolf focuses on the subjective engagement—the feeling. For example, when you're planting a beautiful rose garden, are you into it or does it feel flat and empty to you? We may also consider whether the belief that you're engaging with objective value, or that you are making sense, having an impact, doing purposeful and significant things, is necessary for meaning. I've already shown that subjective belief isn't necessary for meaning. It's not necessary in terms of value, impact, explanation, coherence, purpose, or point. I'll now explain why subjective feelings of engagement are not

---

[22] Wolf, *Meaning in Life and Why It Matters*, p. 65.

[23] Wolf, *Meaning in Life and Why It Matters*, p. 16.

[24] Wolf, *Meaning in Life and Why It Matters*, p. 26.

[25] Wolf, *Meaning in Life and Why It Matters*, p. 20.

[26] Wolf, *Meaning in Life and Why It Matters*, p. 20. Wiggins argues for a weaker form of objective-subjective meaning, as he is much less confident about objective value than Wolf. (See Wiggins, "Truth, Invention, and the Meaning of Life.") He argues for an ill-defined middle ground that "allows the world to impinge upon but not to determine the point possessed by individual lives" (p. 378).

necessary for meaning either (though, as with beliefs, they can add to or enhance meaning).

The objective-subjective view of value and meaning avoids the absurdity of being wrong about value such that a life devoted to your goldfish is meaningful because you mistakenly think it is. But it doesn't avoid absurdity in the other direction: it doesn't avoid the absurdity of judging your time spent saving children from abusive parents as meaningless just because that's how it (erroneously) feels to you. Just as you can be wrong about value by engaging with less than valuable pursuits, such as counting blades of grass while feeling that is valuable and meaningful, you can be wrong about value by engaging in valuable pursuits, such as discovering the cure for a debilitating disease, while feeling that your efforts are worthless and meaningless (or simply not feeling that your efforts are valuable or meaningful). If being mistaken about value can mean your activity is meaningless even though you mistakenly feel it isn't, that logic works the other way as well: being mistaken about value can mean your activity is meaningful even though you mistakenly feel it isn't. Subjective feelings of attraction or engagement are not necessary for Everyday Meaning.

So why doesn't Wolf see this? Why does she add subjective engagement to her otherwise objectivist account of meaning? Wolf finds subjective engagement necessary for meaning because, she says, if your meaningful efforts are unfulfilling to you, then your life is not "satisfactorily meaningful."[27] This is true in a way: those kinds

---

[27] Wolf, *Meaning in Life and Why It Matters*, p. 111. Another reason why Wolf requires subjective engagement for meaning is connected to her metatheory of value, which is not our subject of inquiry, but is intriguing, and under-appreciated. According to Wolf, meaningfulness is not reducible to self-interest or morality and is "a third sort of value a life can possess" (p. 2). On this view, our actions or efforts can be motivated by self-interest, morality, or this third category of value: meaning. Fulfillment is a key component of this domain of value in which we do meaningful things out of love and resulting in fulfillment. E.g., she says love/fulfillment explains the good of visiting my friend in the hospital better than the alternatives, i.e., good for me, or morally good (pp. 49–50). Because Wolf finds that value theory can't provide adequate space for reasons of fulfillment, which are reasons of meaning, she argues for a third addition to what she takes to be an overly restrictive view of value. From this perspective, we can see why Wolf

of meaningful efforts won't be *satisfyingly* meaningful because you won't be satisfied. But they will still be meaningful. Something will be missing, surely, and something you probably care a lot about, namely, your own satisfaction. Yet it's not as if your satisfaction counts for nothing on an objectivist view of value because on all the central theories of objective value, a person has value, and their feelings and experiences have value as well.[28] In this way, personal, subjective thoughts and feelings of engagement, emptiness, happiness, fulfillment, depression, anguish, etc., all have objective value and a role in making your efforts and pursuits more or less meaningful. Time spent engaging with objectively valuable pursuits will be meaningful whether you feel that way or not, but it will be more meaningful if you find it fulfilling or otherwise satisfying because subjective experiences and feelings have objective value. The objectivist view of value and meaning correctly accounts for subjective beliefs, experiences, and feelings without having to grant special and unearned subjective authority to individuals about what is valuable. It avoids both the error of deeming your blades-of-grass-counting meaningful because you feel it is and the error deeming your cancer-curing meaningless because you feel that way, while also noting that pursuits that are subjectively experienced as fulfilling and meaningful are more objectively meaningful than those

finds subjective engagement necessary for meaning since fulfillment is subjective. I'm not persuaded by Wolf's argument for a third domain of value because I don't agree that the current value landscape restricts value to self-interest and morality. I think value is broad and encompasses all that is valuable for all the reasons things can be valuable. That includes reasons of personal well-being, abstract value such as truth or beauty, and interpersonal values, all of which can include both moral and non-moral reasons and also the reasons of fulfillment that Wolf thinks are left out (*Meaning in Life and Why It Matters*, pp. 49–50, 115).

[28] The welfare of a person is central to Aristotelian virtue ethics, which aims at well-being (Aristotle, *Nicomachean Ethics*, Book X, chapter 8). The intrinsic value of a person that demands treatment of persons as ends in themselves is central to Kantian ethics (Kant, *Groundwork for the Metaphysics of Morals*, chapter 2). The subjective happiness of persons is considered by most Consequentialists to have intrinsic value. (See Mill, *Utilitarianism*, chapters III and IV.) In this way, the subjective well-being of a person is valued in objective value theories.

same pursuits without those positive subjective thoughts and feelings.[29]

Subjective Meaning

For meaning subjectivists, however, it is *only* the subjective experience that determines meaning.[30] Subjectivists about meaning tend to be motivated by the intuition that meaning is closely connected to feelings of fulfillment and/or to personal well-being, or that meaning is a good and that good has to redound to the person.[31] They reason that since meaning is good for the person, objectivism is false because prudential value has to connect to what the person cares about in order to be good for that person.[32] Therefore, the reasoning goes, a meaningful life has to be appealing to the person living it[33] and fulfilling in ways that don't need to be objectively valuable.[34]

And, usually, people do feel fulfilled or otherwise satisfied when engaging in meaningful pursuits. But it need not be so, as we can easily imagine, and may well be acquainted with, people devoted to significant, impactful, valuable, and purposeful pursuits without feeling attracted to, engaged, or fulfilled by them. Detachment from

---

[29] Metz notes this as well (*Meaning in Life*, pp. 196–197).

[30] See Chesire Calhoun, *Doing Valuable Time: The Present, the Future, and Meaningful Living*, Oxford University Press, 2018, chapters 1 and 2; Jens Johansson and Frans Svensson, "Subjectivism and Objectivism About Meaning in Life," *The Oxford Handbook of Meaning in Life*, Landau, Ed., Oxford University Press, 2022, pp. 43–57; and W. Jared Palmer, "Meaning in Life and Becoming More Fulfilled," *Journal of Ethics and Social Philosophy* 20 (2021): 1–29, among others.

[31] See Johansson and Svensson, "Subjectivism and Objectivism About Meaning in Life," pp. 43–57; Palmer, "Meaning in Life and Becoming More Fulfilled"; and Daan Evers and Gerlinde Emma van Smeden, "Meaning in Life: A Defense of the Hybrid View," *Southern Journal of Philosophy* 54 (2016): 355–371.

[32] See Johansson and Svensson, "Subjectivism and Objectivism About Meaning in Life," pp. 46–47.

[33] See Evers and van Smeden, "Meaning in Life: A Defense of the Hybrid View," p. 369.

[34] See Palmer, "Meaning in Life and Becoming More Fulfilled," pp. 5–6.

valuable activity is a common symptom of depression, which is a common condition.[35] It doesn't render meaningful activity meaningless;[36] it just sometimes makes it feel that way.

Imagine Jonas Salk, on his deathbed, lamenting his meaningless career. "But you developed the polio vaccine, preventing countless cases of death or lifelong paralysis!" we say to him. "So what?" he replies. "Who cares? Polio, shmolio." What is our next move in this exciting deathbed conversation? Obviously, we might try to correct Salk's failure to appreciate his meaningful achievement as meaningful by trying to help him recognize or appreciate the value, impact, significance, purpose, and point of his meaningful activity. What we will not say is, "If you can come to be engaged or fulfilled by what you've done, only then will your efforts have been meaningful." Instead, we'll try to get him to see that his efforts are already meaningful. Alternatively, if we are having this sort of conversation with, say, a human traffic investigator, undramatically lying around on her regular bed, complaining about how unfulfilling and meaningless her work is, we might encourage her to choose a pursuit that she does find fulfilling since, as we noted, subjective feelings are one part of objective meaning and there are many meaningful activities to pursue.[37] What we will not do is agree with the human traffic investigator that her work is meaningless or claim that her work will only be meaningful if she feels fulfilled by it. And the opposite holds as well: we can imagine people engaged in efforts that are not meaningful while feeling fulfilled by them nonetheless.

[35] See American Psychiatric Association, *Diagnostic and Statistical Manual of Mental Disorders, Fifth Edition, Text Revision (DSM-5-TR)*, 2022, section on Depressive Disorders.

[36] Though it does detract from the meaningfulness because the subjective element is missing, as explained earlier.

[37] What if you have a choice between pursuing something very objectively meaningful that doesn't feel fulfilling to you and a less objectively meaningful activity that does resonate with you—which to choose? I don't think there is one answer to this question because I don't think all values are commensurable. Within the permission space of permissible moral activity, self-interest, and objective meaning and value, there is freedom of choice and not necessarily one clear "winning" choice.

If the delighted grass-counter is your husband or your grown child, will you be happy for them to have discovered a meaningful pursuit? Proud to see them so fulfilled? Doubtful. You might instead worry that your loved one has lost his mind.

Defenders of meaning subjectivism might agree that the fulfilled grass-counter has some internal mental or emotional pathology.[38] In fact, some subjectivists respond to the charges of absurdity posed by the fulfilled grass-counter by denying that a "normal" person would find trivial or pointless pursuits meaningful, saying things like: ". . . the life of a (very) *broadly normal adult human* [italics hers] cannot be meaningful to her if it is devoted to the keeping of a single, ordinary goldfish or to the counting of blades of grass."[39] But why not? Tellingly, we don't hear much from meaning subjectivists on this topic. It is taken as obvious. I agree: it's obvious. Why wouldn't a normal person find grass-counting meaningful? Obviously, because it's not! It's pointless, insignificant, and not valuable. Oops. I think we have just returned to meaning objectivism.[40]

Some resist objectivism about meaning because they see objective value as part of morality and meaning as separate from morality.[41] I agree that meaning is not the same thing as morality.

[38] See Calhoun, *Doing Valuable Time*, p. 43; and Nomy Arpaly, "Desire and Meaning in Life," *The Oxford Handbook of Meaning in Life*, pp. 356–370, 364–367.

[39] See Arpaly, "Desire and Meaning in Life," p. 365.

[40] Some argue that meaning is subjective even if value is objective because meaning involves subjective decisions about how to spend one's days. Harry Frankfurt can be interpreted to be arguing along these lines ("The Importance of What We Care About," *Synthese* 53 [1982]: 257–272). Calhoun explicitly argues this (*Doing Valuable Time*, pp. 35–44). Calhoun judges all assessments of meaning "fundamentally subjective" because we adopt ends for our own reasons. For Calhoun, the check on absurd meaning errors such as counting blades of grass comes from an individual's "normative outlook," which must survive reflection, including reasons not dependent on subjective perspective. She deems it unimaginable for counting blades of grass to survive the reflection of "any psychologically normal adult," yet she resists saying that the reason it wouldn't survive reflection is because it's grounded in patently mistaken values, even though her "reasons for anyone" standard seems to invoke an objective standard.

[41] See Calhoun, *Doing Valuable Time*, p. 43, and Wolf, *Meaning in Life and Why It Matters*, pp. 49–50.

As I've gone to great lengths to note, meaning includes but is not limited to moral value, or even all value. Meaning includes explanation, significance, impact, purpose, point, and all value (not only moral value). However, this does not entail that the value characteristic of meaning must refer to subjective value. We can accommodate the correct observation that meaning is not confined to moral value while remaining objectivists about the value characteristic of Everyday Meaning.

For those wary or skeptical of value objectivism, there is another way to retain sufficient non-absurdly subjective value for Everyday Meaning, and that is the concept of "good as 'Good-for'" or value as relative not to a subjective perspective but, rather, as relative to the kind of entity in question.

Good-For Meaning

Is music good? Is sunlight good? Is company good? To answer these questions, we might ask: "Good for whom?" Visual arts may be good for a person but probably not for a plant. Sun may be good for a plant but catastrophic for a vampire. Company is good for social beings, like people and dogs, but bad for tigers, who thrive in solitude. It's pretty easy to grasp the concept of "Good-for,"[42] and it is one way to explain how things can be non-subjectively good or bad, whether or not there exists non-relative objective value. For any functional system, we may say that whatever promotes, enhances, or maintains its function is good for it.[43] "Good-for" is objectively good relative to a *kind* of being. (Good, period, is

---

[42] Nevertheless, there is much debate, mostly in relation to questions regarding well-being, about exactly how to define "Good-for" and its uses. See, for example, Guy Fletcher, "The Locative Analysis of *Good For* Formulated and Defended," *Journal of Ethics and Social Philosophy* 6 (2012): 1–27.

[43] See Korsgaard, "On Having A Good," p. 418.

objectively good; neither subjective nor relative.) If you think that humans are a kind of being, we can then ascertain which kinds of things are good for or valuable for that kind of being. Aristotle famously thought this and it is built into his concept of flourishing and excellence (virtue).[44] Aristotle analyzes the kind of being we are—what is special or unique about humans? What distinguishes us from other entities?—to determine what our function is and what will help us flourish, and this analysis forms the basis for his view of virtuous living for humans as a life that realizes human moral and rational capacities.[45]

Some deny that people have anything in common in this sort of objective and inclusive way:[46] each person is like a snowflake; no two are exactly alike. Yet even snowflakes have characteristics in common: they're white, they're wet, they melt in the heat, etc. It is hard to deny that the same goes for people, that some things are good for all people, e.g., nourishment, the ability to exercise creativity, engage in social relationships, be free of oppression, etc.[47] You need not dogmatically insist that every child must learn a musical instrument and play a sport (why?) in order to acknowledge that people have some things in common to their functional systems such that certain things promote or prevent excellent functioning. Using the concept of "Good-for" allows us to delineate things that are good for people regardless of personal perspective without making claims to non-relative objective value. It allows us to avoid

---

[44] See Aristotle, *Nicomachean Ethics*, Book I, Sections 7 and 13.

[45] See Aristotle, *Nicomachean Ethics*, Book I, Sections 7 and 13.

[46] Sartre maintains that "it is impossible to find in each and every man a universal essence that can be called human nature" (*Existentialism Is a Humanism*, p. 42).

[47] Amartya Sen and Martha Nussbaum argue for an objective conception of human well-being, based on the Aristotelian view of human good as the capability to exercise human functionings. See Sen, *Commodities and Capabilities*, Oxford University Press, 1985; and Nussbaum, "Human Capabilities, Female Human Beings," *Women, Culture, and Development*, Jonathan Glover and Martha Nussbaum, Eds., Oxford University Press, 1985.

absurdly subjective accounts of value for Everyday Meaning even in the absence of non-relative objective value.[48]

"Good-for" is a way of thinking about value that doesn't demand belief in objective value yet is still non-subjective enough to avoid the Everyday Meaning absurdities we run into if we adopt a subjectivist view of value. Unlike value objectivism, which can inspire skeptical challenges,[49] a minimum of "Good-for" value is hard to deny[50] without seeming preposterous and having to deny that a ready supply of oxygenated air is good for people or that it is good for people to have the opportunity to learn about their environment. "Good-for" reasoning allows for some individual variation as well, insofar as we differ. Acknowledging the differences among us, despite our commonalities, allows for subjective engagement with what resonates, with what each person finds subjectively somewhat more or less fulfilling, from the menu of what is "Good-for" people in general (e.g., music lessons are good for one kid but a jump rope is better for another). In this way, just as value objectivists can accommodate the derivative and subsidiary role that subjective engagement plays within a non-subjective value theory, the "Good-for" value theorist can as well.

[48] Street argues for value that isn't mind-independent but doesn't lead to nihilism or meaninglessness ("Nothing 'Really' Matters"). Korsgaard goes further, arguing that without an interested party having a good, i.e., without a locus of goodness or a "Good-for," we can't even understand what good means; and that the condition of 'having a good' is prior to the good itself" ("On Having a Good," pp. 411–412). This doesn't entail that things are only good as a *means* toward some end. Rather, it means that once there are entities that *have* a good, being that kind of entity morally constrains how others may treat you. (Korsgaard argues this last part most directly in *Fellow Creatures: Our Obligations to Other Animals*, Oxford University Press, 2018.)

[49] See note 15 for prominent challenges to value objectivism.

[50] Yet it is denied nonetheless, though not in the direction of subjectivism. Thomas Hurka argues that "Good-for" is vague and adds nothing that we can't get from the concept of simply good ("Against Good For," *Philosophical Quarterly* 71 [2021]: 803–822). He argues that in order to compare Good-for A and Good-for B, you need simply-good and, once you have that, "Good-for" doesn't add anything. If Hurka is correct, we are back to value objectivism, but it's not clear that we can't compare Good-for A with Good-for B based on how the thing in question affects the functional systems A and B, and without appealing to "simply good."

Fulfilling One's Human Potential

According to both the objectivist and the "Good-for" conceptions of value, it's good for people to fulfill their positive human potential and exercise their capabilities for positive human functioning. In other words, good for people to exercise their awesome moral, intellectual, creative, social, and emotional capacities. (Let's call these "higher" functionings.) Higher human functionings include various artistic, creative, intellectual, and social disciplines and pursuits. It is therefore a broad category open to a wide variety of efforts. (One might consider some of the more impressive athletic feats and disciplines to be a form of bodily art or an expression of a form of creativity, for example.) Efforts and pursuits aimed at or grounded by these "higher" human functionings are more valuable and, in that way, more meaningful than spending your days admiring your goldfish, caring for your basic physical needs, or being a farmer who buys more land to grow more corn to feed more hogs to buy more land.[51] Positive efforts centered on "higher" human functionings engage more deeply and with more valuable values on both objectivist and Good-for accounts of value. They are therefore more meaningful in terms of value. They are also more meaningful in that efforts or pursuits that engage with higher human functionings tend to allow for greater impact and significance because the values, purposes, and points that provide the framework for impactful and significant efforts or pursuits are worthier. Thus, creating beautiful art, caring for your children, reading literature, or singing in your church choir will have greater impact and significance than eating a piece of cake or bathing.

Because pursuits involving higher human functions are generally more valuable and therefore more meaningful for people, following John Gray's recommendation to live more like a cat, which he describes as a life free of worries, free of anxiety about the world,

---

[51] See Wiggins, "Truth, Invention, and the Meaning of Life," p. 342.

just being in the world without the burdens of human consciousness,[52] is not the route to meaning. Although he is right to note, as did Camus,[53] that meaning is not a problem for cats, the solution to the problem of meaning is not to attempt to give up the quest, curl up on your sofa, and live like a cat. You're not a cat, and to aim to live as if you were is futile, contrary to meaning, and a waste of your human potential.

This doesn't mean that we all have to be intellectual snobs or drink dry wine rather than beer. (Both, always both.) But it does help explain why John Stuart Mill objected to Jeremy Bentham's hedonistic utilitarianism as "pig philosophy," for not ranking human capacities higher, as more valuable and more meaningful, than mere animalistic pleasures.[54] Because there is no shortage of valuable pursuits—art, love, knowledge, creativity, truth—there are many ways to engage with Everyday Meaning. Freedom, autonomy, and the human capacity for choice are "high" human functions and supremely valuable. This weighs in favor of pursuing vocations and avocations that resonate with you and pursuing, from among the many meaningful pursuits available, the ones that suit your individual tastes and talents.

Some of us are more ambitious, more capable, or more drawn to dazzling or more heroic efforts than others. Achievements that have exceptional impact and significance are extraordinarily meaningful. We won't all have that extraordinary degree of Everyday Meaning because, by definition, we can't all do extraordinary things. (If we did, they would be ordinary.) In some ways it's preferable to be unexceptional because exceptional achievement

---

[52] See John Gray, *Feline Philosophy: Cats and the Meaning of Life*, Picador/Farrar, Strauss, and Giroux, 2020, pp. 1–7.

[53] See Camus, *The Myth of Sisyphus*, pp. 51–52.

[54] See Mill, *Utilitarianism*, chapter II. Mill argues for ideal rather than hedonistic Utilitarianism, though it's Thomas Carlyle who is credited with using the term "pig philosophy" to critique hedonism. (Carlyle is widely quoted as deeming hedonism "a doctrine worthy only of swine," but none of the many conflicting citations I tracked down were accurate.) See also Mill, *On Liberty*, J. W. Parker & Son, 1859.

or renown often comes at a price: a price of privacy, psychological distress, and sacrifice of whatever may have been neglected to achieve the extraordinary, sometimes including other meaningful pursuits, such as intimately loving relationships.[55] That's why Joshua Glasgow advocates for ordinary, forgettable lives and against the urge toward what he calls the significance impulse, particularly as significance relates to living a meaningful life.[56] Glasgow argues against aiming at important achievement for meaning.[57] He emphasizes that you can live a meaningful, flourishing life as an ordinary person, usually more so than someone whose efforts are aimed at extraordinary achievement.[58] It would not be incorrect to characterize him as arguing for underachievement rather than overachievement as a meaning-enhancer. (If only he could have had a few words with your mother.)

And it is true that importance per se is not meaningful, but only if we define importance as exceptionality,[59] and not if we define importance as significance. The argument against importance and in favor of insignificance seems more applicable to aiming for fame and glory (which are superficial aims and perhaps not of genuine value) than to aiming at importance, defined as impact or significance tied to genuinely positive contributions or achievements. There is value in living an *ordinary* life, not an *insignificant* life. Importance refers not only to exceptionality, which is not necessary for meaning, but also to impact and significance, which are characteristics of Everyday Meaning worthy of our efforts. An "ordinary" everyday life of loving relationships and productive work that contributes to one's community is significant and important;

---

[55] See A. J. Plucker and J. J. Levy, "The Downside of Being Talented," *American Psychologist* 56 (2001): 75–76; Thomas Joiner, *Lonely at the Top: The High Cost of Men's Success*, St. Martin's Press, 2011; and Tyler Cowan, *What Price Fame*, Harvard University Press, 2000; among many others.

[56] Joshua Glasgow, *The Significance Impulse*, Oxford University Press, 2024.

[57] Glasgow, *The Significance Impulse*.

[58] Glasgow, *The Significance Impulse*.

[59] Glasgow, *The Significance Impulse*.

certainly meaningful. But the extraordinary impact and significance of genuinely positive extraordinary contributions or achievements, such as Martin Luther King Jr.'s impact on justice, or Dr. Jonas Salk's role in eradicating polio, are indeed extraordinarily meaningful.

How fortunate that they chose to put forth effort toward these outstandingly significant, impactful, valuable, and purposeful ends. What if they didn't? What if Martin Luther King Jr. decided to be a small-town minister like his father? If Jonas Salk decided to be a librarian? Although being a minister or a librarian is not insignificant or meaningless, wouldn't it be a shame if their outsized talents and abilities were wasted? A meaning misstep?[60]

Waste

Waste has a negative connotation. But what's wrong with it? Waste strikes us as wrong or disgraceful—a *shame*—because it constitutes a failure to properly appreciate value. Failing to appreciate value is similar, though not as blatant, to destroying something valuable for a trivial reason, like using the Notre Dame cathedral for tinder wood, or Van Gogh's *Starry Night* canvas for (very scratchy) toilet paper. Even if there are no competing property claims and you own these treasures free and clear, wanton destruction of value is an inappropriate response to value; a meaning fail. Notre Dame and *Starry Night* have artistic, historical, and cultural value, significance, purpose, and impact. To be blind to all that meaning is to fail to understand, respect, and properly respond to meaning. In the same way, and for the same reasons, wasting opportunities

---

[60] It's possible that outsized ambition and accomplishment contribute to meaning in life but don't always make a person happier. That may depend on how you define happiness. The narrower your definition of happiness, the less likely it is to capture all we care about and the less likely it is to compete with meaning as something worthy for us to prioritize.

for valuable engagement or wasting yourself, since persons have value,[61] is to make a grave meaning error.[62]

This doesn't mean that you have to toil all day every day, putting your all into your work, hobbies, and relationships, wearing yourself out to make sure you don't waste a drop of your potential. Waste involves a flagrant indifference to value, not a failure to maximize opportunities or be perfect. As Iddo Landau has emphasized, it is both narcissistic and cruel to oneself to aim only at perfection, to run only for the gold rather than for the bronze or for the exhilarating feeling of running in the park.[63] But, I might add, run! Do *something* that involves the exercise of your positive human potential. The grass-counter is not only missing the meaning mark by devoting herself to a pursuit that is not valuable, she is throwing her life away,[64] wasting her life. Similarly, if you can eradicate polio, deciding to be a middle-school librarian instead is a waste of your unique abilities; an insult to your human potential. If you could be a middle-school librarian, it is a waste of your abilities to spend your life bagging groceries. To respond to your own talents and abilities without due appreciation of your human potential is to make the meaning mistake of waste.

---

[61] Persons have value on objectivist theories of value (see note 28). It's not as obvious how "Good-for" value theories account for the value of persons (what are persons Good-for?) though I know of no "Good-for" value theorists that don't assume or assert the value of persons. Regardless, "Good-for" theories include opportunities for meaningful engagement as Good-for a person, and that is wasted when those opportunities are squandered.

[62] Frances Kamm similarly argues that wasting one's life displays an incorrect response to value ("Rescuing Ivan Ilych: How We Live and How We Die," *Ethics* 113 [2003]: 202–233). Joel Feinberg argues that failing to fulfill one's natural potential is a waste of one's life, but he doesn't articulate what is problematic about waste ("Absurd Self-Fulfillment," *Time and Cause*, Peter Van Inwagen, Ed., Riedel Publishing Company, 1980, pp. 255–281).

[63] Landau, *Finding Meaning in an Imperfect World*, chapter 3.

[64] Similarly, criminal justice systems that impose life sentences on youth are not only committing a likely injustice of disproportionality and failing to provide opportunity for redemption of a crime, but also the disgrace of throwing away a life, failing to appreciate its value.

Failure

Will some lives include more Everyday Meaning than others? Yes, considering that meaning includes value, explanation, impact, significance, purpose, and point. We will not all have everyday lives that are equally sensible, and we will not all have similar impact or engage in pursuits of equal significance. We will not all live by lofty values, and we will not all succeed in our efforts. The purposes/points for which we strive may not be reached. Even worse, if you never fail, you probably haven't aimed high enough and have therefore failed to respond properly to value. So, either way, failure awaits us all. And it's awful.

Don't believe what you hear. For the most part, failure is as bad as it feels, notwithstanding the efforts of legions of failure fans to put a good spin on it.[65] Failure can transform what might have been a significant achievement into a frustrated effort; what might have made a meaningful impact into a devastation of your struggles, hopes, and dreams. It certainly will not serve whatever purpose you were aiming at and it is usually, of course, crushingly pointless. Let's face it. Failure frustrates meaning and is inevitable. Ain't life grand?

Failure is so corrosively disappointing and so utterly ubiquitous that endless ink is spilled in the popular press, particularly from those who have enjoyed prodigious success, trying to convince us that failure is fine. Henry Ford, the automobile pioneer and magnate, said, "Failure is only the opportunity more intelligently to begin again."[66] Thomas Edison, inventor of the light bulb, the

---

[65] Recent popular books extolling failure include Ryan Leak, *Chasing Failure: How Falling Short Sets You Up for Success*, Thomas Nelson, 2022; and Dan Bongino, *The Gift of Failure*, Liberatio Protocol, 2023. Costica Bradatan, *In Praise of Failure: Four Lessons in Humility*, Harvard University Press, 2023, is a recent philosophical work extolling failure. These works mostly focus on lessons learned from failure or its character-building potential.

[66] Henry Ford in collaboration with Samuel Crowther, *My Life and Work*, Garden City Publishing Company, 1922, pp. 19–20.

phonograph, and many other successful technologies, is famous for saying that he didn't fail but, instead, "found 10,000 ways that don't work."[67] Arianna Huffington, wildly successful author and businesswoman and labeled one of the world's most influential people,[68] assures us that "failure is not the opposite of success, it's part of success."[69] It sure seems easier to stomach failure once you've succeeded.[70] However, although almost every success has failure behind it, not all failures lead to success.

Many think that it is the valued effort, striving, and pursuit that make for meaning, even if nothing comes of it. So long as the pursuit is aimed at an end valued by the person making the effort, meaning is retained even in the face of failure or incompletion, e.g., if the person dies mid-project,[71] because, the thinking goes, striving for a valuable end is sufficient for meaning, regardless of success.[72] Robert Adams notes that "Jesus failed in his crucifixion"[73] and Claus von Stauffenberg failed in his attempt to assassinate Hitler and overthrow the Nazi regime.[74] Yet it would be a misguided affront to label these efforts meaningless. Adams concludes that a life

[67] See Frank Lewis Dyer and Thomas Commerford, *Edison: His Life and Inventions*, Vol. 2, Harper & Brothers, 1919, pp. 615–616.

[68] See Bryan Robinson, "How Arianna Huffington Is Transforming America's Workplace to Benefit You," *Forbes*, January 15, 2020.

[69] Arianna Huffington, May 19, 2019. https://twitter.com/ariannahuff/status/1130 172552352063489?lang=en.

[70] On nearly every "quote" website on the internet, Winston Churchill, the former prime minister of the United Kingdom, who presided over the defeat of Nazi Germany in World War II, is quoted as having said: "Success is stumbling from failure to failure with no loss of enthusiasm." Wondering how well that slogan fares in war, I tried to track it down. According to *Churchill by Himself: In His Own Words*, Richard M. Langworth, Ed., Rosetta Books, 2008, it is "broadly attributed to Churchill but found nowhere in his canon" (p. 892). I too found it nowhere. A scandalous percentage of quotes about failure that proliferate on the internet are false attributions (they fail!).

[71] See Palmer, "Meaning in Life and Becoming More Fulfilled."

[72] See Robert M. Adams, "Comment," Wolf, *Meaning in Life and Why It Matters*; Feinberg, "Absurd Self-Fulfillment"; and Landau, *Finding Meaning in an Imperfect World*, p. 114.

[73] Adams, "Comment," p. 76.

[74] Adams, "Comment," p. 77.

can have meaning not merely in spite of failure but due to a project that has failed; a noble effort.[75]

These arguments are somewhat correct: a meaningful effort is meaningful, regardless of its outcome. It's meaningful in its significance, impact, coherence, and the values, purposes, or points at which it is aimed or by which it is grounded. However, an effort is almost always more meaningful if it succeeds than if it fails. If you're working on a book or raising a child, to fail in those efforts diminishes their meaning: the effort will have less impact, value, purpose, point, explanation, and significance. That's why it's so tragic. Similarly, it's noble, valuable, and meaningful to resist sadistic, megalomaniacal aggression but more meaningful to succeed in those efforts.

Imagine a life of failure: Your love goes unrequited, your marriage fails, you're estranged from your children, your friendships flounder. You fail the licensing exam for your chosen career (over and over), you lose every election you enter, you get demoted, you get fired. You're a moral failure too: you fail to resist the temptation to betray a trust and commit adultery, you can't stop being petty and insensitive no matter how hard you try, you plan to volunteer to help people but you never do. And you're also a garden variety, all-around failure: you kill every plant you try to grow, your singing is not melodic, your needlepoint crooked, your golf atrocious, your cooking revolting, your jokes lame; every team you're on does worse than they'd do without you. Brutal. "A for effort," and kudos to you for your noble striving, but we wish you'd have a modicum of success. Although it is meaningful to use your abilities, to strive to fulfill your human potential and to aim at valued ends, why think that it is just as meaningful to strive and fail as it is to strive and succeed? It isn't. That's why we aim at success! Although it doesn't wipe it out, failure generally diminishes Everyday Meaning.

[75] Adams, "Comment," p. 75.

On the other hand, imagine a life of unmitigated success. Flip our prior example to success, after success, after success in every area of human endeavor. It's difficult to imagine because it is so improbable and, although we might momentarily imagine ourselves enjoying some aspects of that sort of life, we don't want to meet the person who does. Imagine the arrogance, the entitlement, the smugness, the lack of empathy and compassion. Imagine the tedium. For meaningful success, it is necessary to aim high (as discussed), which means sometimes we will fail. Though quite the bitter pill, some failure may help us avoid becoming insufferable, may help us become sensitive and compassionate, and maybe help us learn from our mistakes. Experiencing some failure may add meaning to success because something precarious can be more precious and significant by virtue of being rare and hard won. Things that come too easily risk being easily taken for granted, not as valued, and in that way less meaningful. However, the deeper and more widespread the failure, the more it ravages the most significant and valuable purposes and points toward which one aims or by which one grounds one's efforts, the more that failure undercuts Everyday Meaning.[76] We need to aim high, risk failure, and sometimes fail for Everyday Meaning. Still, overall and for the most part, success is much more meaningful than failure because a successful endeavor usually has more positive impact, significance, point, and coherence than a failed effort.

Of course, some failures are the most significant and impactful aspects of a person's life and, in that way, the most meaningful, e.g., a lost love that colors one's life with painful longing and regret. But the meaning of these sorts of failures—the ones that have negative impact, significance, and value—is negative. Another way

---

[76] Kauppinen argues that success and meaning go hand in hand: "Life is ideally meaningful when challenging efforts lead to lasting success" ("Meaningfulness and Time," p. 346). Velleman argues that it is the narrative arc of success and failure within a life that determine its impact and value ("Well-Being and Time," *Pacific Philosophical Quarterly* 72 [1991]: 48–77).

for meaning to be negative is when the values that are successfully aimed at or by which efforts are grounded are negative values, as we noted earlier. When you aim at negative values or the opposite of value, then, of course, it's good if you fail and more negatively meaningful if you succeed.

Conclusion

For Everyday Meaning, it is important to aim high, try to fulfill rather than waste one's human potential, engage with objectively or "Good-for" valuable projects, efforts, and pursuits, and avoid excessive or extensive failure. Easy? Probably not. Worthwhile? If you are interested in a life with meaning, yes. Barring a miracle (up next!), it is likely the only way.

3

COSMIC MEANING

What Can a Miracle Do for You?

What can a miracle do for you? Let's wave our magic wands, open our minds to miracles, and see how much meaning we can conjure up. Of course, Cosmic Meaning need not be magical, theological, or supernatural. Cosmic Meaning refers to our role and its meaning in the cosmos, including our role as viewed from the cosmic perspective. This includes the purposes or point of the cosmos and our place in it, the value of our role in the cosmos, the impact we have on the cosmos, our significance within the cosmos, and the explanation provided by our cosmic role. All of this may be perfectly natural, though we might expect more Cosmic Meaning to be available through supernatural means.

When considering Ultimate Meaning, we saw that not even supernatural assumptions can change the sad conclusion of its impossibility. When considering Everyday Meaning, we confined ourselves to everyday, natural assumptions since that's the kind of meaning at issue: everyday, regular meaning. When considering Cosmic Meaning, most views are theistic and/or go beyond widely accepted natural explanations, which renders them vulnerable to skeptical challenges. That vulnerability is obvious and not my focus here. Rather than assess *whether* theistic, natural, or supernatural assumptions of Cosmic Meaning are correct, let's consider *what kind* of Cosmic Meaning any of those assumptions could yield: is it mind blowing and awesome or prosaic and lackluster?

Some may lose patience with this approach but, while to dismiss all theistic, supernatural, or natural but factually speculative accounts of Cosmic Meaning as just so much hocus pocus may be tempting to some, doing so fails to seriously contemplate what that sort of meaning could look like. It also fails to explore what many people take to be the most important source of meaning. Therefore, when considering Cosmic Meaning, I will grant all the magic and miracles anyone might want and take up these accounts on their own terms. Unfortunately, even that won't make Cosmic Meaning all that meaningful. As we will see, it doesn't amount to nothing, but it's not great or deep or anything nearly as spectacular as you might expect from a miracle. A surprising, perhaps sobering, but instructive conclusion. For meaning, heaven won't help much at all.

You might think Cosmic Meaning provides us with Ultimate Meaning by providing us with a point for leading and living our lives: e.g., the point of leading a life is to enjoy bliss, realize justice, serve god's perfect purpose, commune with god in the afterlife, or merge into the oneness of the universe. However, as we saw when considering Ultimate Meaning, this sort of cosmic purpose just widens or postpones the problem of pointlessness, leaving us to wonder, once we achieve the bliss, the justice, the achievement of god's perfect purpose, the communion with god, or the merging into the divine or universal whateverness, what the point of the rest of your afterlife is once you get there.[1] (You just moved the tomatoes[2] to the afterlife, so to speak.) Since our lives include their entirety, including any afterlife chapters, the problem of having no valued end separate from it to serve as a point for leading and living it remains. Ultimate Meaning is metaphysically impossible, and when something is metaphysically impossible, we have to accept that reality. Sorry to remind you of that sad fact.

---

[1] See in Chapter 1, sections "Overview" and "Live for Others."
[2] See in Chapter 1, sections "Overview" and "Live for Others."

Purpose

Although Ultimate Meaning isn't possible, maybe Cosmic Meaning is. Cosmic Meaning can't give us Ultimate Meaning, but what can it give us? Can it provide us with a cosmic purpose, a meaningful reason for why we find ourselves in our place or role in the cosmos? If so, maybe it can imbue our lives with purpose. We wouldn't be cosmically here for nothing, good for nothing, useless, purposeless clusters of particles briefly flitting about a tiny corner of the universe. There are both natural and supernatural accounts of our cosmic purpose. Before considering them and evaluating how cosmic purpose might make life more meaningful, let's consider whether cosmic purpose might make life less meaningful.

Demeaning?

Imagine discovering that you were created to provide entertainment to an alien community of sadists who enjoy watching you struggle and suffer and, of course, worry about meaninglessness. You have a purpose, but one that seems contrary to meaning. You're being used instrumentally, as a mere means, by immoral beings, in a way that is contrary to your well-being. Bad all around! Just as with any purpose, a cosmic purpose can contribute to negative meaning if that purpose is contrary to value.

Cosmic purpose may not enhance meaning much either if the purpose is trivial or disconnected from what we care about, even if it's not contrary to value. Nozick argues along these lines, setting a high bar for Cosmic Meaning: he maintains that being here to supply carbon dioxide for plants wouldn't be a meaningful purpose, nor would it do the trick if our purpose was the exercise of our rationality or moral agency, which we do value, in order to make our brains tastier to intergalactic travelers.[3] He thinks that a

---

[3] Nozick, *Philosophical Explanations*, pp. 586–587.

meaningful cosmic purpose would have to be positive and focused on "aspects of ourselves that we prize or are proud of"[4] and use them in ways connected to why we prize them.[5]

I think this goes too far in what is required for meaningful cosmic purpose. While I too would be displeased, maybe even insulted, to play a lowly cosmic role in these sorts of scenarios, those roles would still constitute a minimal kind of Cosmic Meaning. It may not be worth our while to bother living for the sake of plants, but providing life-sustaining air to plants is a purpose consistent with value and doesn't pose a threat to Everyday Meaning. Thus, a cosmic purpose that is valuable but perhaps not worthy of our efforts or even an insult to our preferred status (as star players, say) could provide us with a measure of Cosmic Meaning. Yet, there's still something problematic about it, in addition to the insult. Yes, we might feel insulted by a CO_2-generator sort of cosmic role, especially if we fancied ourselves destined for greater purposes. (Remember the Great Chain of Being? Humans were close to the top![6]) But the problem goes beyond an insult or disappointment to our grand ideas about ourselves. The problem is that just as we should try to actualize our human potential for Everyday Meaning, if our cosmic role failed to do justice to our potential, it would be an example of meaning waste and, in that way, a shame. It would still constitute positive Cosmic Meaning for us, but in a way that includes an insult, a waste, a disappointment.

Some think that any cosmic role not freely chosen would diminish meaning because it would degrade or demean us, using persons as tools[7] rather than as beings capable of fashioning their

---

[4] Nozick, *Philosophical Explanations*, p. 586.

[5] Nozick, *Philosophical Explanations*, p. 587.

[6] See Arthur Lovejoy, *The Great Chain of Being: A Study of the History of an Idea*, Harvard University Press, 1936.

[7] See Kurt Baier, "The Meaning of Life," lecture delivered at Canberra University College, 1957 (reprinted in *The Meaning of Life: A Reader*, E. D. Klemke and Steven M. Cahn, Eds., Oxford University Press, 2008, pp. 82–113).

own purposes.[8] Kurt Baeir says that asking for a cosmic purpose, i.e., asking someone what they are here *for,* treats a person like a *gadget*—here to be used for a purpose not their own, like a garden hose.[9] Jean-Paul Sartre reasons similarly, pointing out that if we're here as the object of a designer, like a knife fashioned by an artisan for a given purpose, then our essence will precede our existence, thereby limiting our self-possession, freedom, and dignity.[10] These arguments rightly note that being created for a purpose can be contrary to dignity because it may treat a person instrumentally, as a tool, rather than an autonomous agent with ends of her own. But they neglect the possibility of being created for the purpose of having or expressing self-creative freedom or the freedom to choose to participate in valuable purposes,[11] be they ones of your own making or purposes you couldn't achieve on your own. (Compare this to intentional procreation: you can create a child to serve as a free field hand or to nurture into an autonomous agent, free to choose her purposes.) Thus, while being created for a purpose can be a case of being treated as a mere means, which is contrary to human dignity and the value of autonomy, it doesn't have to be. If a person is cosmically here to be free to choose her own purposes and/or reflectively endorse purposes given to her as an option, then she may emerge from being created purposefully with her dignity and autonomy reasonably intact.

You might think all this hand wringing over autonomy neglects other values. If happiness is our unchosen cosmic purpose, who cares if we didn't choose it? Freedom isn't superior to happiness,[12] is it? I won't attempt to settle this complex value disagreement

---

[8] See Sartre, *Existentialism Is a Humanism,* pp. 20–22.

[9] See Baier, "The Meaning of Life," p. 101.

[10] See Sartre, *Existentialism Is a Humanism,* pp. 20–22.

[11] Timothy Mawson and Metz argue along these lines. See Mawson, "What God Could (and Couldn't) Do to Make Life Meaningful," *God and Meaning: New Essays,* Joshua Seachris and Stewart Goetz, Eds., Bloomsbury, 2016, pp. 37–58, 39–40; and Metz, *Meaning in Life,* pp. 103–104.

[12] See Joshua Seachris, Metz and Seachris, *What Makes Life Meaningful? A Debate,* Routledge, 2024, pp. 63–64.

here, but consider: Say that instead of discovering you're here to entertain alien sadists with your suffering, you discover you're here to entertain alien non-sadists, who cry at your sorrows and rejoice in your happiness. Would that purpose provide you with Cosmic Meaning, or would the fact that you are, even in this happier case, being used as a mere means to someone else's purposes without your consent or reflective endorsement make this a demeaning purpose contrary to meaning? I think the fact that this purpose renders you a tool, a mere means to someone else's purpose, makes this purpose contrary to meaning even if it coincides with or requires your happiness. If you care more about happiness and less about autonomy and respect, you might disagree. (This differs from being created to provide CO_2 for plants in that exhaling doesn't cost you or treat your deepest emotions and struggles as entertainment. It wastes your potential, which is a meaning waste, but it doesn't otherwise demean your agency, as you would be demeaned if created for entertainment.) There are also purposes we may not be able to achieve on our own and, if those purposes are valuable, the mere fact that we didn't invent them or choose them does not, by itself, render our involvement with them demeaning. You can even be a non-agential subject of a meaningful purpose in a non-demeaning way, e.g., if a charitable foundation is established in your memory. A forced purpose might be still meaningful if the purpose is valuable, e.g., conscripts fighting a just war (some World War II conscripts fighting the Nazis for the Soviets expressed this view).[13] So long as your involvement is with a valuable purpose and doesn't usurp your agency to use you as a mere tool for someone else's purposes alien to yours, it doesn't have to be demeaning. I conclude that in order for a cosmic purpose to be a significant meaning enhancer rather than a meaning detractor

---

[13] Reported to me by Landau, regarding conversations he had with former Soviet conscripts who fought against the Nazis under hard and unfree conditions.

(or a "don't care"), it should be a valuable purpose consistent with human potential. Let's see if we can find one.

Here for the Happiness ☺

Bliss, man. We're in it for the bliss. Many accounts of cosmic purpose, most famously Christian accounts of people created by a perfect god in order to give us a beatific afterlife, hold that our cosmic purpose is perfect happiness.[14] On this view, we are created by a benevolent god for the purpose of enjoying perfect happiness. We trudge through our lives of quiet desperation,[15] usually we have Everyday Meaningful purposes, hopefully we do some good deeds, and then we die and achieve our cosmic purpose of perfect, everlasting bliss, basking in the glory of god, metaphorically sunning ourselves in heaven. That seems appealing, even mouthwatering, like levitating in clouds of cotton candy. But does it sound meaningful? Happiness or bliss is valuable and, in that way, meaningful. But why be created to live a life of suffering if your purpose is perfect happiness? Why not skip this mortal life altogether and go directly to perfect happiness without the unpleasant terrestrial detour? The answer to this question tells us why bliss per se is not very meaningful: unearned happiness is a positive emotional state but it is not, in itself, especially meaningful. It's of value so it's not completely meaningless, but it is not very meaningful (just desirable).[16] Other values can be meaningful in themselves, e.g., love

---

[14] See Keith Ward, "Religion and the Question of Meaning," *The Meaning of Life in World Religions*, Joseph Runzo and Nancy M. Martin, Eds., Oneworld Publications, 2000, pp. 24–25; Stewart Goetz, "Hedonistic Happiness and Life's Meaning," *God and Meaning*, pp. 59–80; Seachris, *What Makes Life Meaningful*, p. 196; and Goetz, *The Purpose of Life: A Theistic Perspective*, Continuum/Bloomsbury, 2012, pp. 7–15.

[15] See Henry David Thoreau, *Walden* (1854), *The Writings of Henry David Thoreau*, vol. 2, Houghton Mifflin, 1906, p. 8.

[16] Metz argues that happiness itself is not meaningful at all, as he thinks is shown by Nozick's famous experience machine example (see Metz, *What Makes Life Meaningful*, p. 174).

or truth, and sometimes they also make you happy. But happiness per se doesn't seem very meaningful. Deserved happiness is more meaningful, and it is to that kind of happiness that accounts of our blissful cosmic purpose refer.[17] If your bliss is just handed to you, you'll enjoy it, but it may not mean very much to you. However, if you earn it, your happiness will be more meaningful because it will be an end that you merited, a purpose realized.

The reason deserved happiness is more meaningful than undeserved happiness is because it results from some other achieved purpose, aim, or even inherently valuable characteristic (e.g., a naturally equanimous character). It's the value of *that* valued end that provides the meaning. The happiness is an added bonus, whose meaning mostly derives from the value of what has been realized or achieved. For example, if your money is handed to you by your hard-working grandfather, it is likely less meaningful to you than if you earn it yourself, but that's because what is valued is whatever you do to deserve the money. The money is not the meaning; the meaning derives from the value of what you do to deserve it. If the kindest kid in kindergarten gets a kindness award which comes with a delicious piece of cake, the happiness she gets from the cake is meaningful mostly because of the valuable purpose it was given to celebrate. The cake is a nice add-on—just as a blissful afterlife would provide a sweet dessert to life, but the cake itself—the blissful afterlife itself—doesn't seem very meaningful or purposeful. If our cosmic purpose is deserved bliss, that bliss itself would be only minimally meaningful. What might be meaningful is what we did to deserve it, but those happiness-deserving acts or attitudes are done in our everyday life and part of our Everyday Meaning.[18]

---

[17] See Thomas Aquinas, *Summa Theologiae* (1265–1274), Fathers of the English Dominican Province, Benziger Bros, trans., 1947, 1a 2ae. 3. 2 ad. 4; Goetz, *The Purpose of Life*, pp. 153–168; and Seachris, *What Makes Life Meaningful*, pp. 194–197; among many others.

[18] The cosmic aspect of those acts may be the justice or reward awarded in the afterlife (see the section "No-nonsense Value," later in this chapter).

Communion

Imagine the deepest, most caring, most intimate and satisfying connection. Love, but to an infinite degree and of a sublime kind. Communion is a name for this unique, transcendent rapport; a relationship with god that's deeper and more meaningful than happiness. Many argue that this is the Judeo-Christian view of our cosmic purpose: to commune with god in the afterlife.[19] It's what John Paul II meant when he said that it is the "fullness of communion with God which is the goal of human life,"[20] and what some think of as the moral of Ecclesiastes.[21] It is also part of the Talmudic description of the afterlife: "In the world to come, the righteous sit . . . enjoying the radiant splendor of the divine presence."[22] We become capable of communing with god through our suffering, faith, good works, worship, etc., in this life,[23] where we begin to develop our relationship with god. Then we die and fulfill

[19] See Aquinas, who says that human beings "attain their last end by knowing and loving God," *Summa Theologiae*, 1a 2ae. 1.8. (The last end consists in the beatific vision, which is where the happiness comes in. Aquinas seems to consider communion a state of perfect happiness—I treat happiness and communion as separate ends.) See also Richard Swinburne, "How God Makes Life a Lot More Meaningful," *God and Meaning*, pp. 149–164; and Philip L. Quinn, "How Christianity Secures Life's Meaning," *The Meaning of Life in World Religions*, pp. 53–68; among many others.

[20] Pope John Paul II, Catechesis at the General Audience, July 21, 1999, https://www.vatican.va/content/john-paul-ii/en/audiences/1999/documents/hf_jp-ii_aud_21071999.html (Website of The Vatican: https://www.vatican.va/content/vatican/en.html).

[21] See Tremper Longman III, "'Meaningless, Meaningless, Says Qohelot': Finding the Meaning of Life in the Book of Ecclesiastes," *God and Meaning*, pp. 231–246, 243.

[22] *The William Davidson Talmud*, Koren-Steinsaltz, trans., Sefaria, *Brachot* (c. 500) 17a: 12.

[23] See Swinburne, "How God Makes Life a Lot More Meaningful," pp. 160–161; Aquinas, *Summa Theologiae*, 1a 2ae. E.s. ad.4; *The New Testament*, King James version, Romans (c. 55–58), 5:3–5 and James (c. 44–48), 1:2–4; Simcha Paull Raphael, *Jewish Views of the Afterlife*, 2nd edition, Rowman & Littlefield, 2009, pp. 120, 288; and Zohar (c. 1250–1305), David Solomon, trans., Margalya Press; Melbourne, 2024, III 53a; among many others. In Islam, the role of worship is paramount, both in this life and in the relationship with god in the afterlife (see Imam Kamil Mufti, "Meaning of Life in Islam," *Arab News*, June 4, 2024, https://www.arabnews.com/islam-perspective/news/868496, and Qur'an [c. 610–632] 51:56, https://legacy.quran.com/, among many others).

our cosmic purpose in an everlastingly fulfilling relationship with a divine being.

Communion seems more meaningful and less superficial than happiness. Unlike happiness, communion isn't just a positive psychological state that we desire; communion is a special kind of intimacy and, like love, is a way of relating to another. Relating usually involves actions, sentiments, and attitudes. So if our cosmic purpose is communion, what happens when we achieve it? Do we just bask in its glow, sizzle in its warmth? As with happiness, that emotional state of feeling closeness does not, by itself, seem very meaningful. It hardly seems like a relationship. For our eternal communion with god to count as a relationship, it has to involve a way of relating. And, indeed, theologians describe communing with god in the afterlife as an infinitely satisfying *relationship*. Richard Swinburne says: "Since God is a being of infinite wonder, it can take beings of finite power an eternity to comprehend him."[24] John Seachris explains that since communion with god is not something you do for the sake of completion (i.e., it is an *atelic* act, valuable in the doing), "relating to an infinite God would be the absolute pinnacle of *atelic* experience: an inexhaustibly good and positive experience that never ends," just as "the wonder of experiencing" the "depths of another person" may be inexhaustible.[25]

But god wouldn't be exploring your depths since an omniscient god knows all about you already. The communing relationship would be one of infinite inequality. We can appreciate an infinite being, we can delight in a perfect entity, we can enjoy the love given to us by an infinitely wise and loving god, regardless of inequality or even partly due to the inequality—the greatness of god constitutes much of the greatness of the relationship with god. But it also unavoidably renders the relationship infinitely unequal, which is off-putting, especially as a purpose. Not all valuable relationships are

---

[24] Swinburne, "How God Makes Life a Lot More Meaningful," p. 160.
[25] Seachris, *What Makes Life Meaningful*, p. 198.

equal, of course. Parent-child relationships are unequal in power and capacity, yet still valuable. However, parents and children are the same kind of being (albeit at different stages of maturity), usually with equal inherent capacity. And, usually, both parents and children benefit from their loving relationship, which grows more equal over time. If we created children intending to keep them in an infantile state, that too would be an objectionably unequal relationship. We can't say that pets and humans are of similar capacity, but both humans and pets are biological animals, with lots in common. Arguably, both humans and pets benefit from their relationship (if not, then that relationship is likely problematic, and it may be problematic regardless). That wouldn't be the case in a human-god relationship. By communing with god, "we are made partaker of the divine nature,"[26] which sounds appealing. But it is also largely a receiving role. We would be the beneficiaries in that relationship, metaphorically sucking forever on god's infinite teat. That kind and degree of inequality[27] can render a relationship negative, of negative value, the presence of beneficent intimacy notwithstanding, especially if we were expressly created for that purpose. Imagining myself sucking forever on god's infinite teat is not an appealing image, even if god lovingly pats my head while I do it (and even if god likes it—god shouldn't want this sort of relationship either). It's objectionably unequal and in that way inconsistent with the positive value of intimate relationships.

Not all are equally troubled by inequality in relationships, but this extreme lopsidedness is not just a problematic relationship. Worse, and more to the point, in terms of purpose, it's kind of

---

[26] John Owen, *Communion with God: Fellowship with the Father, Son, and Holy Spirit* (1657), chapter III, Section 4.3.

[27] Guy Kahane thinks this gives us reason to hope that god doesn't exist. He argues that god's existence would curtail our "*independence*," making us childlike and objectionably servile. He takes servility to be bad even with a benevolent master because it "involves a failure of self-respect . . . a failure to recognize one's true moral status" (see Kahane, "If There Is a Hole, It Is Not God Shaped," *Does God Matter? Essays on the Axiological Consequences of Theism*, Klass J. Kraay, Ed., Routledge 2018, pp. 95–131, 112–113).

pathetic: we are *partakers*; destined not for greatness but to render ourselves capable of appreciating or partaking in someone else's greatness—"enjoying the[ir] radiant splendor."[28] That's not a purpose worthy of our efforts or potential. Although there's nothing inherently objectionable about appreciating or communing with something far greater than oneself, e.g., being inspired by nature or taking a class in order to better appreciate sophisticated works of art, to have your entire existence predicated on that derivative sort of purpose would be demoralizing. That's all you're for? To appreciate or partake in something else? It's almost like having no real role at all—like being cast as audience in your theater group's play. Communing with god in the afterlife is not a purpose worthy of us, and the relationship is a mixed bag: you get the beneficent intimacy but in ways that render it somewhat distasteful and contrary to other important values. (Even if we assume an imperfect god, the nature and abilities of an infinite, brilliant, being powerful enough to be a god would still yield a profoundly unequal relationship.)[29] Because communing with god in the afterlife involves negative value and is a purpose unworthy of human potential, it is not a promising route to Cosmic Meaning.

Merge into Ultimate Reality

An alternate view of human cosmic purpose regarding a relation to the divine involves merging into the mind of god, infinity, or ultimate reality: You return from and disappear back into whence you came, like a wave returns to the ocean, and all of your suffering is

---

[28] Talmud, *Brachot* 17a: 12.

[29] If we assume a flawed god-light entity, then the afterlife loving relationship would be more similar to earthly love, which is valuable, and therefore meaningful. But it's not infinitely meaningful as an eternal *purpose* due to its limitations which prevent continual progression without rendering the love "too much," and contrary to value. See the section "Everlasting Value," later in this chapter.

ended (as are you).[30] You're able to achieve this union or reunion upon dying by being a good person here on earth: being compassionate, honest, not materialistic or egoistic, etc.[31] This conception of human cosmic purpose is central to many versions of Buddhism (*nirvana*)[32] and Hinduism (*moksha*),[33] and it is also found in some views of Judaism[34] and perhaps Taoism.[35] A common theme to these conceptions of human cosmic purpose is that earthly life is a travail of suffering caused by separation or alienation—the "heart-wrenching sorrow of separation from God."[36]

If the disease is separation, it stands to reason that reunion is a cure. Thus there is a clear logic to this account of cosmic purpose. But does it describe a meaningful cosmic purpose? To find your way home and disappear? To what end? You go back from whence you came and by ceasing to exist as a self in this process of reintegration you thereby end your suffering. That's less anguishing than continuing to flounder about aimlessly, like a forlorn lost soul.

[30] See John Hick, "The Religious Meaning of Life," *The Meaning of Life in World Religions*, pp. 269–286; Keith Ward, "Religion and the Question of Meaning," *The Meaning of Life in World Religions*, pp. 11–30, 21; and Masao Abe, "The Meaning of Life in Buddhism," *The Meaning of Life in World Religions*, pp. 153–161, 159–160.

[31] See Waka Takahashi Brown, "Introduction to Buddhism," *Stanford Program on International and Cross-Cultural Education*, December 2002, https://spice.fsi.stanf ord.edu/docs/introduction_to_buddhism; Runzo, "Meaning and Asian Religions," *The Meaning of Life in World Religions*, pp. 105–108; and Abe, "The Meaning of Life in Buddhism," pp. 160–161.

[32] See Obayashi, Ed., *Death and the Afterlife: Perspectives of World Religions*, Praeger, 1991, Part III: Death and the Afterlife in Eastern Religions.

[33] See Hick, "The Religious Meaning of Life," pp. 269–286.

[34] See Matt, *The Essential Kabbalah: The Heart of Jewish Mysticism*, Castle Books, 1997.

[35] There are many references in encyclopedic articles to this view in Taoism (see Wikipedia, "Taoism," subheading *Soteriology and Religious Goals,* https://en.wikipe dia.org/wiki/Taoism#cite_ref-FOOTNOTERobinet199750_62-0; Jessica Mousseau, "Taoism Beliefs and Holidays," *Diversity Resources*, https://www.diversityresources. com/taoism-beliefs-and-holidays/; and "Taoism," *National Geographic* Education, Encyclopedic Entry, https://education.nationalgeographic.org/resource/taoism/) but I could not trace these summary articles to primary Toaist texts expressing this view (even when following their citations—the works cited did not express this view in Taoism as far as I could discern).

[36] Runzo and Martin, "Love, Relationships, and Religion," *The Meaning of Life in World Religions*, pp. 179–184, 181.

But nature offers us an end to suffering as well, via biological death. How much more meaningful is it to merge into the mind of god and become one with ultimate reality than it is to rejoin and become part of the earth via decomposition, "ashes to ashes" and "dust to dust"?[37] The only difference is that you don't have to behave well, grow spiritually, or renounce your ego during this life to ensure the end of your suffering and your return to the universe upon death. Perhaps that speaks more directly to the value of morality and the virtuous life rather than to the meaningfulness of being assigned the cosmic purpose of finding your way home. If our cosmic purpose is to return from and disintegrate into whence we came, that is hardly inspiring. It doesn't seem like a particularly meaningful purpose. (GPS, anyone?)

Value

Some think that the universe itself aims at value and that this is the purpose of the universe, i.e., cosmic purpose.[38] This is different from considering the value of our cosmic role or our cosmic value.[39] The argument here is that the universe *itself* has a purpose, and that its purpose, its aim, is moral value. Considering all the random suffering caused by the universe itself—mudslides, cancer, earthquakes, floods, and "how does the baldness fit in?"[40] —you might conclude that the universe is a terrible marksman. If it's aiming at value, it sure seems to miss a lot. Its misses notwithstanding, some

---

[37] *The Book of Common Prayer* (1549), Anglican Liturgy Press, 2019, "Burial of the Dead/The Committal," p. 261.

[38] See Philip Goff, *Why: The Purpose of the Universe*, Oxford University Press, 2023; and Tim Mulgan, *Purpose in the Universe: The Moral and Metaphysical Case for Ananthropocentric Purposivism*, Oxford University Press, 2015.

[39] See the section "Value," later in this chapter.

[40] In the TV series *Seinfeld*, the character George Costanza (played by Jason Alexander) says this in response to Jerry Seinfeld saying, ". . . it's all part of a divine plan." See *Seinfeld*, "The Apartment," Season 2, Episode 10, first aired 4/4/1991. Written by Peter Mehlman.

argue that the universe's physical laws are fine-tuned toward life, which they take to be objectively valuable, and that this fine-tuning for life cannot be accidental or a result of non-agential causes.[41] The fine-tuning for life argument is based on the understanding that the "standard model" of particle physics includes constants (e.g., the masses of fundamental particles and the strength of the forces that govern them) required to make the equations of the model work and the odds of those constants required for life are, they say, nearly impossible to have occurred by chance. (E.g., had the strong nuclear force been even .008 higher, most of the hydrogen would have burned off, precluding most of the chemical complexity in the universe, thereby also precluding life, which is chemically complex.)[42] Consciousness is also sometimes cited as best causally explained by intentional rather than accidental forces.[43] Some therefore conclude that the universe has purposes and those purposes include or imply a universe aimed at moral value, since life and consciousness are fundamental to moral value.[44]

If the universe itself intentionally aims at value, whose perspective is this? Who is the agent that is the universe? Tim Mulgan argues for an intentional creator of the universe who is not focused on people. He argues that the suffering we endure shows that people are irrelevant to god's purposes.[45] For similar reasons, Philip Goff also rules out a benevolent god.[46] Instead, he posits "pan-agentialism," as the best explanation for some mysteries in

[41] See Goff, *Why*, pp. 16–46; and Mulgan, *Purpose in the Universe*, pp. 99–129.

[42] See Goff, *Why*, pp. 17–22; and Mulgan, *Purpose in the Universe*, pp. 10, 109–129. There are many ways to challenge these arguments and their conclusions—we can challenge their applications of probability theory, the certainty and completeness of the standard model, what can constitute life, what life can be made of, etc.—but that's not my objective here.

[43] See, Goff, *Why*, pp. 47–84; and Mulgan, *Purpose in the Universe*, p. 25.

[44] Goff, *Why*, pp. 20, 75–76, 131–133; and Mulgan, *Purpose in the Universe*, pp. 346–347. They both seem to assume that Utilitarianism constitutes moral value, but they don't provide any arguments for that assumption (Goff, *Why*, pp. 137–139; and Mulgan, *Purpose in the Universe*, pp. 25–26).

[45] See Mulgan, *Purpose in the Universe*, pp. 1, 220–260.

[46] See Goff, *Why*, pp. 85–110.

quantum mechanics,[47] and according to which agency is everywhere in the universe, such that: "Particles are never compelled to do anything, but are rather disposed, from their own nature, to respond rationally to their experience."[48] Goff further claims that whenever there is indeterminacy, the purposeful laws of the universe will aim at value.[49]

These claims can seem fantastical. An atom-agent? From the incomplete scientific understanding of consciousness and cosmology to a creator that's just not that into you? To be fair, I did say that I would grant all the magic necessary to consider Cosmic Meaning possibilities. But these value accounts of cosmic purpose are supposedly scientific so their implausibility is more problematic. However, even though natural accounts don't really merit the practical leeway given to supernatural accounts since they claim not to need any magic wands, I will grant the premises here an (ill-fitting) magic wand and consider whether this sort of cosmic purpose can provide us with Cosmic Meaning.

You might think a cosmos aimed at value is the most meaningful reality we can hope for. Goff does. He says that a good cosmic purpose to which we can "contribute to through our actions" is "tantamount to winning the reality lottery"[50] because "If we were able to contribute, even in a small way, to the good purposes of *the whole of reality*, that would be as big a difference as you can imagine making and would consequently greatly add to the meaning of our lives."[51]

Why, though? Swooning over "whole of reality" may be a case of confusing cosmic purpose with Ultimate Meaning and concluding that by participating in the purpose of the universe you can be

---

[47] See Goff, *Why*, pp. 55–70. These mysteries include the collapse of the wave function and why systems depart from some predictions associated with quantum mechanics. (You might wonder whether attributing agency to every particle in the universe solves more mysteries than it creates.)

[48] Goff, *Why*, p. 59.

[49] Goff, *Why*, p. 115: Whenever there is indeterminacy, "the teleological law directing the universe towards life will kick in, ensuring that X rather than Y occurs."

[50] Goff, *Why*, p. 4.

[51] Goff, *Why*, p. 4.

part of something greater than or beyond yourself—one of the classic (yet failed) prescriptions for Ultimate Meaning. But there is no route to Ultimate Meaning. The universe's purposes, insofar as you aim at them, are your purposes too and part of or inside of the project, effort, or enterprise of leading your life. They therefore can't provide a point to running that life in the first place.[52] If cosmic purposes are contrary to your purposes or are purposes you don't aim at, then it's hard to see how they would add much meaning to your life.[53] (If I win the reality lottery, I'd be pretty disappointed if the prize is the serving of some alien purpose.)

However, Goff contends that we contribute to the good purposes of "the whole of reality" in an agential way, by being moral, since: "True ethics is a concern to *make reality better.*"[54] Setting aside what constitutes "better" in this context and whether this is what "true ethics" is about, what if there's no cosmic purpose? Do we not then still contribute to the good of reality and make reality better by being moral? When I sacrifice half of my donut to my neighbor, do I not thereby make reality better in the same way and to the same degree as I would if doing so thereby also advanced the aims and purposes of the cosmos? When I devote my Thursday morning to planting wheat or loving my children, am I doing that in an unreal realm, making no difference to reality? Obviously not. *Whatever* we do contributes to reality because that's where we do everything we do and affect everything we affect—right here in reality. So what meaning is added by having the good purposes we have in being moral also be the good purposes of the universe itself? (Who cares about the universe?)

---

[52] See Chapter 1.

[53] If we just happen to play an important non-agential cosmic role, such as providing CO_2 for plants, that could constitute a minimal sort of Cosmic Meaning. Minimal because we have nothing to do with it—the meaning would be merely incidental. Compare: if someone starts a valuable charitable foundation in your name after you die, usually you would have had something to do with it—some relationship or values, *something*. If you truly have nothing but an incidental relationship to that foundation, then it wouldn't lend much meaning to the life you had lived.

[54] Goff, *Why*, p. 138.

If any meaning is added by this kind of cosmic purpose, perhaps it is due to how *much* of reality we contribute—arguably, if we participate in cosmic purposes, we contribute not only to earthly reality but also to *all* of reality; to "the whole of reality," rather than only to the part of reality we affect via our Everyday Meaningful projects and purposes. Having a greater effect can be more meaningful in terms of impact and significance. However, in fact, the effect here is not greater in terms of impact and significance because who is affected and what difference the effect makes is the same whether there is cosmic purpose or not. Your half-donut eating neighbor is the same infinitesimal part of the cosmos whether the purposes furthered by your generosity are everyday only or also cosmic. She's the same fraction of the whole of reality affected or made better by your half-donut gift. Therefore, how much of reality we contribute to by being moral cannot be the meaning difference that the value view of cosmic purpose makes. The only difference, then, is that if there are cosmic purposes, then there's some other agent involved, i.e., the cosmos itself, whose purposes you serve by splitting the donut. So contributing to a cosmic purpose is like helping your cousin pitch a tent—contributing to someone else's valuable project or a joint valuable project—i.e., joint Everyday Meaningful purposes. I don't see why or how the fact that in the cosmic purpose case the other agent is the universe itself makes this more meaningful or meaningful in a different way than Everyday Meaningful purposes. (Who cares about the universe?)

In order for the purposes of the universe itself to add Cosmic Meaning to our lives, we would have to be meaningfully connected to the universe itself and its purposeful intentions.[55] Then the fact

---

[55] Maybe that's what the expression "one with the universe" is intended to convey. But that union—that connection—needs to be spelled out in order to see whether it can give us Cosmic Meaning. I argue here against this possibility. A caring universe is more like a god—an agent who is involved in the universe and who cares about you. We have already considered godly cosmic purposes and found them wanting in terms of Cosmic Meaning.

that our purpose is also the purpose of the universe might be meaningful in virtue of our meaningful connection to the universe itself. For example, if I write the most creative work of fiction ever written, that can be meaningful to me for my own purposes, for the pride of my family, for the country that provided the conditions of freedom and security for my work, and even for all of humanity that can read it. If the purposes of my family, my country, and my fellow humans include the art I create, then the meaning of my purpose in creating it may be enhanced insofar as the purposes of my family, my country, and humanity matter to me. Since my family, my country, and other people care so much for me and are connected to my own work and purposes in various ways (as just outlined), my purposes are enhanced by also being their purposes (and vice versa). We cannot say the same about a universe that doesn't seem to care much about us (even on these views that claim the universe itself is purposeful) and to which it would be very difficult to personally relate. The meaningful connection between ourselves, our purposes, and the purported purposes of the universe is missing. (If we're talking about the purposes of a universe that does care about us and to which we are personally connected, that's something similar to a god-like entity, whose cosmic purposes we have already considered.)

What's the connection, then, between valuable cosmic purposes and meaning? Mulgan says that the reason cosmic purposes should matter to us—should be significant, and in that way meaningful for us—is that the morally valuable reasons inherent to cosmic purposes "(partly) *constitute*" human well-being.[56] In other words, we should care about cosmic purposes because they're moral purposes constitutive of human good. If moral purposes are an integral aspect of our well-being, they

---

[56] Mulgan, *Purpose in the Universe*, p. 343.

will be valuable and significant to us, i.e., meaningful. But we can value morality directly for this reason, whether it is also a cosmic purpose or not. No meaning is lost by valuing morality directly and leaving the universe out of it. If the universe has its own purposes, they don't seem to confer Cosmic Meaning to us. (All together now: Who cares about the universe?)

Let us then consider cosmic value directly as a source of Cosmic Meaning.

Value

Value is a crucial characteristic of meaning and the source of much of our Everyday Meaning. Valued ends provide us with everyday points and purposes; provide explanation for many of our everyday efforts, projects, and pursuits which aim at valued ends; and partly determine the impact and significance of the meaningful efforts we engage in. Beyond the part played by value in Everyday Meaning, some think that cosmic value—value based on our role in the cosmos or value from a cosmic perspective—provides us with Cosmic Meaning due to its perfect nature, its everlasting duration, its ability to makes sense of some value dilemmas, and its providing us with value from a cosmic perspective.[57]

---

[57] See Scott Davison, "God and Intrinsic Value," *Does God Matter?*, pp. 40–45; John Cottingham, "Theism and Meaning in Life," *European Journal for Philosophy of Religion* 8 (2016): 47–58; Seachris, *What Makes Life Meaningful*, pp. 144–155; Mulgan, *Purpose in the Universe*, pp. 7–15; Goetz, *The Purpose of Life*, p. 32; Kant, *Critique of Practical Reason* (1788), Werner S. Pluhar, trans., Hackett Publishing Company, 2002, II 2, p. 113; Charles Taliaferro, "The Expansion and Contraction of the Meaning of Life," *God and Meaning*, pp. 137–147; Mawson, "Theism and Meaning in Life," *The Oxford Handbook of Meaning in Life*, Landau, Ed., Oxford University Press, 2022, pp. 229–242; Cottingham, "Meaningfulness, Eternity, and Theism," *God and Meaning*, pp. 123–136; and Brooke Alan Trisel, "How Human Life Matters in the Universe," *Journal of Philosophy of Life* 9 (2019): 1–15; among many others.

Perfect Value

Say there's a maximally valuable being. Arguably, a universe that included that sort of entity would be more valuable than one that didn't because it would include infinitely more value; value of an infinite degree and of an infinite kind (by including the perfect characteristics of immutability, simplicity, and atemporality).[58] In this way, the existence of a perfect god may be taken to translate into a more valuable world, a world with more cosmic value and, therefore, more Cosmic Meaning.[59] But we may wonder how this makes our lives more Cosmically Meaningful. Merely coexisting in a more valuable universe doesn't tell us how that cosmic value reaches us or pertains to us.

One way we might incorporate perfect cosmic value into our existence is by participating in its purposes by aiming at it aspirationally, but that seems no different from the ways in which we aim at value in our everyday lives and thereby engage with Everyday Meaning, nor different from how we might aspire to perfect goodness even if it didn't exist in the universe. It is therefore hard to see how the bare existence of a maximally valuable being would enhance the Cosmic Meaning in our lives just by being there.[60]

Maybe we can get Cosmic Meaning out of a perfect being by engaging in a relationship with it. Relationships are often meaningful (purposeful, valuable, significant, impactful, etc.), so maybe relating to a perfect god would be cosmically meaningful since it would connect us to infinite cosmic value. Alas, we have already

---

[58] See Metz, *Meaning in Life*, p. 99.

[59] See Davison, "God and Intrinsic Value," pp. 40–45.

[60] Metz provides a further argument against this kind of cosmic purpose, arguing that god's perfect qualities of atemporality, simplicity, and immutability "are incompatible with purposiveness" because purposes are temporal and changeable, involving goal-directed activity (see Metz, *Meaning in Life*, p. 106).

noted that a relationship with a perfect being is fraught with imperfections of its own.

Many think that a perfectly good god is necessary for objective value, which, in turn, is necessary for Everyday Meaning. On this view, the existence of perfect cosmic value makes both Everyday Meaning and Cosmic Meaning possible because it provides the ground for objective value.[61] In my view, there are persuasive arguments for the existence of objective value regardless of cosmic value.[62] But if those arguments weren't persuasive, I don't see how the existence of a maximally valuable god would help because deeming an entity maximally valuable implies that we already have independent standards for what counts as maximally valuable, i.e., for what meets the criteria, for what actually is valuable. You might think that value is *set* by god, i.e., that something is only good because it is so designated by god.[63] But that's really not a reason for deeming something good—an arbitrary designation is not a reason for deeming something good. Presumably, an omniscient god would designate things as good for the reasons that the things were indeed good, i.e., for the reasons independently applicable. I conclude that a perfectly good god is neither necessary nor sufficient for objective value. (Although this debate remains quite live in the literature,[64] I find the logic conclusive.)

[61] See Cottingham, "Theism and Meaning in Life," *European Journal for Philosophy of Religion* 8 (2016): 47–58; Seachris, *What Makes Life Meaningful*, pp. 144–155; and Mulgan, *Purpose in the Universe*, pp. 7–15; among many others.

[62] See Chapter 2, section "Subjective or Objective Meaning?"

[63] This is similar to the question famously explored in Plato's *Euthyphro* dialogue: Is something good because the gods deem it good, or do the gods deem something good because it is good? See Plato, *Euthyphro* (c. 380 BC), *Plato: Five Dialogues: Euthyphro, Apology, Crito, Meno, Phaedo* (c. 387–400 BC), G. M. A. Grube, trans., Hackett Publishing Company, 2002, 10a.

[64] For recent insights into this debate, see Harriet A. Harris, *God, Goodness, and Philosophy*, Routledge 2011; and David Baggett and Jerry L. Walls, *Good God: The Theistic Foundations of Morality*, Oxford University Press, 2011.

No-nonsense Value

When values aren't realized, the world can seem to make no sense. So much senseless suffering, unreasonable miscarriages of justice, and the seeming imbalance of bad things happening to good people. Cosmic value, particularly cosmic justice, can right this imbalance by rewarding the virtuous and punishing the wicked in the afterlife. Everyone gets their just deserts and the world makes sense. To many, the jarring unfairness of miserable good people and happy terrible people is deeply disturbing, even disorienting. If a morally reprehensible person lives a life just as happy as a morally upstanding person, then you might think "life seems deeply absurd."[65] Therefore, some posit that, "God exists to make sure that happiness and morality meet and embrace in the afterlife. If they do embrace, then things fit together as they should in the end because the desire for perfect happiness is fulfilled."[66]

It's a romantic picture: the embrace of happiness and morality in heavenly skies. Kant, not known as a romantic, shares this vision. Although Kant argues that happiness and virtue are not logically or causally bound,[67] he finds this problematic because he views morality as practical rationality and happiness as a practical human end.[68] Since there is no harmony of happiness and morality in this life, where happiness can be a matter of chance, Kant argues that it makes sense for there to be an afterlife where this harmony can be achieved.[69] Similarly, the Hindu and Buddhist doctrine of *Karma*,

---

[65] See Goetz, *The Purpose of Life*, p. 32.

[66] See Goetz, *The Purpose of Life*, p. 178 (for Goetz, the happiness is perfect because it is proportioned to virtue/desert). And see Kant, *Critique of Practical Reason*, II 2: 113 for a similar view.

[67] Kant, *Critique of Practical Reason*, II 2: 113.

[68] Kant, *Critique of Practical Reason*, II 2: 113.

[69] Kant refers to this state of deserved happiness, where happiness is proportioned to virtue, as the *summum bonum*, or the highest good for which we should strive. Since it can't be achieved in this life, in order to be promoting something achievable (since "ought implies can"), we need god to accomplish this for us in an afterlife. See Kant, *Critique of Practical Reason*, II 2:110–113; and II 5: 124–125. Mackie critiques this "ought implies can" reasoning, arguing that just because we should strive for something

i.e., that your status of fortune in this life is determined by your right actions and attitudes in a past life and will determine your status of fortune in your next life, is a system of cosmic justice wherein the scales of justice match a person's well-being.[70]

Yet why assume that well-being and happiness *should* coincide? Why does it make more sense or defy explanation any less for a charitable person to have a headache than for a miserly person to have one? A headache has nothing to do with generosity. Cosmic justice only solves a problem or makes more sense if you assume that being good and faring well should go together. But right action and good fortune are not the same thing, so why would one cause or guarantee the other? The Stoics knew this. That's why they told us that virtue is its own reward.[71] Virtue can still be otherwise rewarding sometimes and, to an extent, it often seems to be: if you're kind and industrious, you're likelier to get along well with others and have good relationships and work habits, which contribute to success and satisfaction in many areas of life. But that doesn't mean you won't be betrayed by a friend, or chronically depressed, or that your child won't be murdered or die of a brain tumor. Why would it? Only if you assume that this is the more "sensible" universe. If you remove that unwarranted assumption, then your virtue makes sense even if your house is flattened by a cyclone because virtue is justified by its own value and doesn't prevent cyclones. You do the right thing because it's the right thing to do. To act morally in order

doesn't mean it has to be achievable—the ought here is "strive," the "can" is we can strive for the *summum bonum* (see Mackie, *The Miracle of Theism: Arguments for and Against the Existence of God*, Oxford University Press, 1983, pp. 106–110).

[70] See Joseph Runzo, "Meaning and Asian Religions," *The Meaning of Life in World Religions*, pp. 106–107; and A. R. Wadia, "The Philosophical Implications of the Doctrine of Karma," *Philosophy East and West* 15 (1965): 145–152.

[71] See Marcus Tullius Cicero, *Treatise On the Commonwealth* (c. 58–43 BC), Francis Foster Barham, trans., Edmund Spettigue, 1841–1842, *De Legibus* [Laws] 1.48. Incidentally, it was also Cicero who coined the term *summum bonum*, the highest good, which he argued was virtue. See Cicero, *De finibus* (45 BC), Walter Miller, trans., Harvard University Press, 1913, Book II, 37 ff. Kant disagreed (see note 69).

to achieve good fortune is like expecting to feel full after giving your meal away to the indigent. You might feel good, and full of benevolence, but your stomach will register as empty because it is. If you do the right thing to escape misfortune, it is you and not the cosmos that is lacking in sense because you seem to be ignoring much of what we know about cause and effect, and connecting things that are not practically, scientifically, or even conceptually tethered.

We may reasonably be resentful when other moral *agents* act unjustly toward us because they're not meeting their moral obligations to us (presumably). That's unjust and perhaps a disruption of the social contract upon which we may reasonably depend. You might include god as an agent whose natural system makes you suffer the "slings and arrows of outrageous fortune"[72] and think he ought to make that up to you in the afterlife. Perhaps cosmic justice can help us with these problems, though it's not simple to see how (and it won't have anything to do with explanations or making sense). To illustrate: Say I spend most of my life in prison for a crime I didn't commit because a corrupt group of people conspired against me for fun. They had a good laugh. I die in prison and I'm buried in the prison yard where I spent my time being bullied by people there for crimes they did commit. God knows, that's all very unfair. And god does know: in heaven, my name is cleared, my reputation is restored, and I enjoy heavenly bliss. Those responsible for my unjust suffering are duly punished. Does that undo the original injustice? I still spent my life in jail, an injustice that remains. But maybe it's "made up" to me by my restored reputation, blissful afterlife, and, of course, the suffering of my tormentors. Here, finally, we may have arrived at a way for cosmic value to be Cosmically Meaningful to us. (Though not because it adds sensible or explainable value to the cosmos. It adds, restores, or provides a more functional version

---

[72] William Shakespeare, *Hamlet* (1603), Early American Imprints, Series 1, no. 27692, 1794, Act III, Scene One.

of justice, which is a value, so it's more meaningful in terms of the value of justice.)

However, after a very long while the suffering of my earthly tormentors becomes itself unfair. They have come to see the error of their ways, they have apologized, they have suffered, and there's nothing more they can do to redress their wrongs. Their further suffering seems unjust. God knows this too. So their punishment is over and eventually they too enjoy eternal heavenly bliss. (It's unjust to let any earthly action have much eternal effect since that seems disproportional, so eventually everyone will have to be given the opportunity to improve their station in the afterlife. Given forever, it's likely we then eventually all end up in the same blissful state.) The people who suffered more natural evils are given special afterlife perks too but not forever, because that would be unfair to those who suffered fewer natural evils since the difference in their suffering was not infinite. If we assume a just, eternal afterlife, then we probably all end up the same after a period of punishment, atonement, and improvement that pales into insignificance over the course of eternity.[73] (If you think that periods of suffering are not erased or made insignificant by subsequent good of any length of time, then afterlife justice can't work to redress earthly injustice.) So even cosmic justice in the afterlife may not fix the so-called nonsense of justice unserved, happiness finding a home in the wrong people, natural evils, etc. Karma fares no better in this regard because it too eventually leads either to eternal suffering, which seems unjust, or to ending up in the same state of nirvana, an eternal state compared to which the finite time that came before is insignificant. Thaddeus Metz raises the possibility of a finite afterlife where justice is served, over, and done,[74] like a comforting epilogue to a

---

[73] For more on this topic, see Metz, *What Makes Life Meaningful*, p. 192; Mawson, *Monotheism and the Meaning of Life*, Cambridge, 2019, p. 53; and Metz, "Comparing the Meaningfulness of Finite and Infinite Lives: Can We Reap What We Sow if We Are Immortal?" *Royal Institute of Philosophy Supplement* 90 (2021): 105–123.

[74] Metz, *What Makes Life Meaningful*, p. 121.

disturbing novel. I'm not sure if all that metaphysical work is worth the trouble for a quick settling of accounts, but it's a possible route to gain an additional measure of justice without veering into injustice or undoing the rectification. Thus, cosmic justice can potentially provide us with a better working version of justice, though its value as a settling of accounts epilogue to life is less than most views of the afterlife imagine (since it is finite, limited, and delayed), and it doesn't contribute to the explanation aspect of meaning.

Everlasting Value

A crucial difference between everyday value and cosmic value is that cosmic value can last forever, assuming an infinite afterlife. When something valuable lasts forever, its value may persist and can therefore be more meaningful due to its perpetual value, enduring impact, and eternal significance. It's often taken as obvious that enduring value is more meaningful than temporary value. If something is valuable, why would you want it to stop?[75]

Because, at some point, it's enough already. The love grows too sweet, the justice irritatingly exacting, the beauty overstimulating. Thus, although value can conceivably last for an infinite duration, it is harder to conceive of it continuously growing in value. That's not to say it would become tedious—it's just that it couldn't continue to grow in a positive way because there seems a limit to how much value can grow before backfiring. In order for everlasting value to remain positive, we would have to stop the love from growing before it becomes cloying or suffocating, the justice before it becomes nitpicky and tyrannical, the knowledge before it becomes overwhelming or irritatingly detailed, etc. And then, to

---

[75] See Taliaferro, "The Expansion and Contraction of the Meaning of Life," pp. 137–147, 145. Goetz agrees (as does nearly everyone else), arguing that the intrinsic goodness of that which is intrinsically good gives us reason to hope it never ends (see Goetz, "Hedonistic Happiness and Life's Meaning," *God and Meaning*, pp. 59–80, 64).

prevent a reduction or diminishment of value, and seeing as more of it would be too much, freeze that epitome of value in its optimal state. It would then be a pleasant state, but its meaning would be somewhat arrested since you're not doing anything; all is static, stagnant. In a way, its own kind of death. Arguably, that would be more meaningful than biological death, which stops your experience of value completely, and almost certainly not in any optimal state. (I'll talk about death and the relationship between transience and meaning in the next chapter.) While everlasting cosmic value cannot be dismissed as meaningless, it's not infinitely more meaningful in quality (only in duration) than everyday value because in order to remain valuable it's hard to imagine it continuing to grow without tipping into negative value. If all a miracle can give us is a static state, even one put into stasis at the ideal value point, that is a meaning disappointment. Not meaningless, but not all that meaningful either.[76]

Value from a Cosmic Perspective

If a godlike entity values us, some say that would make us cosmically valuable because we would then matter in this expansive way, from the point of view of the being whose eye sees all. This can simply be because god's loving care "raises us to such an extent" that we are infinitely valuable from an eternal perspective,[77] or because our valuable actions matter eternally because they matter to an eternal being.[78] Another way we might be cosmically valuable is

---

[76] This reasoning applies to the view of the afterlife as one where people grow in their godlike nature. See *The New Testament*, 2 Peter (c. 62–64) 1:4 and 2 Corinthians (c. 53–55) 5:17. Whatever qualities you are developing—compassion, wisdom, justice—at some point, you will reach the optimal level of these qualities, etc.

[77] See Mawson, "Theism and Meaning in Life," p. 240.

[78] See Cottingham, "Meaningfulness, Eternity, and Theism," *God and Meaning*, pp. 123–136, 123.

if we are valuable to the cosmos itself in virtue of some of our valuable characteristics or contributions.[79]

It's nice to be valued, which can include love, care, and respect—all forms of value that are usually meaningful when executed in ways that are not contrary to value, e.g., smothering. Being valued by god is one way to be valued and would provide us with this form of cosmic meaning. Of course, we have no shortage of valuers here on earth with us and, in most societies, many of our fellow earth-dwellers value us. How much meaning it adds to our lives to have god on the list of those who value us depends on the kind of god and how that god values us. The security and infinity of god's love are a special and important valuing and, therefore, meaningful, but we might wish there wasn't that sort of overshadowing, paternalistic, meddlesome being in our lives at all. You might worry that god's valuing us includes aspects of negative value: Many versions of god are all-seeing and all-knowing, which can be seen as the most extreme version of stalking.[80] Being god's precious child is a way to be meaningfully cosmically valued, but it renders us children, contrary to the value of independence. A perfect god should do a perfect job of valuing you, thereby solving this problem.[81] But a perfect god and a god that values you perfectly seem in tension with each other since omniscience is part of perfection so an all-knowing god will know all about you (stalker!), and omnibenevolence is part of perfection and an all-good god might sometimes need to interfere with human agency in order to maintain the goodness of the universe (meddler!), etc. An imperfect god is unlikely to value you perfectly, since, being imperfect, he might not know how, or might not be powerful or good enough to do so, etc. Being valued by a

[79] See Trisel, "How Human Life Matters in the Universe," p. 4; and Guy Kahane, "Our Cosmic Insignificance," *Nous* 48 (2014): 745–772.

[80] Kahane argues that because an all-knowing god would invade our privacy, we have reason to wish that no such god exists (see Kahane, "If There Is a Hole, It Is Not God Shaped," *Does God Matter*, pp. 95–131, 95).

[81] See Michael Tooley, "Axiology: Theism Versus Widely Accepted Monotheisms," *Does God Matter*, pp. 46–69.

flawed god may be more similar to being valued by a person: valuable, but not because there's something distinctively cosmic about it. Therefore, what being valued from the cosmic perspective amounts to and whether the Cosmic Meaning derived from being valued by god is positive or not is something of a toss-up.

Another potential benefit of being valued by god is that since our valuable actions matter to god, they matter forever because god is forever.[82] This is a different kind of everlasting value, in which what persists is the valuer rather than the valuable effects of the valued effort itself. So long as someone still cares that you kissed your baby, that kiss retains value; so long as someone still remembers your song, that song retains value. This eternal cosmic value may blunt the effects of time's wearing away at meaning to some extent. God cares and god's caring lasts. On the flip side, negative value persists as well because god remembers the negative value of your ignoring your friend's phone call long after your friend has forgotten about that minor slight.[83] So this form of cosmic value has its dark side.

Finally, we have value from a cosmic perspective, irrespective of god, due to the value we add to the cosmos. This too must include both the positive and negative value we add to the universe.[84] Arguably, our moral, rational, and creative capacities are intrinsically valuable; valuable on Earth (contributing to Everyday Meaning) and in the cosmos (contributing to Cosmic Meaning). It's not clear to me why we should care very much about the value we contribute to the cosmos per se, as opposed to the value we contribute to Earth. Assuming that we are a valuable part of the

---

[82] Trisel, "How Human Life Matters in the Universe."

[83] We can imagine a god that only remembers the good, but the inauthenticity of that sort of memory adds negative value and, since so many good and bad things are mixed together or are good for one and bad for another, even a god might have a hard time accomplishing this sort of memory trick.

[84] Benatar, for example, argues that people are so bad and add so much negative value to the world as to argue in favor of human extinction (*Better Never to Have Been: The Harm of Coming Into Existence*, Oxford University Press, 2006, p. 224).

cosmos, how cosmically significant that value is may depend on what else is out there. I turn now to that question.

Impact and Significance

Impact

How significant something is, i.e., how much it matters, often is dependent on impact. We likely have little impact on the cosmos, which appears incomprehensibly vast and governed by powerful physical forces. The planets maintain their orbits, the sun its nuclear reactions, the black holes do whatever it is they do, and we have no impact on any of it. Human impact seems more local, confined to planet Earth and its environs (and individual impact is even more localized). As for our impact on Earth, we may worry that we're on course to ruining it by killing, eating, and burning nearly everything on it. Eventually, we might turn Earth into a dead planet. Yet what's one more dead planet in a universe littered with them? Even our most extreme Earthly impact would likely have negligible impact on the cosmos overall.

Unless we're the only place in the cosmos teeming with life, love, passion, art, morality, genius, and incredible beauty. If we ruin *that*, then we will have had a significant impact on the cosmos because we will have destroyed the most valuable place in the universe. That's one way we could have significant cosmic impact— negatively. We could have positive cosmic impact by making or keeping our corner of the cosmos valuable. There's a limit to this impact because humans aren't the only source of life, love, passion, art, genius, and beauty on Earth. Other life forms seem to love, be creative, and have culture and abilities we likely don't fully know or appreciate.[85] And there have been other forms of life fairly similar

[85] Andrew Whiten, "The Burgeoning Reach of Animal Culture," *Science* 372 (2021): 6537; Thom Scott-Phillips and Christophe Heintz, "Animal Communication in

to us (Neanderthals, for example), produced by forces and causes irrespective of humans.

Significance

Absolute or intrinsic significance can come from the nature of the thing itself, e.g., a person or a gorgeously red rose; relative significance depends on context, e.g., the broken knuckle on your finger is insignificant when you've also been shot in the face. Guy Kahane claims that while value can be both intrinsic and relative, cosmic significance is "importance ... all things considered"[86] (i.e., relative to all things) and, consequently, our cosmic significance depends on how cosmically unique we are.[87] He therefore concludes that our cosmic significance depends how alone we are as intelligent beings in the universe and how much we can claim to be *standing out* relative to the rest of the cosmos.[88] If we're not alone in the universe, then, he says: "Our significance would be massively diluted. ... And things would be worse if our greatest achievements pale in comparison to those of numerous more advanced civilizations."[89]

Linguistic and Cognitive Perspective," *Annual Review of Linguistics* 9 (2023): 93–111; and Björn Ólafsson, "New Research on Animal Communication Shows Their Cultures Are Often Complex and Cumulative," *Sentient Science*, May 1, 2024, among many others.

[86] See Kahane, "Our Cosmic Insignificance," p. 750. Bertrand Russell goes further in thinking of significance as only relative, arguing that because our lives are small and transitory we cannot think of them as significant (see Russell, "A Free Man's Worship," 1903, *The Basic Writings of Bertrand Russell 1903–1959*, Robert E. Egner and Lester E. Denonn, Eds., Simon and Schuster, 1961, pp. 66–72). This too neglects intrinsic significance and assumes, without sufficient reason, a direct and proportional relationship between size, duration, and significance. In response to Russell, Williams argues that there's no cosmic lens from which to assess significance and, therefore, our lives are significant so long as they are significant to us, from our point of view (see Williams, "The Human Prejudice," *Philosophy as a Humanistic Discipline*, Princeton University Press, 2006, pp. 135–154, 137–145).

[87] Kahane, "Our Cosmic Insignificance," pp. 750–762.

[88] Kahane, "Our Cosmic Insignificance," p. 459.

[89] Kahane, "Our Cosmic Insignificance," p. 762.

This perspective neglects intrinsic significance, which does not depend on how many things there are that can be considered similar to you. Although there are billions of people in the world, Kahane is wrong to conclude that we are each, therefore, "terrestrially insignificant"[90] because significance—how much something matters—has both an intrinsic and a relative component. There's no shortage of people in the world, "plenty of fish in the sea," yet each person matters. Each person, like Walt Whitman, "contain[s] multitudes";[91] each person, a world,[92] because each person has unique, untransferable, unfungible, and intrinsic value. You can't kill a person and claim you did something insignificant because there are billions of other people. There is an intrinsic kind of significance, just as there is an intrinsic kind of value because how much something matters cannot be divorced from its value. Generally, the more valuable something is, the more significant it is: the more it matters if you lose it, destroy it, ignore it, create it, nurture it, etc. Intrinsic significance doesn't disappear no matter how widely you pan out—even as far out as the entire cosmos—because it is inherent in the thing itself. Therefore, since we are intrinsically significant, we are significant wherever you find us. In this way, we have cosmic significance because we are significant in and of ourselves, and therefore significant anywhere, including the cosmos within which we reside. Does this make our lives more Cosmically Meaningful? I don't think so because it doesn't change how significant we are. It just reflects a fact about where that significance is located: in the cosmos.

---

[90] Kahane, "Our Cosmic Insignificance," p. 762.

[91] See Walt Whitman, "Song of Myself," stanza 51, *Leaves of Grass*, Rome Brothers, 1855 (titled in 1891, in a later edition).

[92] This biblical concept is traced to the creation of mankind from one man, Adam, in *The Old Testament*, The Contemporary Torah, Jewish Publication Society trans., Sefaria, Genesis (c. 1400 BC/disputed) 1:26–27; and *The New Testament*, Acts (c. 60–90) 17: 26–27. See Talmud, *Sanhedrin* 37a (c. 450–550), based on Mishna, Koren-Steinsaltz, trans., Sefaria, *Sanhedrin* 4:5 (c. 100–300).

However, there's also a relative aspect to significance. If we are the only planet with self-aware beings on it, that would make us very cosmically significant, just like the fact that there is only one *Mona Lisa* makes it more significant than if Da Vinci had created hundreds of identical *Mona Lisas*. Since we don't know whether the cosmos is filled with advanced civilizations, moral, creative, and loving beings or filled with light, rock, and dust, we cannot yet know how relatively cosmically significant we are. Should we hope for the dust world so that we are not mere dust in the wind in cosmic comparison? Being cosmically relatively significant in this way would give us more Cosmic Meaning in this respect but at the cost of living in a cosmos with significantly less cosmic value overall (which is how we get to be relatively so cosmically significant). Thus our relative cosmic significance would come at a high cost of cosmic value and would not be worth that meaning price. It would be like wishing that the oak tree in your front yard was the only oak tree on earth so that it would have more relative significance. The cost of that trade-off is the loss of the value of all the other oak trees (and whichever other ecological losses would follow from that). Spare us such cosmic significance.

Finally, on some conceptions of god, we might be relatively cosmically significant in the eyes of god or because of how god created the universe. If god created the universe for us, we would be the most important entities in the cosmos because we would be the reason the cosmos exists at all. We would occupy the center stage, be the main character, be extremely cosmically significant. We would be so important because, presumably, we would be the very *purpose* of the cosmos. But what could that purpose be? Our quest for cosmic purpose did not yield great Cosmic Meaning. Being cosmically significant due to our purpose cannot be more Cosmically Meaningful than the meaning afforded us by our cosmic purpose. (The same goes for our value as seen from the cosmic perspective. The extent to which our value from the cosmic perspective makes us cosmically significant in a meaningful way depends on the nature of our cosmic value, which, as we have seen, has both positive and negative aspects.)

Another meaning advantage that our occupying center stage in the story of the universe might provide is the implication that there may be a *story* of the universe, a unifying explanation of the universe and our existence within it.

Explanation

Many theistic accounts of the cosmos contend that theism gives us an explanation for the universe and our lives within it. Seachris argues that "scripture instantiates a redemptive-historical narrative" that gives us meaning by "narrating ultimate origins, purpose, value, significance, pain and suffering, futility, death, and ultimate ending."[93] Scripture is "god's story," which helps us make sense of the world.[94] Similarly, Timothy Mawson says that theism gives us a meaningful explanation of the origins of the universe because the theistic explanation provides an intentional explanation for our creation[95] (which is to choose to freely return god's love and be morally good, making the choice to do our duty),[96] and a happy ending of communion with god in the afterlife.[97] If theism can best explain the origins of the universe, the purpose and point of our lives, and provide an ending that redeems/explains all of our suffering, that would be a powerfully meaningful explanation.

[93] Seachris, "The Meaning of Life and Scripture's Redemptive-Historical Narrative: Illuminating Convergences," *God and Meaning*, pp. 13–34, 22.

[94] Seachris, "The Meaning of Life and Scripture's Redemptive-Historical Narrative," p. 24.

[95] See Mawson, *Monotheism and the Meaning of Life*, pp. 12–13.

[96] Mawson, *Monotheism and the Meaning of Life*, pp. 33–34.

[97] Mawson, *Monotheism and the Meaning of Life*, p. 42.

Explained Origins?

The beginning of the story of the cosmos is, as yet, a natural mystery because we don't have a naturalistic account of it. The closest we come to a naturalistic account of the origin of the universe is the Big Bang theory, which posits that matter was compacted into a small point of infinite density and heat (i.e., the Singularity) that began expanding.[98] That is a theory of expansion, however, not truly a theory of origin. In simple terms, we might think that the Big Bang had to occur *after* the beginning of the universe because before the Big Bang, there had to be something to bang. (Whence the Singularity?) The same problem applies to positing god as the creator or originator of the universe: what causes or creates god? Since the universe is everything that exists, including any forces or gods that may exist, it is especially difficult to explain its origin.

The physicist David Deutsch argues that the causal explanation of something doesn't have to precede it in time but can, instead, consist of multiple things happening at different times, including past and future times.[99] If we accept this view, then the question of what preceded god or what preceded the Singularity has less undermining force against those origin accounts, but this applies equally to both accounts. Deutsch further argues that there can be no "bedrock principle" that explains everything else because then what would explain that?[100] There is a compelling logic to this point. Thus, god is no more bedrock than any other explanation because what would explain god? Perhaps god is self-caused, always existent, or self-explanatory. However, as Hume wondered,

[98] See Joseph Silk, *The Big Bang*, 3rd edition, W. H. Freeman and Co., 2000, preface.

[99] See David Deutsch, interviewed by Jim Holt, *Why Does the World Exist?*, Liveright, 2012, p. 126.

[100] See Deutsch, interviewed by Holt, *Why Does the World Exist?*, pp. 125–126. This can be seen as a refutation or denial of the classic "Principle of Sufficient Reason," which holds that for everything, there must be a reason (or a cause). See Gottfried Wilhelm Leibniz, *The Monadology* (1714), Robert Latta, trans. (1898), independently published, 2024, Section 32.

if god can be self-caused, always existent, or self-explanatory, why can't the universe itself be self-caused, always existent, or self-explanatory?[101] The natural account in this case might be simpler, because it posits fewer causes and events (since it does not add god to any of the natural events and processes we already know about) and also because it doesn't appeal to anything "extra" beyond empirically verifiable natural forces. Simpler need not always be more accurate, but it's generally a point in favor of an explanation (for many reasons: it has fewer ways to go wrong and posits no more than necessary—e.g., the engine propels the train, so bells and whistles don't best explain why the train runs, even if they adorn the train, since we have already explained, via the engine, why the train runs).

While the jury is still out on our cosmic beginnings, theistic explanations of the origins of the universe seem no more explanatory than non-theistic explanations, and no account I am aware of provides a complete or satisfactory explanation of the origins of the cosmos. But perhaps a view of the origin of the cosmos that includes intention will provide us with an explanation for why we are here—a reason for the origin of the cosmos. The "why" rather than the "how" of it—the point or purpose of the universe.

Explanatory Purpose/Point

As we have already discussed, we can engage with meaningful purposes within our everyday lives and engage in efforts that have a point—a valued end—and achieve Everyday Meaning.[102] That doesn't give us Ultimate Meaning, and neither can god.[103] Cosmic purpose does not yield very significant or unequivocally positive

---

[101] See Hume, *Dialogues Concerning Natural Religion* (1779), Part IX.
[102] See Chapter 2.
[103] See Chapter 1.

cosmic meaning, so it cannot give us much of a cosmically meaningful explanation either.

An Explanatory, Redemptive End?

But maybe the end will explain it all. The good will be rewarded, the evil punished, and we will persist in everlasting love, bliss, communion with or incorporation into the mind of god or ultimate reality. I've already gone through the problems with these happy endings in terms of purpose and value. It's not easy to imagine an end that provides a significantly meaningful, positive, and sensible explanation of the universe, no matter how much magic sauce we allow into the mix.

Furthermore, if you think that, generally, the ends don't justify the means, there is reason to be even more skeptical of the possibility of a happy ending that makes sense of an intentional cosmos. Consider the mind that would fashion a universe populated with sentient beings designed such that they must stalk, hunt, kill, and eat each other in order to survive. No matter what happens next, that is already nothing short of diabolical. If that's the opening act, I cannot imagine an encore or second act that will supposedly, somehow, redeem it all because I don't think any end can justify those means. Perhaps I lack imagination. That's not a throwaway line. Happy endings tend not to be spelled out. There's a reason why "and they all lived happily ever after" is the formula for a happy ending—it's an open, blank end, left to be briefly and hazily imagined because happy endings are hard to imagine ("happily *ever* after" is not actually an *end* at all). It's hard to conceive of any way to fill in an end to the cosmic story such that all that came before is explained and all that comes after is meaningfully happy.

Does cosmic explanation give us Cosmic Meaning? It has not yet been demonstrated to do so to a significant degree. A natural explanation of the cosmos would provide facts about the universe, but it's not clear why those facts would be particularly meaningful to us. Arguably, a theistic cosmos would make less sense than a natural cosmos because theism implies that this confounding, often excruciating, sometimes beautiful, universe is an intended *plan*. Furthermore, a supernatural, theistic cosmos gives us a world that "contains *genuine magic*,"[104] which makes understanding the cosmos harder because magic defies explanation, thereby "undermining intelligibility."[105] It is therefore hard to see how a theistic universe makes more sense or is more explanatory—at this point it is a promissory note. We have good reason to doubt it can be profitably cashed out.

Conclusion

Our foray into wizardry is over: "Wands down!"

What did we get? In a word (okay, two), underwhelming meaning. We did not get Ultimate Meaning, or a point for leading and living our lives because nothing can give us the metaphysically impossible. We did not get an inspiring cosmic purpose because bliss per se is not very meaningful, communion with the divine is a purpose not worthy of our potential and includes objectionably unequal elements, merging with the divine relieves suffering but does not seem like a very meaningful purpose, and no value beyond our everyday meaningful purposes is added if they turn out to be also the purposes of the universe itself. We did not get great Cosmic Meaning in terms of cosmic value either, because the existence of perfect value doesn't do much for us (beyond communion, which has its problems), value from a cosmic perspective has negative aspects, everlasting value is limited in its meaning, and balancing the scales of justice is both limited and likely overshadowed

---

[104] See Stephen Maitzen, "The Problem of Magic," *Does God Matter?*, pp. 132–146, 139.
[105] See Maitzen, "The Problem of Magic," p. 140.

by eventual equality in an eternal afterlife (and has nothing to do with making sense). Our cosmic impact is likely negligible. Our intrinsic cosmic significance is not meaningfully different from our earthly intrinsic significance. We don't yet know our relative cosmic significance, but we should hope for it to be low so that we have a more valuable cosmos overall. Finally, we don't have persuasive reasons to hope for an explanation of the cosmos that gives us satisfactory explanatory Cosmic Meaning.

We must therefore conclude that even if we assume theism, or supernatural wonders, Cosmic Meaning is not all that positive or pivotal to meaning in our lives; certainly not the game changer we might have anticipated. (Cosmic, yet "meh.") However, if we assume an afterlife, at least we don't end when we die, leaving open the possibility of everlasting meaning, however imperfect that turns out to be. Although Cosmic Meaning doesn't seem super fantastic or crucial, it may afford us a happy ending, or—better yet— no ending! One of the deepest appeals of theology and its potential for Cosmic Meaning is the promise of an afterlife such that death is not our end. How much more meaningful would that be? What is the relationship between death and meaning? I turn now to that question.

4
DEATH

It's Overrated

One thing you might notice as you get older is that people die with stunning regularity. You wake to news of deaths daily. This author: dead; your brother: dead; that former head of state: dead; your neighbor: dead; that notorious criminal: dead. Him too? Yes, him too. Everyone. Every single one. That will include you, of course. Slowly, the fact of your own mortality becomes a little more real. That might lead you to seize the day and make the most of the time you have left. Or it might lead you to wonder why you bother so much with your flash-in-the-pan, mere moment in time, life. That's what happened to Tolstoy. He wondered:

> Sooner or later there will come diseases and death (they had come already) to my dear ones and to me, and there would be nothing left but stench and worms. All my affairs, no matter what they might be, would sooner or later be forgotten, and I myself should not exist. So why should I worry about these things?[1]

Life's finitude bothered Tolstoy so much that he resolved to adopt religious faith to connect to the infinite afterlife, even though he considered religious belief "irrational" and "monstrous." Otherwise, he could not justify the efforts in his life or the things he cared about. He clearly found death a threat to Everyday Meaning.

---

[1] Tolstoy, *A Confession*, Section IV, 1882.

And he is hardly alone. Some argue that death drains life of meaning,[2] while others argue that it is death that makes life meaningful.[3] Many argue that it does both.[4] Aphorisms about death and meaning abound, though it is often impossible to find their source. "The meaning of life is that it stops," Franz Kafka supposedly said.[5] "The fact that we die is the most important fact about us,"[6] says Todd May.

Why, though? What is it about death that makes it seem so central to issues of meaning? This is different from questions regarding the badness of death. Considerations of the badness of death often focus on the fact that death deprives you of future good[7] and also annihilates you.[8] Consideration of the goodness of death can include the fact that it deprives you of future suffering—finally, a release! As Schopenhauer says: "The great opportunity to no longer be I."[9] Death is a release, an end to life, which seems like an important, consoling fact we can cling to in the worst of times.[10] This too shall pass. Without death, life is a forever sentence, and that might

---

[2] See Tolstoy, *A Confession*, Section IV; Benatar, *The Human Predicament*, chapter 5; and Landau, *Finding Meaning in an Imperfect World*, p. 85; among many others.

[3] See Martin Hägglund, *This Life: Why Mortality Makes Us Free*, Profile Books, 2019, pp. 49, 68, 191, 200, 204; Williams, "The Makropolous Case: Reflections on the Tedium of Immortality," *Problems of the Self*, Cambridge University Press, 1973, pp. 82–100, 82; Nussbaum, *The Therapy of Desire*, Princeton University Press, 1994, p. 229; Scheffler, *Death and the Afterlife*; and Simone de Beauvoir, *All Men Are Mortal* (1946), Leonard M. Friedman, trans., Norton, 1992, pp. 192–193; among many others.

[4] See Todd May, "Death, Mortality, and Meaning," *Exploring the Philosophy of Death and Dying*, Michael Cholbi and Travis Timmerman, Eds., Routledge, 2021, pp. 157–161, 157; May, *Death*, Acumen 2009/Routledge, 2014, chapters 1 and 2; and Heidegger, *Being and Time*.

[5] This quote is widely attributed to Kafka, but as far as I can tell, it's not sourced to any of his works. See https://www.goodreads.com/quotes/49827-the-meaning-of-life-is-that-it-stops; kafka-online.info; https://www.theviennareview.at/archives/2012/franz-kafka-the-meaning-of-life-is-that-it-stops; and many others. All attribute the quote to Kafka. None say where he says this.

[6] May, *Death*, p. 4.

[7] See Nagel, "Death," *Mortal Questions*, Cambridge University Press, 1979, pp. 1–10.

[8] See Benatar, *The Human Predicament*, pp. 103–121.

[9] See Arthur Schopenhauer, *The World as Will and Representation* (1818), Vol. 2, E. F. J. Payne, trans., Dover (NY), 1958, p. 508.

[10] During a rough patch in my life, I used the following only half-joking mantra to help me fall asleep: "I am a finite being. My suffering will end." Schopenhauer would

feel like a trap or a prison.[11] Being annihilated has its benefits. In many spiritual traditions it is a coveted goal, of sorts: to lose your ego—the source of your earthly suffering—and merge into the infinite or the mind of god.[12]

For our purposes, we don't need to focus on the goodness or badness of death itself. I'll focus on what death means for the meaning of our everyday lives. Since, as we have already established, nothing can affect the Ultimate Meaning of our lives (the end-regarding justifying reason, the valued end, or the point of leading a life at all),[13] I will consider death mostly as it pertains to Everyday Meaning, with the exception of my discussion of annihilation. (Since death ends the life you lead, I'll discuss the meaning implications of annihilation as it pertains to both Ultimate Meaning and Everyday Meaning.) Recall that Everyday Meaning includes the value and significance in our everyday lives, including values such as beauty, morality, love, and truth; and the significance of engagement with them. This includes the purpose (i.e., the reason for which something is done) and point (i.e., justifying valued end) of much of our meaningful, everyday lives, which aim at these valued ends. It includes the impact we have on others and on the world around us, as well as the explanation of some of our meaningful activities and pursuits.[14] While death does present some meaning

have approved. He argued that a positive aspect of death is that it releases us from suffering (*The World as Will and Representation*, pp. 468–469).

[11] Even if we envision an immortal life that you could end by choice, it would be a choice much harder to make because you would have no idea what you were cutting yourself off from, given your otherwise infinite existence.

[12] See Obayashi, *Death and the Afterlife*, Part III: Death and the Afterlife in Eastern Religions; and Matt, *The Essential Kabbalah*. See also Chapter 3, section "Purpose."

[13] See Chapter 1.

[14] Whether death has implications for Cosmic Meaning may depend on one's view of the nature of Cosmic Meaning. If your view of Cosmic Meaning depends on the afterlife or our mortal nature, then death might be necessary for Cosmic Meaning. If your view of Cosmic Meaning depends on people being permanent, live fixtures of cosmic value, then death may diminish Cosmic Meaning. If you think that Cosmic Meaning is not all that important, then you won't have reason to care much about whether and how death affects Cosmic Meaning.

problems, it's not nearly as salient to meaning in our lives as many seem to think. It is time, and not death, that plays the role often attributed to death: necessary for most meaning (not sufficient, but necessary, for most meaning), yet undermining of meaning.

How Death Is (Supposedly) Needed for Meaning

Narrative Meaning, Shape, and Trajectory

In order for our lives to make sense to us, which is a crucial aspect of Everyday Meaning (explanation), you might think that we need to be able to get some sort of handle on it as a whole, as something graspable, and with something we can recognize as a plotline. In this way, via its role in lending our everyday lives coherence, explanation, and a form of value, narrative value can be seen as part of Everyday Meaning.[15] Without death, you can imagine life trailing off into a shapeless incoherent blob of sorts and, therefore, many argue that death is what gives life its stages, shape, trajectory, and the ending needed for narrative coherence and meaning. Martin Hägglund says: "My death is the horizon of my life—it renders intelligible all temporal regions of my life."[16] May agrees, arguing that immortality would render our lives "shapeless."[17] Heidegger has been interpreted as having this view as well.[18] Samuel Scheffler

---

[15] I take no position as to whether narrative value is *necessary* for Everyday Meaning, but I can see it playing a role in the explanation characteristic of Everyday Meaning, and, insofar as it is valuable, in the value characteristic as well.

[16] See Hägglund, *This Life*, p. 200.

[17] May, "Death, Mortality, and Meaning," p. 160.

[18] See Heidegger, *Being and Time*, Part II. Some interpret Heidegger as giving death a central role in shaping the meaning of our lives. See Benjamin Mitchell-Yellin, "How to Live a Never-Ending Novella (Or, Why Immortality Needn't Undermine Identity)," *Exploring the Philosophy of Death and Dying*, pp. 131–136, 132; Kiki Berk and Joshua Teply, "Sartre and Heidegger on Death and Meaning in Life," *2nd International Conference on Philosophy and Meaning in Life*, 2019, Waseda University (unpublished manuscript); and Theodor Adorno, *Metaphysics: Concepts and Problems*, Edmund

argues that without death, life would be drained of meaning because accomplishment and fulfillment depend on *stages* of life, and without death, life would be one long unending stage.[19] David Velleman explains:

> When your life comes to a close, it becomes fully specific. . . . Until people circumnavigated the Earth, they lived somewhere in the midst of somewhere or other. In order to see where they stood, they had to close the circle. Similarly, closing the circle of one's life is necessary to seeing it as the particular life one has lived.[20]

Sartre mentions this need for an ending as well, noting that one might think that death relates to the meaning of one's life as the "resolved chord at the end of a melody."[21] Closure. People like closure precisely for this reason: a tale with an ending can be understood, assimilated, and perhaps then finally stop poking at you with its jagged jutting pieces and trapping you into its gaping, unpredictable holes. Narratives help us understand our lives by making them intelligible by selecting, distilling, ordering, and unifying the

Jephcott, trans., Rolf Tiedemann, Ed., Stanford University Press, 2000, pp. 129–137. Others dispute this and argue that Heidegger views death as less central to meaning (see May, "Death, Mortality, and Meaning," pp. 157–158; May, *Death*, chapter 1; and Adam Buben, "Heidegger and the Supposed Meaninglessness of Personal Immortality," *Journal of the American Philosophical Association* 2 [2016]: 384–399). Which interpretation is correct? Having read every word of *Being and Time*, I tend toward the view that Heidegger views death as central to the shape, trajectory, and meaning of human life. But Heidegger is not exactly a clear writer, so who knows?

[19] See Scheffler, *Death and the Afterlife*, p. 96.

[20] Velleman, "Dying," *Think* 11 (2012): 29–32, 32. Connie Rosati, following Velleman, argues that a narrative has to be viewable as a whole and only a life that ends can meet this criterion (see Rosati, "The Makropolous Case Revisited: Reflections on Immortality and Agency," *The Oxford Handbook of the Philosophy of Death*, Ben Bradley, Fred Feldman, and Jens Johansson, Eds., Oxford University Press, 2013, pp. 355–390).

[21] Sartre, *Being and Nothingness* (1943), Sarah Richmond, trans., Washington Square Press, 2018, p. 690. Sartre rejects this view because he views death as not part of life but, instead, its final boundary. See Kiki Berk and Joshua Teply, "Sartre and Heidegger on Death and Meaning in Life."

features of our lives.[22] An understandable life is more meaningful than an incoherent, shapeless life that resists explanation.

Yet it's really time, and not death, that gives shape to our lives by allowing for sequence, which allows for a narrative. Before, during, after; yesterday, today, tomorrow. Plotlines play out in time, but they need not end in order to be understandable or meaningful. Without time marking out our lives, it's hard to fathom life at all because we live in the fundamentals of the present, the past, and the future. It is nearly impossible to imagine timeless meaningfulness. You might conjure up a hazy vision of existing in a timeless state of pure joy, or a more dystopian vision of unmitigated sorrow. Could we exist in a timeless state of both joy and sorrow? Only if the two contradictory emotions occurred simultaneously since there cannot be a sequence without time. Yet even a state of pure love or unmitigated joy sounds more like a drug trip than a meaningful life. How meaningful can it be if that's all that's going on? No striving, no hoping, no succeeding, no failing—some of the crucial markers of meaning could not occur without time because they are oriented in the past as it relates to the present as it relates to the future. Even love loses much of its meaning in the absence of time because love without time would lack the element of faithfulness that characterizes deep and enduring love, which shows itself by persisting for better or for worse through time. Without time, it's hard to conceive of much of what we take to make our lives meaningful. Time is needed for most meaning. However, so long as we live in time, even if we lived forever, much of what makes our everyday lives meaningful could remain. Without death, we would not have the final stage of lives, but that doesn't entail that we would have no stages at all.[23] Without death, we wouldn't have a completed narrative of our lives, with a final ending, but we might

---

[22] See Helena de Bres, "Narrative and Meaning in Life," *Journal of Moral Philosophy* 15 (2018): 545–571.

[23] See Niko Kolodny, "That I Should Die and Others Live," Scheffler, *Death and the Afterlife*, pp. 159–176.

still have something like a serial or, if you keep it exciting enough, a soap opera.[24] A very long and unending story, but still, a story, with a narrative structure, and day-to-day Everyday Meaning.

Of course, there are some elements of a narrative that will be missing from a never-ending story. In an ongoing saga, we may never be sure of a person's character: the seeming cowardice may yet be redeemed; the murderer can turn out to have been framed. An unfinished story can take many unexpected turns. We don't know who won the football game until the clock runs out. Thus, there's an element of narrative meaning that we don't have when we have an ongoing serial instead of a concluded narrative. But the salience of narrative value to meaning lies in its explanatory power. Life stories are more coherent than a chaotic, unconnected series of episodes. Via its role in helping us explain our lives and make them more coherent, narrative is part of the explanation aspect of Everyday Meaning. And we can have enough narrative meaning to lend our lives explanation even if we never see a final chapter. That's fortunate, because many people—maybe even most people—don't get to fully experience their lives coming to an end even in our mortal lives, either because they die unexpectedly or because their mental capacity is too diminished at the end of life for them to fully understand or appreciate the final chapter of their lives.[25] Yet most of our lives can still have narrative meaning and coherence, just as long-running soap operas do (some of which last longer than many lives).[26] Although missing the final chapter of a story is usually not as narratively satisfying as a cohesive ending, some of the best stories leave you wishing for more or have parts that stand on their

[24] See Mitchell-Yellin, "How to Live a Never-Ending Novella"; and John Martin Fischer, *Death, Immortality, and Meaning in Life*, Oxford University Press, 2020, pp. 109–111.

[25] For a subtle discussion of how the end of life affects it meaning, see Helen Small, *The Long Life*, Oxford University Press, 2007, chapter 3.

[26] *General Hospital*, one of the longest serials in recorded history, is currently in its sixty-second season; *Coronation Street*, a British soap, has been running for over sixty years. That's longer than some lives. If these serials didn't maintain an audience by being narratively compelling, it is doubtful they would have lasted this long.

own as meaningful. Without death, we would not have "The End" of our narratives, but we would retain sufficient narrative meaning for the explanation aspect of Everyday Meaning. You don't have to die in order to have a life story; you can have an ongoing, never-ending story that makes enough sense for Everyday Meaning.

Background Meaning Conditions of Risk, Reward, Scarcity, and Limited Resources

In order for our everyday lives to include purposeful, significant, and valuable activity, many insist that we need death so that the background conditions of risk, reward, and value necessary for those characteristics of meaning remain in place. Hägglund goes all in on this idea:

> The risk of death . . . is an intrinsic part of the reasons one has to care about anything and to take responsibility for what happens. Without the risk of irrevocable loss, what happens would have no meaningful consequences and there would be nothing at stake in keeping faith with the ones we love.[27]
>
> What I do with my time only matters to me because I grasp my life as finite.[28]

This is pretty extreme stuff, and you might wonder whether we need to risk death, obliteration, and annihilation in order to have any Everyday Meaning at all. Hägglund seems to be conflating immortality with invulnerability, but they are not the same thing. If we lived forever, all that would secure for us is not dying, and there is no shortage of awful outcomes short of death (and many arguably worse than death). We could easily lose what we have worked

[27] Hägglund, *This Life*, p. 68.
[28] Hägglund, *This Life*, p. 191.

toward, what we love, what we believe in, without dying. Doesn't this happen to live people all the time?

Without any risk at all, it's hard to envision meaningful success or fulfillment. Yet, more vulnerability doesn't always allow for more meaning. Are our lives any less meaningful since the discovery of antibiotics? Do we value having children less, or less meaningfully, now that dying in childbirth and infant mortality stopped being commonplace? If anything, it seems the opposite: the likelihood of our children surviving infancy may allow us not to hold anything back in our attachment and devotion to them, and the fact that women are likely to survive birthing children allows us to invest more fully of ourselves in the process. Some high-risk activities are meaningful to those who engage in them in part because they're risky, e.g., solo mountain climbing, but those are specific kinds of meaning, important to those who find thrill in high risk, probably because of the ways in which high risk can sometimes, for people with atypical temperaments, make the reward feel more significant and valuable. But an immortal life would not be a risk-free life.

Scheffler famously argues that fundamental concepts and values, like health, safety, and security, would be hard to make sense of in an immortal existence because we need the ultimate scarcity of death as a limit or vulnerability, as a background for meaningful decisions and values.[29] Martha Nussbaum agrees, arguing that immortality would make some virtues absent, e.g., courage (since we couldn't risk our lives for anything), or moderation (since our bodies wouldn't be threatened by excess). She says that personal relationships would suffer, since children wouldn't be dependent on parents for survival and there'd be a limit to how much you could sacrifice for a friend. And, she contends, the meaning of our passions and pursuits requires an awareness of the finite nature of our opportunities.[30]

[29] See Scheffler, *Death and the Afterlife*, pp. 97–99.
[30] See Nussbaum, *The Therapy of Desire*, pp. 227–229.

Here too, there seems to be an implicit assumption that an immortal life is an invulnerable one (or one devoid of time). But that's false. Never dying gives us plenty of time for repercussions, no shortage of ways to suffer, and endless time to suffer. Life without death doesn't entail life without risk, so there's no reason to assume we would lack opportunities for courage and sacrifice if we never died.[31] Indeed, in a life without end, some sacrifices could last forever, some courageous acts could risk permanent, everlasting damage. So we need not worry about virtue or risk. Living forever does not do away with these background conditions for meaning.

What about scarcity? Is life more valuable because it is limited? Would the *Mona Lisa* be more valuable if we knew it would fall apart in fifty years? I don't think so. It's more valuable because of its unique nature, but not because it is finite. The same goes for each of us: we are valuable because of our unique and valuable nature but not made more valuable because we will die. I just don't see how that is supposed to work. Some worry that the lack of scarcity of time in an immortal life would make us lethargic, unmotivated to complete that which could always be done tomorrow or the infinite tomorrows thereafter—that Jorge Luis Borges is correct in describing a society of immortals, where everything is in ruins because "where there is time for everything, nothing is urgent to accomplish."[32] Perhaps. But there is also unlimited time to suffer the effects of living in a hovel, providing pressure to fix things. Just because you can fix something tomorrow doesn't mean that you won't tire of living in a ruin today. You might procrastinate more, but immortality does not do away with time pressure or the motivation to fix up your ruin.

So let us reconsider whether death is really needed for the background meaning conditions of risk, reward, and limited resources.

---

[31] Fischer notes this as well. See Fischer, *Death, Immortality, and Meaning in Life*, chapter 6.

[32] See May, "Death, Mortality, and Meaning," p. 159, discussing the Jorge Luis Borges short story, "The Immortal," *Labyrinths*, New Directions Press, 1962.

Without death, would there be no urgency to our projects, no particular reason to follow through on things that would still be there for you tomorrow, no reason to cherish the love you have today? These conclusions overlook the role that time plays in providing us with these conditions. A human life lived in time would be able to have the backdrop of risk, reward, and the forward motion so connected to meaningful activity. Without death, love would still be a risk: Will she love me back? Will it end in heartbreak? What will become of our children, if we are lucky enough to birth them? Time will tell. Starting a project would remain risky: Will it play out as planned, will it end in humiliation or fulfillment? Will it have been worth our efforts? You don't need death to have time pressure or motivation: you need to hire a band in time for the wedding; you need to show your children how much you love them while they are still growing up; you need to fix the fridge before the food spoils; you need to ask the girl out before she leaves the train station. . . . Similarly, the rewards of the risks we take and the things we do with our time would remain meaningful because we would continue to reap those rewards and they would continue to be at risk, not to be taken for granted. We would still have many limitations on our resources, quite possibly more so than we do now since human consumers would persist indefinitely through time. We would have to take care to preserve our planet, to grow sufficient food to avoid hunger and malnutrition, to decide what to attend to now and what can be put off without undue cost. Both risk and reward would remain meaningful without death, and perhaps become even more significant since their effects might last a lot longer and thereby have a deeper, more meaningful, impact.[33] It is

---

[33] Scheffler argues that many of our values are time bound and time-scarcity bound such that without death, we might have no values or an entirely different set of values. However, the absence of death doesn't do away with time, its passage, or its pressure. We would still live in time. It would still be valuable for us to have nourishment, social connection, cognitive stimulation, justice, beauty, etc. So we don't have enough reason to

time, not death, that we need for these background conditions for meaning.[34]

Boredom

But what about boredom? Don't we need death to avoid boredom? Might living forever force us into a bored meaninglessness? This was Bernard Williams's worry. Williams, worried about the tedium of immortality, thought that the only way we could avoid the crushing, meaningless boredom caused by an infinite life would be to change our projects and interests so radically over the course of an immortal lifetime as to cease to be who we once were and thus not be immortal after all. Otherwise, we would eventually run out of things to occupy us, since there is a limit to a person's interests.[35] Death solves this problem for us and, in this way, is thought to be needed for meaning. Without death, we would be bored to death.

If boredom results from having too much time, it can make sense to think that an immortal life would be horribly boring. Is boredom caused by too much time, or just time without anything to fill it? The answer is: neither. You might be bored with something that must be done in exactly the time it takes to do it, e.g., washing the dishes in the fifteen minutes you have before you go to bed. You might find time with nothing to do pleasant, or hardly registering

conclude that our values would be utterly different or nonexistent if we never died. See Scheffler, *Death and the Afterlife*, pp. 97–99.

[34] Lilian Alweiss argues that, according to Heidegger, we need death as a limit to take our finitude seriously, and gain an authentic understanding of time and the possibilities open to us. On this reading, for Heidegger, our open possibilities are only possible because we have the closed possibility of death on the horizon. I think this is a reasonable read of Heidegger. It seems to indicate that Heidegger understands time as necessary for meaning (which is correct), but, as I argue, we don't need death in order to have temporal limits, or the background conditions that time provides us with for meaning. See Alweiss, "Heidegger and 'the Concept of Time,'" *History of the Human Sciences* 15 (2002): 117–132.

[35] See Williams, "The Makropolous Case," pp. 82–100.

as a feeling at all, if you mindlessly stare off into the middle distance as you sit on your front porch for a while. Boredom occurs when we restlessly feel time's passage without being engaged, absorbed, or entertained. The opposite of boredom occurs when we are engaged and fully absorbed without frustration to the point that we get lost in what we're doing and hardly feel the time pass at all. (What has become known as "flow.")[36]

The worry about boredom and immortality is that eventually we will exhaust our interests and therefore be unable to find anything sufficiently absorbing to avoid boredom. "Not another asteroid, world war, fire, orgasm, or dazzling sunset. Yawn," we'd say to ourselves. We have seen it all before. Really? That seems an unlikely reaction. It is more plausible that some pleasures are repeatable rather than exhaustible.[37] I love my coffee every single day, perhaps more so for the fact that it's there for me day after day after day. (And more plausible still if we include repeatable pains, which are unpleasant but usually not boring. Nothing but repeatable pleasures can sound a little boring but that's because it's just pleasure and nothing else, not because it's a repeated pleasure.) Further, in imagining an immortal life, we have to recognize that things would likely continue to change, quite possibly enough to continue to engage us indefinitely. Even once we conquer space, the expanding universe may open new areas of exploration for us. Even if war couldn't kill us, it would likely still be threatening and unpleasant enough to command our attention. We might refresh or further develop old skills (maybe you can forget how to ride a bicycle!), or enjoy taking up something after enough time has passed to make it seem interesting once again. Considering how boredom tends to occur during our current, finite, lifespan is edifying. If

---

[36] The concept of "flow" was proposed by Mihaly Csikszentmihalyi in 1990. See *American Psychological Association Dictionary of Psychology*, 2020, https://dictionary. apa.org/flow.

[37] See Fischer, "Why Immortality Is Not So Bad," *International Journal of Philosophical Studies* 2 (1994): 257–270, 262–266.

people get increasingly bored as they age, that might lend credence to the view that an infinite life will become boring. However, research does not show that. Instead, research shows that boredom invades and recedes over a lifetime depending on opportunities and abilities for absorbing engagement with the world.[38] An infinite life might be unpleasant (just as a finite life often is), but I see no reason why it must be boring, and even less reason to conclude that if it were boring it would have to be meaningless.

Boring and meaningless are not the same thing. Boredom is a psychologically unpleasant state of restless lack of engagement or absorption.[39] Meaninglessness involves lack of value, explanation, impact, significance, purpose, or point. Plenty of boring things are valuable, significant, impactful, purposeful, and pointful. That is why we wash the dishes, fold the laundry, read the same story over and over to our children, and drive to work. Not fascinating, but not meaningless either. On the other hand, we might turn to a meaningless game or diversion to alleviate boredom.[40]

Time is necessary for boredom and will not help alleviate it. Death, on the other hand, will alleviate boredom, but only because it eliminates you as a subject for boredom. But it won't thereby make life more meaningful because boring does not entail meaningless. Therefore, to conclude that death is needed to avoid meaninglessness due to boredom seems unwarranted, and a rather drastic and disconnected remedy for a banal, episodic condition; an overly faithful way to kill time. Overkill, if you will. Maybe we can take up knitting instead? We can easily be bored in a finite life ("Millions long for immortality who do not know what to do with

---

[38] See James Danckert and John D. Eastwood, *Out of My Skull: The Psychology of Boredom*, Harvard University Press, 2020.

[39] Peter Toohey posits that Heidegger thought that the boredom of waiting can help us understand our genuine selves because when we wait, we are deprived of distractions and encounter raw time. The self then has to face itself—pure "being," i.e., reality, and can better reconcile with death. See Toohey, *Hold On: The Life, Science, and Art of Waiting*, Oxford University Press, 2020, pp. 199–200.

[40] Calhoun draws this distinction between meaninglessness and boredom (*Doing Valuable Time*, pp. 119–136).

themselves on a rainy Sunday afternoon"[41]), and plausibly not be bored in an infinite one. Since we're focused on meaning, it is important to note not only that it is unclear that immortality would be tedious but also that tedium does not preclude meaning. Maybe we are prone to the mistake of conflating boredom with meaninglessness because we associate the feelings of emptiness and lack of purpose/point with both boredom and meaninglessness. But they are distinct phenomena, with different causes, different implications, and different remedies. It is therefore incorrect to claim that we need death to avoid a state of bored meaninglessness. We probably don't even need it to avoid boredom, and we certainly don't need it to avoid meaninglessness due to boredom because meaninglessness is not caused by, a result of, the same thing as, or a byproduct of boredom.

How Death (Supposedly) Threatens Meaning

Erosion of Impact (and, Thereby, of Significance and Value)

Just as death is argued as necessary for meaning, it is also thought that death undercuts life's meaning by putting a limit on the impact and significance of our efforts, and eventually wiping all vestiges of our lives away.[42] Why bother working so hard when we and everything that we have done will disappear sooner or later? Even if some of our efforts have impact beyond our lives, eventually it all dissipates and disappears. We leave hardly a trace. Even Landau, a meaning optimist if there ever was one, thinks that death diminishes meaning by blunting the impact, and thereby the

---

[41] Susan Ertz, *Anger in the Sky*, Hodder & Stoughton 1943, p. 134.
[42] See note 2. Many of those who argue that death is necessary for meaning also argue that it undermines meaning (see notes 3 and 4).

significance and value, of our efforts and investments. We are like Sisyphus, rolling the rock up the hill, knowing all the while that it will then roll back down. But, he argues, transience does not exclude value. So long as the floor we sweep stays clean for enough time for the work to make it worth it, sweeping the floor retains value.[43] That seems reasonable and is consistent with how most people feel about housecleaning. It is indeed less meaningful because it is bound to be undone—its impact is limited—but it's still somewhat valuable, and somewhat meaningful, if it lasts long enough (though how long is long enough probably varies according to the factors of expectation, effort, and purpose, as I will explain shortly). The existential psychologist Irvin Yalom finds the fact of our impact being undone by death deeply unsettling and recommends thinking of how who we were and what we did will ripple through time, like a pebble thrown into a river.[44] Both Landau and Yalom seem to think that the ways in which our mortal nature diminishes the meaning in our lives leave us in need of some solace: the floor is clean for a *while*, you will ripple out a *bit*. But what makes the fact that something doesn't last a problem for meaning?

Let's think about eating an ice cream cone, building a sand castle, and building a house. None of these things last forever, yet how much their transience diminishes the meaning of our efforts or engagement with them varies considerably. I suggest it varies depending on our expectations, the purpose of our investment (which can include how much we need it), how much work we put into it, and how hard that work is. We don't expect or even really want the ice cream to last forever. That's not the point of eating ice cream. If we kept eating it—the endless cone—it would diminish the pleasure because it would be too sweet, too cold, too boring. It's not intended to be permanent. It's the break from regular food

---

[43] See Landau, *Finding Meaning in an Imperfect World*, chapters 5 and 6.

[44] See Irvin Yalom, *Staring at the Sun: Overcoming the Terror of Death*, Jossey-Bass/Wiley, 2009, chapter 4.

or work; its transience is consistent with its purpose, our expectation, and the effort we put into eating it (we don't even have to chew). It is usually not too much work to get one, which makes it easier to get another one when the desire arises again. When we build a sand castle, we expect it to last the day, until the tide comes in and sweeps it away. It's fun, intended as play, and its impermanence allows us to return the next day and use the same sand to vary our design. But if the tide comes in early, or someone kicks over the sand castle, we may feel our work was for naught. It has not served its purpose, we didn't get a chance to finish and admire it, and it did not meet our expectations for how long it was supposed to last. (We also had to watch it be destroyed, which adds insult, and which would not happen if we built it, admired it, and went home.) When we build a house, its purpose is permanent shelter (which we need), it is very hard work, it is expected to last a lifetime or two, and, for most people, requires more money than they planned or can afford to pay. If it is destroyed in a fire five years later, it's a disaster, a tragedy, a trauma. We put a lot of work into it, invested resources, expected it to last, and did not have much fun along the way.

Is everyday life like an ice cream cone, a sand castle, or a house? It's way too much work for a cone or a sand castle, and for most people a lot less fun. That leaves the house. The house that we know is destined for rubble. Because everyday life is hard work, with a lifetime of investment, engagement, hopes, dreams, failure, and more work still, the fact that it all eventually comes to nothing does not sound like great news for meaning. At least we expect to die. Imagine if we didn't. Imagine if we found out about death at twenty-one years old, all at once, instead of the way that we grow up with death all around us—the bugs, our pets, our grandparents, our house plants, our food—such that there is no time of the dreadful reveal: "Ta-da! You die! He dies! We all die!" It is hard to imagine this, but my guess is that could cause a crisis of meaning even harder to bear than the ones we face already.

However, maybe we are mistaken about the purposes of the things we do and care about in our everyday lives. We know they won't last, so why think of their purposes as including longevity or permanence? Why not let the transience of life and all we engage with in it to sink in and change our attitudes about its purposes? Don't get too attached to anything because it is all quite temporary.[45] Live in the moment, and for the moment. Many religious traditions, philosophical advice, and pop-psychology movements seem to embrace this approach, exhorting us to live in the moment.[46]

But there is a limit to how well this approach can work. First, as we have already noted,[47] a life truly led that way would likely seem fragmentary, lacking coherence and agency; almost animal-like rather than human. Second, we are forward-looking creatures, probably evolutionarily evolved that way so that we take care to see what's coming and not get killed by it. Focusing only on the present can cost us, because the future is coming, whether we attend to it or not, so best be prepared. Finally, even if umbrellas would miraculously show up in time for the rain, existing in the present would present its own meaning conundrums. Meaningfulness and timelessness—the constant-present—are not natural bedfellows. Conjure up again that timeless state of pure love; picture floating on a sea of downy clouds. Dreamy! For a bit. It's hard to see these states

[45] "Attachment is the root of all suffering" (*The Middle Length Discourses of the Buddha*, Bhikkhu Bodhi and Bhikkhu Nanamoli, trans., Wisdom Publications, 1995, p. 868). Detaching may help you feel life's losses less acutely but at the cost of being detached from life. If you don't get attached to things, how can you love them, care for them, grow them, enjoy them, etc.? The cure here is arguably worse than the disease.

[46] Examples: The Buddha (see *The Teaching of Buddha: The Buddhist Bible: A Compendium of Many Scriptures Translated from the Japanese*," 1934, The Federation of All Young Buddhist Associations of Japan); the Stoics—see Marcus Aurelius, *Meditations of Marcus Aurelius* (c. 171–175), Meric Casaubon, trans., Philaletheians, 2013, Book XII; existential psychologist Rollo May (see Rollo May, *Man's Search for Himself*, W. W. Norton & Company, 1953, p. 227); and contemporary mindfulness proponents (see Ekhart Tolle, *The Power of Now: A Guide to Spiritual Enlightenment*, New World Library, 2004).

[47] See Chapter 1, section "Why Care?."

that sound sort of like pleasant drug trips being pleasant forever, and nearly impossible to imagine them as meaningful. We need the progression of time for what most of us can recognize as meaning.

Yet, here too, it is time, and not death, that threatens meaning by eroding the impact of our lives. Time erodes meaning, as we can see by considering what would become of us if we never died. If we lived forever, we would live to see what time does to our accomplishments, commitments, and efforts.[48] That might be a fate worse than death. Time erodes impact and significance. Whatever we put so much care and effort into a hundred, or a hundred thousand, years ago would be hardly a memory now, with the added torment of watching this process play out and knowing that it would be the future of our current engagements and passions. The paintings burned, the justice reversed, the books forgotten, the love lost, the symphony no one has played in ten thousand years, the friendships petered out. Like Simon de Beauvior's immortal Fosca, having seen our prior work dissipated, erased, or reversed, we too might come to think that there's no point to doing anything; that "it's not worth the trouble."[49]

Generally, the harder something is to achieve and the more its purpose is enhanced or achieved by permanence, the more its meaning is diminished by its eventual destruction. Because death ends our lives, to whatever extent expediting the fact of all of our investments and engagements coming to nothing, it seems to diminish the meaning in our lives. But we really don't need death for this problem, as we note when we imagine living forever. It may seem like death erodes, eradicates, and even nullifies everything we do, but not only is this an exaggeration—that kiss isn't nullified

---

[48] As Schopenhauer noted: "Time is that by virtue of which everything becomes nothingness in our hands and loses all real value." See Schopenhauer, "On the Vanity of Existence" (1818), *Essays and Aphorisms*, R. J. Hollingdale, trans., Penguin Books, 1970, p. 51.

[49] See de Beauvoir, *All Men are Mortal*, p. 14.

or made meaningless just because it already happened and doesn't last—to the extent that it's true, it is a function of time. In the absence of death, time alone would eventually wear away at the effects of our efforts and engagements, thereby diminishing the impact and significance, and challenging the purposes and point, of much of what we do and care about.

Endless time presents meaning problems: erosion of purpose, erosion of impact, erosion of significance, erosion of value—erosion is an effect of time. I suspect that's why many religions have views of the eternal afterlife as not subject to time, not in time; absent the element of time at all.[50] It's very hard to imagine what that sort of existence would be like or whether it would be a way we might want to exist. It is even harder to imagine that sort of existence as meaningful. Religion has not convinced me of its supernatural promises, but at least it knows what the problem is (in this respect—it does not seem to recognize the meaning problems posed by timelessness).

Annihilation of Self

But death annihilates *you*. Being annihilated poses a meaning challenge similar to the challenge posed by the erosion of the impact, and thereby the significance and value, of our efforts and engagements, except that instead of what we do or care about, we ourselves are eliminated. Death is like the tide that comes in and sweeps away not only the sand castles you built, but the *you*—the very self—that built them. It wipes you out, obliterates you, literally turns you to dust. In this way, death is widely argued to undermine

---

[50] See *The New Testament*, Revelations (c. 95–96), 10:6 (Christianity); Raphael, *Jewish Views of the Afterlife*, p. 356 (Judaism); Nerina Rustomji, *The Garden and the Fire: Heaven and Hell in Islamic Culture*, Columbia University Press, 2009, p. 77 (Islam); and Steven Collins, *Nirvana: Concept, Imagery, Narrative*, Cambridge University Press, 2010, p. 31 (Hinduism and Buddhism).

meaning.[51] Shelly Kagan explains that this can be seen as not only horrifying, but an insult to human nature and its lofty, valuable, and meaningful potential: "That something as amazing as us, as exalted and valuable as we are, could end up something as lowly and unimportant as a piece of rotting flesh."[52] It is hard to have an impact if you aren't there to do anything. Hard to contemplate meaningful personhood that is reduced to rotting meat. Hard to have meaning when you don't exist. These all seem like plausible reasons to conclude that death sabotages the meaning in (and even of) our lives because it annihilates us.

In order to evaluate this view, let's separate the problems of insult and loss from the possible meaning problems posed by annihilation. Death can seem an insult to the kinds of beings we take ourselves to be, i.e., beings with a rich mental and moral existence and value. To be reminded that we are mere organisms that die and decompose can feel like a loss of dignity or status. That loss of dignity can imply a devaluation, which can thereby be taken as a diminishment of meaning. However, we can easily be reminded of our status as bodies by everyday living and digestive activities, which include no shortage of rot and decomposition. So I'm not so impressed by the special insult of death in this regard, though death does demonstrate our status as meat pretty emphatically.[53] Being annihilated involves a loss of your life and yourself, which can be very sad and unfortunate if you value your life and yourself, as most people do. It is a loss, which we can see as a negative aspect of death. But it's not necessarily a loss of meaning. Mortality only

---

[51] See Benatar, *The Human Predicament*, pp. 102–110; May, *Death*, p. 36. (He's pretty explicit: "Death makes life meaningless by being our end, with nothing left of us; it annihilates us without any further purpose.") See also works of existential psychology, which place fear of death/annihilation at the center of the human psyche, including Yalom, *Existential Psychotherapy*, Basic Books, 1980; and Ernest Becker, *The Denial of Death*, Free Press/Simon & Schuster, 1973. For a more personal, literary account, see Julian Barnes, *Nothing to Be Frightened Of*, Knopf, 2008.

[52] See Shelly Kagan, *Death*, Yale University Press, 2012, p. 279.

[53] For a more poetic version of this point, see Jonathan Swift, "The Ladies Dressing Room" (1732), *Swift: Poetical Works*, Oxford University Press, 1967, p. 318.

threatens meaning if being eternal is more meaningful than being finite. It is not clear that this is always the case, e.g., a rock lasts a lot longer than you do but is not therefore more valuable or meaningful; an ice cream cone, as discussed earlier, would not be more meaningful if it lasted forever. In order to evaluate how the fact that we are destined for annihilation via death affects the meaning in and of our lives, we may consider the ways in which being transitory, or temporary, can affect the meaning of the entity in question.

As discussed, the harder something is to achieve and the more its purpose is enhanced or achieved by permanence, the more its meaning is diminished by its eventual destruction. As I've shown, life, including the lives we lead, overall, has no purpose,[54] so dying cannot get in the way of the purpose of our lives. The things we do in our lives that give us Everyday Meaning are not negated by our eventual annihilation. (Time is what erodes the meaning of the things we do, as just discussed.) The *Mona Lisa* is not less meaningful, impactful, significant, or valuable because Da Vinci is dead. Being alive does demand considerable work. However, since that work is ultimately pointless anyway, it is not less meaningful for us that we do this work for a finite amount of time. You might think the opposite: since leading and living a life is ultimately pointless and difficult, at least it doesn't go on forever. As for the things we work at in our lives, the Everyday Meaning of that work—the devotion to our children, the beauty of our art, the valuable usefulness of the pipes laid down to provide the city's residents with indoor plumbing—is not diminished by the mortal nature of the person who does the work. That leaves our expectations. We do expect to die, but it's hard to internalize this knowledge because being alive is all we have ever known. Still, we expect to die. We are temporary

---

[54] Because without a purpose—a reason for which something is done—there can be no point, no valued end (since the valued end would also serve as a reason for the effort or activity). Like many characteristics of meaning, purpose and point are connected (see Introduction).

things that have no purpose and are not expected to last. Therefore, death does not make our lives not meaningful by annihilating us.

However, death does impose an Everyday Meaning limit and a loss, and perhaps a bit of an insult as well. Since death ends our efforts and engagements with Everyday Meaning, it presents a limit point for our Everyday Meaning—a *time* limit. There is thus a time limit to our meaningful engagements, a time limit to how much we can grow, change, achieve, and renew. Furthermore, since death annihilates us, and we are valuable due to our nature as conscious beings with awesome intellectual, moral, and creative capacities, it is a loss of value when a person dies (most people). The value of the person is not thereby eliminated, just as the value of the *Mona Lisa* would not be eliminated if it didn't last forever. But the loss of something valuable that would continue to be valuable if it persisted presents a loss of meaning since value is an aspect of meaning.

However, it is not certain that we wouldn't eventually feel some sense of annihilation even if we never died. If you lived forever, could you maintain the personality, psychological memory, and psychological continuity that provide the scaffolding for your sense of self such that it feels like it is you that is living forever?[55] Would it still feel like you singing your favorite song in a billion years? It can be difficult to imagine. You might no longer enjoy singing at all and lord help us if we are still listening to you singing that same song. It's likely that you too would have tired of it. Personality changes over time,[56] and over infinite time it is seems possible that it could change so greatly as to make the person you are now so radically different from who you will be fifty million years from now as to make it hard for it to feel like it is *you* that is living forever.[57] It is also hard to imagine that our memories would extend back far enough

---

[55] Williams, "The Makropolous Case," pp. 82–100.

[56] See Matthew A. Harris, Caroline E. Brett, Wendy Johnson, and Ian J. Deary, "Personality Stability from Age 14 to Age 77 Years," *American Psychology and Aging* 31 (2016): 862–874.

[57] See Williams, "The Makropolous Case," pp. 82–100.

to maintain the psychological connectedness[58] and continuity generally thought to be an important part of what most take to be themselves, at least not without significant biological upgrades.[59] I am referring here to a subjective sense of self, not to objective or external criteria for personal identity, since persisting while feeling as if you were annihilated is still a loss to the person experiencing it. If we lived long enough, could we remain similar enough and psychologically connected over time as to feel like ourselves forever? That could be a challenge because personalities change and memories fade over the course of a short life. An infinite life would presumably be similarly rife with changing and forgetting.[60] It's one thing to feel different from the boy you once were, as many older adults do without feeling as if they have been annihilated, but feeling radically different and/or having almost no memory of what or who you were like thirteen million years ago might make you feel so alienated from that distant self as to not feel personally like it is you that is living forever. We might have overlapping chains of psychological connection, just as we do now, giving us a sufficient sense of self, even over eons.[61] But perhaps not. Perhaps, eventually, we might come to feel that time itself annihilates us. If we lived forever, we would be spared the brutal way we are just blanked out of existence by death. But we might experience our pseudo-annihilation in a more agonizing way, seeing it coming, and living

[58] See Sydney Shoemaker, "Identity, Properties, and Causality," *Midwest Studies in Philosophy* 4 (1979): 321–342; and Shoemaker, "Personal Identity: A Materialist's Account," Shoemaker and Swinburne, *Personal Identity*, Wiley-Blackwell, 1991.

[59] See Shaun Nichols and Michael Bruno, "Intuitions About Personal Identity: An Empirical Study," *Philosophical Psychology* 23 (2010): 293–312.

[60] I am assuming a relatively stable human nature. If we instead develop microchips or genetic modifications that allow us to remember (and care about) things forever, that might prevent the kind of annihilation of self that seems otherwise possible over infinite time.

[61] If we have sufficient overlap, we can retain narrative value/meaning by seeing our lives as a serial, as discussed earlier. If we would eventually become a different person to ourselves, we might see our lives as a series of stories. Either way, immortality would not do away with narrative meaning. Thanks to Rom Gruman for helpful suggestions on this point.

through the process again and again. We might watch as each of our "selves" fades over time, again and again, knowing with each successive cycle that whatever makes us feel like ourselves will eventually wear away. The sands of time themselves might do us in, if we lived long enough.

We may wonder whether we might be able to adjust our expectations, efforts, and engagements to an evolving, ever-changing subjective sense of self. After all, the gradual changes to our personalities over time now don't usually cause a distressing sense of lack of sense of self, or annihilation. So why assume that we could not adapt to feeling like a series of selves over the course of an infinite life? Perhaps indeed we could, though why would that be different in terms of meaning than our present situation where current people die and new people are born? Furthermore, if we could adjust our sense of self that way, maybe we could adjust our current view of ourselves such that we internalize the idea of ourselves as temporary, like a balloon or a butterfly (or, for that matter, any living thing). Maybe then the fact of our eventual annihilation would feel less disruptive, and thereby less of a threat to Everyday Meaning, because it would feel like less of a loss of value and explanation. Regardless of how we might adapt, though, if annihilation presents a deep meaning problem, doing away with death may not fully resolve the ways in which time might present us with similar problems.

The Specter of Death

Let's remember that we don't just die of old age when we are ninety-five years old. Death is a constant threat. We live with death looming over us, in its shadow, under its threat. Some claim that this precarious-making specter-of-death fact of life both enhances and diminishes life's meaning.[62] Many argue that the specter of

---

[62] See Heidegger, *Being and Time*, pp. 302, 311; and May, *Death*, pp. 104–114.

death enhances life's meaning by making life risky, thereby, rewarding; and scarce, therefore uniquely valuable.[63] However, as argued earlier, we don't need death for risk or scarcity so it is unwarranted to consider the specter of a death a meaning enhancer. We have more than enough of the risk, reward, and scarcity elements necessary for meaning without needing death to add any more in order to make life meaningful. As with so many other things, the pessimists are right on this one: the specter of death diminishes life's meaning by threatening to cut us off at any time, before we have done our work, had a chance to play, raised our children, grown up; indeed, often before we have had much of a chance to live at all. Death hangs over our heads. It's a wonder we can carry on under these conditions at all, and some psychologists argue that suppressing our awareness of this specter, and our eventual death, is a primary human psychological drive.[64]

By bursting in unannounced, uninvited, often while we are busy living and planning for the future, we might think of an untimely death as a case of someone knocking over our sand castle when the sun is still high in the sky and we are engrossed mid-build. By subverting our purposes and negating our impact, the sand-castle-kicker diminishes the meaning of our day at the beach. When he was about three years old, apropos of nothing, my son declared: "You should have a good and happy life and not die in the middle."[65] An apt blessing. Dying "in the middle" threatens the meaning in our lives by cutting us off prematurely and unexpectedly, thwarting our everyday purposes, and diminishing the impact and significance of our everyday engagements. Because we work so hard at life and expect it to last a human lifespan, as argued earlier, the fact that

---

[63] See Hägglund, *This Life*, pp. 44–68; Nussbaum, *The Therapy of Desire*, pp. 227–229; May, *Death*, pp. 104–114; and Heidegger, *Being and Time*, p. 311.

[64] See Becker, *The Denial of Death*; Yalom, *Staring at the Sun*; and Sheldon Solomon, Jeff Greenberg, and Tom Pyszczynski, *The Worm at the Core: On the Role of Death in Life*, Random House, 2015.

[65] Joey Gruman, 2010.

life ends is more similar in its meaning implications to a house that burns after 150 years or so than to a sand castle that gets swept away with the tide, or even knocked over mid-build. The specter of death hounds our lives by constantly threatening to burn our house down while we still plan, expect, and need to live in it. This is consistent with my earlier suggestion that transience diminishes meaning to the extent that we work hard for the transient thing in question, expect it to last, and its transience is at odds with its purpose.

To belabor this metaphor, if our house burns, i.e., we die, when we've lived a "lifetime," it's far less a threat to the meaning in our lives than if it burns a lot earlier. If you "suddenly" die at ninety-five, the meaning loss posed by the abruptness of death does not seem to apply. I suggest that is because you have already lived an expected lifetime, even though it was probably difficult and it was definitely ultimately pointless. Still, you had your Everyday Meaning—your terrestrial horrors, escapades, and occasional delights—and living forever wouldn't solve your meaning problems anyway. A timely death is therefore not a great threat to meaning. But an untimely death is. (And it used to be commonplace: for most of human history, infant mortality, maternal mortality, war, and infection killed most people before they reached middle age. The human lifespan was not much shorter—those who lived long lives lived nearly as long as the long-lived do now—but most people didn't make it through to a natural human lifespan.)

What makes the specter of death a terrible threat to meaning is not that death occurs at all but that it often occurs without rhyme or reason, at any time, almost always too soon (life is indeed too short for optimum meaningful engagement),[66] and frequently before the business of living a human life is anywhere near done. Living with the specter of death, knowing that you and everyone you care about can die at any moment—can die "before their time"—threatens the

---

[66] See Weinberg, "Why Life Is Absurd: A Consideration of Time, Space, Relativity, Meaning and Absurdity (Yep, All of It)," *New York Times*, January 11, 2015.

meaning of our lives because it threatens to cut us off before we have accomplished the meaningful things we strive for. The children unraised, the manuscript unfinished, the love unexpressed. There is no upside to this sword of Damocles, and the better we get at keeping it at bay with seatbelts, antibiotics, and peace, etc., the more meaningful our lives can be. But time will come for our meaning in the end, one way or another, through erosion of impact, value, purpose, and significance, whether we die or not.

Conclusion

As we have seen, it is time, and not death, that provides for the narrative shape and trajectory that is important to meaning. It is time, and not death, that allows for the background conditions of risk, reward, and limited resources necessary for most meaning. It is time, and not death, that erodes the impact, significance, and value of our investments, efforts, and engagement. It is therefore not clear exactly how the fact that we die diminishes the meaning in or of our lives, except that it precludes further opportunities to engage with meaningful activity by limiting our time and enacts an abrupt loss of self. In this way, death presents a limitation and an abrupt loss for Everyday Meaning. The most significant meaning problem posed by death is that it comes too early and it comes whenever; no rhyme or reason. To the extent we can extend healthy human life (add a hundred years or so) and mitigate the specter of death, we will have a better shot at meaningful lives.

Its star billing notwithstanding, death is not the ghost that haunts our meaningful ambitions. We would have our meaning possibilities and our meaning problems whether we were mortal or not. It is time, and not death, that lends life its shape yet eventually wipes us and our deeds out, undercutting the meaning of our lives. Somewhat surprisingly, when it comes to meaning, death may be a less brutal way to have to face our meaning limitations because, although we know it's coming, we are spared having to watch as our past projects, loves, passions, and accomplishments spin out into meaninglessness. So don't blame or laud death as a meaning-maker or a meaning-slayer. Regarding meaning, for the most part death just does what time would do eventually anyway, but perhaps more mercifully. If you're going to have your commitments, relationships, and efforts eventually come to nothing, it's easier if you don't have to watch. It's less agonizing to die. Death is a marker of time: it tells you when your time is up, and takes you out of time and into nothingness (most likely). Time's the bitch, my friends: can't have meaning with her, can't have meaning without her either. Recognizing that time is what makes life both meaningful and not meaningful allows us to obsess a little less about death and reconcile with the fundamental element of our lives: the time we have to live.

5

TIME

Timing Is Everything...

The Time-Meaning Conundrum

Time is the fundamental element, currency, resource, backdrop, flow—the soup of our lives: "Time, not life, is what we live;"[1] "... We're in the swim, sinking in time, until finally we drown and go."[2] We speak of time elliptically, metaphorically, poetically, scientifically, but almost never clearly. It's frustrating and can be disturbingly surprising to realize that we have a hard time directly explaining the stage on which (or is it in which or of which?) our lives play out. Perhaps that's why we have so many metaphors for how time is the element and currency of our lives; for how we *live time*: we spend time, save time, waste time, burn time, kill time, do time, serve time, buy time, even steal time. Perhaps tellingly, we don't trade time. It's a bedrock value, yet not quite subject to exchange. It can seem so personal: in you,[3] of you, some go so far as to say it *is* you.[4] But what is it, and how does it relate to meaning?

[1] Samantha Harvey, *The Shapeless Unease: A Year of Not Sleeping*, Grove Press, 2020, p. 72.

[2] Philip Roth, *The Dying Animal*, Vintage Books/Random House, 2001, pp. 147–148.

[3] Both Aristotle and Kant speak of the inner sense of time, a "counting soul" of sorts (see Eva Brann, *What, Then, Is Time?* Rowman & Littlefield, 1999, pp. 35–93 and note 45).

[4] Heidegger is commonly interpreted as having this view—that we are, fundamentally, time (see Brann, *What, Then, Is Time?* p. 197). See also Oliver Burkeman, *Four Thousand Weeks: Time Management for Mortals*, Farrar, Straus, and Giroux, 2021, p. 217: "... we are nothing but moments"; among many others.

Whatever else we might say or be unable to say about time, it is crucial to meaning. Time allows for the dynamism so central to meaningful living. The arrow of time allows us to use our memory and our current state to project ourselves into the future,[5] and engage meaningfully with our environment. If we had no ability to predict or foresee the effects of our actions in time, what point would there be in taking them? Why bother reaching into the pool now to pull out the drowning child if pulling the child out did not predict the child being out of the water and back in breathable air for the future? Why bother reaching into the pool to pull out the drowning child if time had no predictable direction, such that by pulling the child out *after* she fell in, you gave her a chance to start breathing again and continue living into her future? Most meaningful activity requires at least some selection among possible futures,[6] which provides us with a way to express, engage with, or appreciate value. The direction of time provides us with a way to have an impact. It makes it possible for our lives to be explicable and to have a sensible trajectory, rather than a chaotic jumble. It allows us to pursue ends of value, to act with purpose, and to do things for a point. You do something now so that something else will happen, or be a certain way, in the future. Most meaningful activity requires the arrow of time.[7] More fundamentally, meaningful acts (in fact, all acts) are performances unfolding in time.

Without time, it is very difficult to see how we could have much meaning. But time also erodes meaning by eroding the impact, significance, and thereby the value of our meaningful engagements, efforts, and pursuits. Not entirely. As we have discussed, that kiss

---

[5] What the neuroscientist Dean Buonomano calls "mental time travel." See Buonomano, *Your Brain Is a Time Machine: The Neuroscience and Physics of Time*, W. W. Norton & Company, 2017, chapter 11.

[6] See Pierre Uzan, "The Arrow of Time and Meaning," *Foundations of Science* 12 (2007): 109–137, 125.

[7] See Uzan, "The Arrow of Time and Meaning"; see also Chapter 4.

isn't meaningless just because it happened already and is securely in the past; the fun you had while watching the ballgame didn't last but it wasn't supposed to and it was indeed a fun time (the activity met its expectation and purpose, and it was not much work—its transience is not a challenge to its meaning according to the measures of how transience affects meaning).[8] And, as Landau noted, it will always be true that you loved your mother, and just because Martin Luther King Jr. and Jack the Ripper are both dead and gone, that doesn't mean that their lives had no meaning or had equal significance and value.[9] Transience doesn't exclude meaning.

But it wears a lot of it away, given enough time, especially for efforts that are difficult and for purposes that include longevity. The swept floor gets dirty again, friendships fade, the justice we worked so hard to gain slips away and our society reverts to injustice or oppression. The art we created gets destroyed in a natural disaster (or one of our own making), the books go out of print, the music we created goes out of fashion and fades from memory. Relationships fall apart or grow apart. As we noted, time eventually wears away the effects of our efforts and engagements, thereby diminishing the impact and significance, and challenging the purposes and point, of much of what we do and care about. In five thousand years (probably a lot less), both Martin Luther King Jr. and Jack the Ripper will have faded into insignificance. Their deeds, their accomplishments, both for good and for ill, will not endure and it will eventually be as if neither had ever lived. Thus, given a long enough view, everything eventually seems to come to something close to nothing, and that does detract to some degree from our efforts, especially when those efforts were difficult and aimed at purposes intended to have lasting effects, as we have recognized.[10]

[8] See Chapter 4.
[9] Landau, *Finding Meaning in an Imperfect World*, pp. 85–87.
[10] See Chapter 4.

Thus Schopenhauer laments, somewhat melodramatically:

> *Time* and that *perishability* of all things existing in time that time itself brings about is simply the form under which the will to live, which as thing in itself is imperishable, reveals to itself the vanity of its striving. Time is that by virtue of which everything becomes nothingness in our hands and loses all real value.[11]

Time, and more specifically, the very dynamism that allows for meaning, also gives rise to the erosion process by which meaning drains out. Time is necessary for meaning since only within time can you engage with meaning, yet time also erodes meaning by wearing away the fruits of our meaningful engagement. Hence, the conundrum.

The constant flux and change—the entropy that governs our lives—is a source of stress and suffering, and can lead to crises of meaning.[12] Your swept floor will soon be dirty again, your children will eventually die, the work you did will soon be undone and forgotten, as will you. Whole philosophies and ways of life have been developed to mitigate this aspect of the human condition.[13] Life is deeply unstable, not just because lots of things are precarious and unreliable but because eventually *everything* changes, erodes, dissipates, and disappears. The evanescent nature of our existence can make meaning feel slippery, faithless; a phantom. The inherent instability of everything makes trauma—the reeling, shocked emotional reaction to abrupt change or loss—"all pervasive" . . . a "fact of life."[14] The facts of time, i.e., the ever-changing and decaying

---

[11] Schopenhauer, "On the Vanity of Existence," p. 51.

[12] As we saw with Tolstoy (see Chapter 4).

[13] See section "What Can We Do About It?" The psychiatrist Mark Epstein interprets Buddhism this way (see Epstein, *The Trauma of Everyday Life*, Penguin Books, 2014). Some interpret Existentialism and Existential psychotherapy similarly (see Yalom, *Existential Psychotherapy*, and *Staring at the Sun: Overcoming the Terror of Death*). One can read Heidegger this way (Heidegger, *Being and Time*).

[14] See Epstein, *The Trauma of Everyday Life*, pp. 1–3.

nature of our existence, the ferment and flux and entropy of life, challenge our meaningful aspirations.

Time is inherently a double-edged sword. "Time heals all wounds," "this too shall pass"—but "all good things come to an end." The dynamism of time allows for meaning. Yet it is also a cause of erosion of meaning and the trauma of everyday life. We want the meaning, but we don't want it to crumble. Yet it seems that time saddles us with both: it provides us with opportunity for meaningful engagement, but it also wears away a good deal of our meaningful achievements, commitments, and projects. That is the time-meaning conundrum, and we cannot get a firm grip on meaning and our struggles with it without confronting it. It is time to face off with Father Time and see what we can make of this paradoxical, bittersweet, vexing, soothing, traumatic meaning conundrum: Time.

Time? What Time?

Start talking about time and its effects and you might be waved off by skepticism about time being real at all, being merely relative, or only existing in a subjective, manipulable, dubious haze. So how big a conundrum can it pose? This skeptical attempt to minimize the time-meaning conundrum will not succeed because, as I will explain, even the most scientifically bare-bones conception of time—entropy—is enough to generate the time-meaning conundrum. That's really all you need. But, for the recalcitrant time skeptics who might still worry about the reality of time and, therefore, the reality of the time-meaning conundrum, I will also explain how physics, biology, and neuroscience provide an objective basis for our experience of time, and some insight into some of the ways in which we may experience temporal illusions. Although time is difficult to understand, it is firmly a part of reality; both the reality of the world and the reality of human experience.

Entropy

The second law of thermodynamics tells us that while heat can move from a hot object to a cold object, it will not spontaneously move from a cold object to a hot object.[15] (Bear with me! No equations, I promise.) An implication or part of this law is *entropy*, i.e., the fact that disorder increases rather than decreases within an isolated system such as the universe (which is why you can't unscramble an egg).[16] Although entropy may seem to just tell us boring things about how molecules move between hot and cold environments, it is a scientifically accepted basis for a lot of what we call or experience as time. It shapes our experience and gives us a direction of change and an arrow of time, of sorts; *a movement in only one direction.*[17]

Living entails a thermodynamic direction. Life itself can be characterized as the entropic process of moving energy from the hot sun to the cold earth.[18] Eating is a process of consuming an ordered form of energy and then "rejecting a disorganized form of energy (heat) into the cosmos."[19] You can only do this if you have a thermal imbalance between the hot source providing

[15] This law was formulated by the physicists William Thomson and Rudolph Clausius. See https://www.britannica.com/science/second-law-of-thermodynamics.

[16] See Jim Lucas, "What Is the Second Law of Thermodynamics?," *Live Science*, February 7, 2022; and *Libretexts/Chemistry*, "2nd Law of Thermodynamics," August 15, 2020, https://chem.libretexts.org/Bookshelves/Physical_and_Theoretical_Chemistry_Textbook_Maps/Supplemental_Modules_(Physical_and_Theoretical_Chemistry)/Thermodynamics/The_Four_Laws_of_Thermodynamics/Second_Law_of_Thermodynamics.

[17] Entropy is accepted science, as is the asymmetry of the direction of time. There is less agreement regarding how global or absolute the arrow of time is (see section "Time? What Time?").

[18] This is how the renowned physicist Ludwig Boltzmann characterized it ("The Second Law of Thermodynamics," 1886, *Theoretical Physics and Philosophical Problems*, Brian McGuiness, Ed., Reidel Publishing Company, 1975, p. 24). The physicist Carlo Rovelli reasons similarly, incorporating twenty-first-century physics and quantum mechanics into his theory of time, yet still concluding that ". . . Life is this network of processes for increasing entropy"; Rovelli, *The Order of Time*, Riverhead Books, 2018, p. 162.

[19] Uzan, "The Arrow of Time and Meaning," p. 117.

the ordered energy and a cold source absorbing disorganized energy.[20] The arrow of time gives us life, so to speak, and it also gives us opportunities for meaningful engagement. Meaningful engagement requires entropy—i.e., *change in a predictable and irreversible direction*—so that you can, for example, compose music, then record it, then have others listen to it, etc. So that you can crack the egg, scramble it, and then eat it (though entropy doesn't tell you if the chicken came first). Entropy provides us with the possibility of change in an irreversible direction, which we need for meaningful action. Change in an irreversible direction is one part of the physical law of entropy. But entropy also entails that things fall apart,[21] so entropy is also the process by which so much meaning is lost. Entropy entails that everything tends toward increased disorder,[22] making the effort we put into bringing order into our lives something of a losing proposition. Entropy takes life and opportunity for meaningful engagement away since we, and everything we do and care about, age and decay in one direction.

Time is notoriously difficult to describe, yet it governs our lives and pervades our experience. That's probably why one of the most quoted statements about time is from St. Augustine, capturing this dichotomy: "What, then, is time? If nobody asks me, I know. If I want to explain it to him who asks, I don't know."[23] Despite this difficulty, all we need to generate the time-meaning conundrum is entropy, which necessitates change in a predictable and irreversible direction (so we can do meaningful things) and the inevitability of decay (so the meaningful things we do don't last and we ourselves

---

[20] Uzan, "The Arrow of Time and Meaning," p. 117.

[21] See Lucas, "What Is the Second Law of Thermodynamics?"; *Libretexts/Chemistry*, and pretty much anywhere else.

[22] Since there are more disordered states for a system to be in than there are ordered states, random interactions lead to greater disorder. (Lucas, "What Is the Second Law of Thermodynamics?"; and *Libretexts/Chemistry*).

[23] St. Augustine, *Confessions* (c. 400), E. B. Pusey, trans., Project Gutenberg, 2023, Book XI, chapter XIV.

don't last), and is shown by the second law of thermodynamics.[24] So the time-meaning conundrum cannot be easily dismissed. All it takes to generate it is entropy.

Yet we can go further than entropy in addressing the time skeptic's resistance to the time-meaning conundrum (though entropy is sufficient to generate the conundrum): Time is real *and* relative. Our physical sciences provide evidence for the reality and objectivity of the irreversible and directional nature of time, and our life sciences point to the objective basis for how we experience time. For those skeptical enough about the nature and reality of time to be tempted to dismiss the time-meaning conundrum, I will briefly provide the most basic of thumbnail sketches describing the ways in which time is real and relative (to space, perceptual apparatus, and other factors) so that it's clear that these skeptical worries don't present grounds for dismissing the conundrum. This will involve a bit of the metaphysics of time and some empirical information about time and our perception of it. For those not gripped by time skepticism or who are otherwise uninterested in the vagaries of time, feel free to skip the rest of this section and go on to the next section, where I discuss what we can do about the time-meaning conundrum.

Does Time Flow or Stand Still?

One way to capture the various ways to conceive of time is to consider what led J. M. E. McTaggart to conclude that time is not real.[25] In his famous 1908 paper, McTaggart divided theories of time into what he called A-theory and B-theory. The catchy names—A and B (Thing 1 and Thing 2?[26])—stuck. A-theory is the view that there is

[24] See Lucas, "What Is the Second Law of Thermodynamics?"; *Libretexts/Chemistry*, and pretty much anywhere else.

[25] J. M. E. McTaggart, "The Unreality of Time," *Mind* 17 (1908): 457–473.

[26] Thing 1 and Thing 2 are the names Dr. Seuss had the cat give his helpers in the classic children's book, *The Cat in the Hat*, Random House, 1957.

an absolute past, present, and future, and that time is like a classic arrow of time timeline, wherein every point in time has an absolute position and time *passes*.[27] B-theory is the view that time is tenseless, and fully analogous to space: just as objects are distributed through space, events are distributed through time.[28] Thus, events are not past or present (absolute) but earlier or later than each other (relative, just as things are taller or shorter relative to each other). "Here," a location, and "now," a point in time, are local, and relative. B-theory is tenseless (there's no past/present/future, just earlier/later relations) and presents a "block universe view of time," i.e., a four-dimensional, unchanging "block," in which all times exist and there is no basis for singling out a time as "present." According to B-theory, "none of the dynamic features of time are real."[29] It's a kind of *Slaughterhouse-Five* view of the universe, where there is no privileged present and time is static, leaving us no particular reason to cry at a funeral, as Kurt Vonnegut's narrator explains: "… The dead person is in bad condition in that particular moment, but … the same person is just fine in plenty of other moments."[30]

McTaggart found both A- and B-theory implausible, and it is easy to agree with that assessment. A-theory contradicts physics because Einstein showed that time is not absolute, but relative such that there is no objective or fixed present. The Special Theory of Relativity shows that simultaneity—whether two events occur in the "present"—depends on the frame of reference in which they are measured.[31] The Lorentz time dilation of Special Relativity Theory tells us that clocks at rest in different reference frames that are in motion with respect to each other will have different times

---

[27] See Simon Prosser, *Experiencing Time*, Oxford University Press, 2016. Most A-theorists argue that only the present is real, a view known as "presentism" (see Prosser, *Experiencing Time*, pp. 5–7).

[28] Prosser, *Experiencing Time*, pp. 1–2.

[29] Prosser, *Experiencing Time*, pp. 1–2.

[30] Kurt Vonnegut, *Slaughterhouse-Five* (1969), Dial Press, 2009, p. 34.

[31] Prosser, *Experiencing Time*, pp. 18–19, and any basic physics textbook written after the dissemination of Einstein's Special Theory of Relativity.

elapsed when they return to the same place.[32] Even more simply put, Einstein showed that time passes more quickly at higher elevations.[33] So time is not absolute and A-theory cannot be correct. Its contradiction of settled science makes it a non-starter.[34]

But that's not why McTaggart rejects A-theory.[35] He finds that A-theory contradicts itself, which is an even worse thing for a theory to do than to contradict something else, even if that something else is settled science. McTaggart argues that A-theory is contradictory because no event can be past, present, and future but every event is so at one time. (To respond to that contradiction by saying that no event is past/present/future at the *same* time, you must already assume that time passes, which is what A-theory is supposed to show rather than assume.)[36]

So much for A-theory. But B-theory is deeply problematic as well because it doesn't include change, which McTaggart took to be necessary in any theory of time ("time involves change")[37] and which I have argued is central to meaning. Thus, McTaggart rejects B-theory. Many philosophers reject B-theory due to its lack of dynamism: It doesn't seem to account for the human experience of change and succession;[38] it doesn't explain our experience

[32] Hyperphysics, "Time Dilation," Georgia State University, 2024. http://hyperphysics.phy-astr.gsu.edu/hbase/Relativ/tdil.html.

[33] See Rovelli, *The Order of Time*, pp. 10–17.

[34] Some contemporary A-theorists argue that Special Relativity Theory tells us that *measuring* simultaneity is relative but not that there is no absolute simultaneity. Some also argue that there exists a privileged time frame that defines absolute simultaneity but doesn't appear in physical measurements (see Prosser, *Experiencing Time*, p. 19). However, this defense seems to contradict settled science (again, see any contemporary physics textbook or encyclopedia, https://en.wikipedia.org/wiki/Special_relativity).

[35] McTaggart's rejection of A-theory could not be due to its contradiction of settled science because the science it contradicts was not yet discovered, let alone settled, at the time. McTaggart's paper preceded Einstein's discoveries about spacetime.

[36] McTaggart, "The Unreality of Time," pp. 466–470. Prosser argues that A-theory is unintelligible because there is no property such as the passing of time (*Experiencing Time*, p. 54).

[37] McTaggart, "The Unreality of Time," pp. 466–470, 459.

[38] William James, *The Principles of Psychology*, Henry Holt, 1890, pp. 628–629. Shoemaker argues that it is conceivable to detect time without experiencing change ("Time Without Change," *The Journal of Philosophy* 66 [1969]: 363–381). But some take

of temporal motion (the past recedes, the future approaches);[39] it doesn't account for our different attitudes toward the past and the future (we are relieved or nostalgic about the past; we dread or anticipate the future).[40] Some even argue that we must reject B-theory and embrace A-theory even though A-theory contradicts Special Relativity because, without dynamism, we cannot have meaning.[41] (That's quite the pill to swallow! Ignore what seems to be empirically true because we need meaning.) B-theorists respond to the criticisms about its view of time as static by arguing that our experience of dynamism is illusory.[42] But this view seems to contradict not only human experience but basic science as well, since entropy gives us both change (dynamism) and an irreversible direction of change (see earlier discussion). B-theory also does not seem to allow for the indeterminacy of quantum mechanics.[43]

Because we have reason to reject both A-theory and B-theory, McTaggart concludes that time is unreal.[44] If it were true that time is "unreal," then we might wonder whether it's time to rethink lots of our thoughts about meaning. Maybe give up on it entirely.[45] But

Shoemaker to have begged the question (see Denis Corish, "Could Time Be Change?" *Philosophy* 66 [1969]: 363–381).

[39] See Peter van Inwagen, *Metaphysics*, Westview Press, 2nd ed., 2002, p. 64.

[40] See A. N. Prior, "Thank Goodness That's Over," *Philosophy* 34 (1959): 12–17; and David Cockburn, *Other Times: Philosophical Perspectives on Past, Present, and Future*, Cambridge University Press, 1997, chapter 2. Nagel responds by arguing that although we are relieved when a bad thing is over, our reasons for action remain timeless (see Nagel, *The Possibility of Altruism*, Princeton University Press, 1970, p. 71). Prosser has a similar response (see Prosser, *Experiencing Time*, chapter 3), as do many others.

[41] See Ned Markosian, "Meaning in Life and the Nature of Time," *The Oxford Handbook of Meaning in Life*, chapter 11.

[42] See L. A. Paul, "Experience and the Arrow," *Chance and Temporal Asymmetry*, A. Wilson, Ed., Oxford University Press, 2015; James Tartaglia, *Philosophy in a Meaningless Life*, Bloomsbury, 2016, pp. 141–143; and Prosser, *Experiencing Time*, p. 30, and chapters 6 and 7. Buonomano discusses some time illusions but rejects the view of time's dynamism as entirely illusory (see Buonomano, *Your Brain Is a Time Machine*, chapters 4 and 9).

[43] For a defense of B-theory, see Prosser, *Experiencing Time*.

[44] See McTaggart, "The Unreality of Time."

[45] We might agree with Taylor, that to deny time is to "suggest that our rejoicings and sorrowings rest upon illusion" and "would rob our lives of all meaning." See Taylor, "Time and Life's Meaning," *The Review of Metaphysics* 40 (1987): 675–686, 675.

McTaggart's conclusion seems overly hasty. If we look at scientific evidence, we will see that time is real, dynamic, and relative (both to space and to the perspective/nature of the perceiver); real, but perhaps a bit local in its deterministic behavior (at extremely high speeds, or at the quantum level, time can be funky).[46]

Time Is a Dynamic Relation

Historically, time in human society has functioned as a measurement of regular motion or change, such as the movement of the sun in the sky, the movement of sand through an hourglass, or, more recently, the rate of decay of certain atoms (atomic clocks).[47] Roughly speaking, our measurement of time has always included a rate of change that occurs to objects in space with regularity.[48]

Einstein discovered that time and space together form the gravitational field, which is not perfectly uniform across the universe because it is curved or warped by mass.[49] Space and time exist, and are quite real, but they are not independent of each other; they are relative to each other.[50] At the quantum level, the tiniest of particles

[46] See Rovelli, *The Order of Time*, chapter 5.

[47] See David Rooney, *About Time: A History of Civilization in Twelve Clocks*, W. W. Norton & Company, 2021.

[48] Because anytime you have an object, you have mass, and mass exerts and responds to gravitational force. See "Newton's Law of Gravitation," *The Physics Classroom*, https://www.physicsclassroom.com/class/circles/Lesson-3/Newton-s-Law-of-Universal-Gravitation, and pretty much any other current introductory physics text.

[49] See Richard Feynman, *Physics Lectures*, 42 "Curved Space," CalTech, https://www.feynmanlectures.caltech.edu/II_42.html#Ch42-SUM, or any basic physics text. We can think of spacetime as the bounce mat of a trampoline. Imagine putting a heavy bowling ball in the middle of the mat. It would sag downward and curve underneath the ball, due to the mass of the ball. And if you then added a tennis ball, the tennis ball would roll toward the bowling ball, i.e., toward the greater mass (see Dave Farina, *Professor Dave Explains*, "General Relativity: The Curvature of Spacetime," https://www.youtube.com/watch?v=R7V3koyL7Mc).

[50] Rather than a drawing on a canvas, the world includes layers and forces that flex and stretch against each other, e.g., clocks slow down near something massive because the gravitational field curves spacetime and time passes more slowly due to that curvature. See Rovelli, *The Order of Time*, pp. 76–77; and Christopher S. Baird, "Does Time Go Faster at the Top of a Building Compared to the Bottom?," *Science Questions*

or the most minute scale of reality, time seems to behave less uniformly or hardly at all.[51] The indeterminacy of quantum mechanics entails that just as between one appearance or measurement and another an electron has no precise position,[52] spacetime fluctuates as well such that it is only determined at certain instants, when it interacts with something else.[53] Thus, we can conceive of time as a "network of relations."[54] However, at our scale, the differences in speed at which time passes relative to distance from mass are too small to register to us.[55] Thus, for us and in our area of our universe, time behaves pretty uniformly and predictably.[56] Yet even at the quantum level, some physicists argue that because measuring an electron forces it into a definite location from which it is not possible to go back, quantum mechanics includes time irreversibility, the flow of time; an arrow of time.[57] Thus, at a minimum, we can think of time as perhaps a tad local in its deterministic and flowy behavior. And even this minimalistic view of time doesn't make time, entropy, or the direction of change any less real. Just as, to

with Surprising Answers, June 4, 2013, https://www.wtamu.edu/~cbaird/sq/2013/06/24/does-time-go-faster-at-the-top-of-a-building-compared-to-the-bottom/#:~:text=Gravitational%20time%20dilation%20occurs%20because,the%20slower%20time%20itself%20proceeds.

[51] For the gravitational field, the minimum is called the Planck scale, which tells us that at the minute scale of time, i.e., 10^{-44} seconds, "the notion of time is no longer valid" (Rovelli, *The Order of Time,* pp. 82–84). The spatial analogue, Planck length, is around 10^{-33} centimeters, "the minimum limit below which the notion of length becomes meaningless" (Rovelli, *The Order of Time,* p. 86).

[52] This is an implication of Heisenberg's famous Uncertainty Principle (see Werner Heisenberg, "On the Perceptual Content of Quantum Theoretical Kinematics and Mechanics," *Z. Physics* 33 [1925]: 879–893).

[53] This is basic to quantum mechanics. See Rovelli, *The Order of Time,* pp. 86–90, or any current quantum mechanics basic text.

[54] See Rovelli, *The Order of Time,* p. 90.

[55] See Rovelli, *The Order of Time,* p. 197.

[56] As opposed to time near a black hole, where paradoxical spacetime things may occur due to the extreme force of gravity exerted by the great, compact mass; e.g., some argue that in a black hole you have to move toward the present rather than the future to exit it, even though this is impossible (see Rovelli, *The Order of Time,* p. 55).

[57] See George Ellis, "On the Flow of Time," *FXQi,* 2008, https://arxiv.org/pdf/0812.0240.pdf, p. 1.

be simplistic but accurate, the fact that there is no absolute up or down in the universe doesn't mean that the upstairs bedroom of your house is not up or above your basement.

Time is also relative to the kinds of organisms we are and to our perceptual apparatus. Organisms with faster metabolisms and smaller body sizes perceive time more quickly than organisms with slower metabolisms and larger body sizes.[58] When sensory information is processed slowly, time feels faster; when it's processed quickly, time feels slower because if you perceive slowly, things are happening faster than you can perceive them, like a blur. If you perceive quickly, you perceive more things happening within a span of time, so it seems like you're slower relative to those perceptions.[59] This explains why the fly evades your swat: it sees it coming; the movement of the swatter is perceived as slower by the fly than it's perceived by you.[60]

Time also feels differently to us relative to how absorbed we are in what we're doing, how painful something is, how dangerous it is, and whether we are perceiving an event as it happens or in our memory of the event.[61] When we are engaged in a task, "lost in thought," absorbed in what we are doing, time can fly by without our even noticing it,[62] but when we are waiting in line, time seems to pass more slowly as we do nothing but attend to its passing.[63] When

---

[58] See Kevin Healy, Luke McNally, Graeme D. Ruxton, Natalie Cooper, and Andrew L. Jackson, "Metabolic Rate and Body Size are Linked with Perception of Temporal Information," *Animal Behavior* 86 (2013): 685–696.

[59] See Burgundy Bug, "How Animals Perceive Time," *The Burgundy Zine*, April 16, 2020.

[60] Healy et al., *Animal Behavior*.

[61] As Buonomano points out: "Prospective timing is a true temporal task in that it relies on the brain's circuits," but retrospective timing is "an attempt to infer the passage of time by reconstructing events stored in memory" (*Your Brain Is a Time Machine*, p. 60).

[62] See Philip A. Gable and Bryan D. Poole, "Time Flies When You're Having Approach-Motivated Fun: Effects of Motivational Intensity on Time Perception," *Psychological Science* 23 (2012): 879–886; and Ritu Agarwal and Elena Karahanna, "Time Flies When You're Having Fun: Cognitive Absorption and Beliefs About Information Technology Usage," *MIS Quarterly* 24 (2000): 665–694; among many others.

[63] See Robert E. Hicks, George W. Miller, and Marcel Kinsbourne, "Prospective and Retrospective Judgments of Time as a Function of Amount of Information Processed,"

something is painful, we attend to it and usually have an emotional response, both of which can make its duration seem longer than it actually was.[64] Trying to suppress our emotions, which we might sensibly try to do while in pain, can also make an event seem to last longer.[65] When something is dangerous, we pay more attention as well, and time can seem to slow down, as is commonly reported by people recounting life-threatening experiences.[66] Finally, we may remember events temporally differently than we perceive them at the time. An example of this is the "holiday paradox" wherein a delay at the airport seems to take forever while waiting, and a fun day flies by while you're having your bit of fun, but, in memory, the opposite is true.[67] In memory, the delay is but a blip, yet you remember all the details of the fun day and it seems long in your memory. Empty time seems long in passing but short in retrospect. This is because engaging stuff flies by since we're not thinking about the time but, retrospectively, the duration of activities "is estimated in part by the number of events stored in memory,"[68] and waiting, as annoying as it is, is still only one looooong event.[69] The opposite happens with retrospective timing—the more cognitively

The American Journal of Psychology 89 (1976): 719–730; and Richard A. Block, Peter A. Hancock, and Dan Zakay, "How Cognitive Load Affects Duration Judgments: A Meta-analytic Review, " *Acta Psychologica* 134 (2010): 330–343.

[64] See Amadine E. Ray, George A. Michael, Corina Dondas, Marvin Thar, Luis Garcia Larrea, and Stephanie Mazza, "Pain Dilates Time Perception," *Scientific Reports* 7 (2017): 15862.

[65] See Kathleen Vohs and Brandon J. Schmeichel, "Self-Regulation and the Extended Now: Controlling the Self Alters the Subjective Experience of Time," *Journal of Personality and Social Psychology* 85 (2003): 217–230.

[66] See lbert von St. Gallen Heim, "Remarks on Fatal Falls" (1892), Russell Noyes, Jr., and Roy Kletti, trans., *Omega—Journal of Death and Dying* 3 (1972): 45–52; Leah Campbell and Richard Bryant, "How Time Flies: A Study of Novice Skydivers," *Behavior Research and Therapy* 45 (2007): 1389–1392; and Burkhard Bilger, "The Possibilian: What a Brush with Death Taught David Eagleman About the Mysteries of Time and the Brain," *The New Yorker*, April 18, 2011, 54–65, among many others.

[67] See Buonomano, *Your Brain Is a Time Machine*, p. 60.

[68] See Buonomano, *Your Brain Is a Time Machine*, p. 60.

[69] See Buonomano, *Your Brain Is a Time Machine*, p. 60. The fun day also gets more memory priority because it is more novel than a delay.

demanding an experience is, the longer it seems to have taken in retrospect.[70]

Illusions and distortions of time notwithstanding,[71] time is fundamental to our brain processes and, indeed, to every cell, which has a circadian rhythm even when deprived of light.[72] Your cat may not be able to tell you what time it is, but it knows if you left it overnight because it can assess a time interval.[73] One of the brain's main jobs is to learn from the past and predict the future so that you can survive and reproduce in your changing environment.[74] The brain's internal sense of time allows us to understand speech, appreciate music, plan for the future, and recall the past. Prosody, the rhythm of speech, requires a sense of time so that we can understand the difference between "grade A" and "gray day."[75] (The brain's sense of time, of expected interval, is why we cannot understand speech or appreciate music that is extremely slowed down or sped up).[76] Everyday activities, such as gauging when you can safely cross a street or where to put your hand to catch a ball, require the brain to tell time. Catching the ball demands a sense of both space and time and a rudimentary expectation of their interaction. In fact, evidence indicates that organisms borrowed spatial neurocircuits to provide for an understanding and use of time,[77] leading to the fascinating speculation that perhaps we think of space and time as inherently connected scientifically because our brain is so structured biologically.[78]

[70] See Buonomano, *Your Brain Is a Time Machine*, p. 62.

[71] For an extensive discussion of temporal illusions, see Buonomano, *Your Brain Is a Time Machine*, chapter 4.

[72] Buonomano, *Your Brain Is a Time Machine*, p. 36.

[73] James G. Heys and Daniel A. Dombeck, "Evidence for a Subcircuit in Medial Entorhinal Cortex Representing Elapsed Time During Immobility," *Nature Neuroscience* 21 (2018): 1574–1582.

[74] See Buonomano, *Your Brain Is a Time Machine*, chapter 2.

[75] See Buonomano, *Your Brain Is a Time Machine*, p. 32.

[76] See Buonomano, *Your Brain Is a Time Machine*, pp. 99–100.

[77] See Geoffrey Lee, "Temporal Experience and the Temporal Structure of Experience," *Philosopher's Imprint* 14 (2014): 1–22, 17–18; and Buonomano, *Your Brain Is a Time Machine*, p. 178.

[78] Buonomano, *Your Brain Is a Time Machine*, p. 178.

Thus, we may conclude that time is real but relative; both objective and somewhat subjective: fundamental on the outside in terms of being part of the basic physical laws and processes of the universe and fundamental on the inside in terms of being basic to the structure of our brains, and to our experience of and in the world. There is no escaping it and, as we will soon see even more clearly,[79] that sort of cure would be far worse for meaning than the disease.

Before we move on, a quick shout out to some of the many great minds of history that clued in to the deep mysteries and truths of time long before empirical tools could show them to be on to something: to Plato, who distinguished between external and internal time and noted the mysteries and paradoxes of time;[80] Aristotle, who said that time is dependent on change;[81] St. Augustine, who recognized the mystery of time[82] and also that the past/future are in the mind and that's how we can become aware of duration even though the past doesn't now exist and neither does the future;[83] Newton, who thought that time was motion (which is the change that entropy describes—molecules moving from hot to cold);[84] Kant, who theorized that time was inside us, as the way our brains are structured to perceive and experience the world;[85] Leibniz, who said that time is a relation which abstracts from the nature of change;[86] Shakespeare, who knew that time was relative;[87] Hegel,

[79] See section "What Can We Do About It?"

[80] Plato, *Timeus* (360 BC), Donald J. Zeyl, trans., Hackett Publishing Company, 2000. See also Viktor Ilievski, "Eternity and Time in Plato's Timeus," *Živa Antika* 65 (2015): 5–22.

[81] Aristotle, *Physics* (c. 384–322 BC), C. D. C. Reeve, trans., Hackett Publishing Company, 2018, Book IV: 10–14.

[82] St. Augustine, *Confessions*, Book XI, chapter XIV.

[83] St. Augustine, *Confessions*, Book XI, chapters XXXIV–XXXVI.

[84] Sir Isaac Newton, *Principia Mathematica* (1686), Andrew Motte, trans., Daniel Adee, 1846, p. 77.

[85] Kant, *Critique of Pure Reason* (1781), Norman Kemp Smith, trans., St. Martin's Press, 1965, Part I, Section 2, Time, pp. 74–78.

[86] Leibniz, *Metaphysical Foundations of Mathematics* (1714), Leroy E. Loemker, trans., University of Chicago Press, 1956, p. 1083.

[87] William Shakespeare, *As You Like It* (c. 1600), Project Gutenberg, 1998, Act III, Scene 2 (Rosalind says, "Time travels in divers paces with divers person").

who argued that the idea of time develops from space;[88] Husserl, who argued that memory is crucial to our sense of time;[89] and Proust, who keyed into the relationship between time, subjectivity, and memory.[90]

What Can We Do About It?

Dismissing the time-meaning conundrum by facilely denying the reality of time is unwarranted. We have to face the fact that time is necessary for meaning yet time erodes meaning. What can we do about it? Let's examine some of the possibilities. Will any of them work? No. (Of course!) However, we can tease out some insights from these failed attempts and thereby make progress toward coping with things as they are. (For purposes of this discussion, the kind of meaning referred is to Everyday Meaning and "life" refers to "everyday life," not to the project, effort, or enterprise of leading a life.)

Forget Time and Live in the Present

As we have noted,[91] focusing on the present is something that has been recommended throughout centuries of recorded history and across divergent cultures as a way to cope with the crushing existential angst and crises of meaning caused by our awareness of the inexorable march of time, inevitable decay, and all the ways that time

[88] Wilhelm Friedrich Hegel, *Encyclopedia of the Philosophical Sciences*, Part II: Philosophy of Nature (1830), A. V. Miller, trans., Oxford University Press, 1970, Sections 257–259.

[89] Edmund Husserl, *Phenomenology of Internal Time Consciousness* (1904–1905), James S. Churchill, trans., Indiana University Press, 1964, Section two.

[90] Marcel Proust, *Remembrance of Things Past*, Volume One (1913), C. K. Scott Moncrieff and Terence Kilmartin, trans., Vintage Books/Random House, 1981, "Swann's Way," pp. 3–52.

[91] See Chapter 4, section "How Death Supposedly Threatens Meaning."

can erode meaning. This has some commonsense appeal. Dwelling on past disappointments and failures or constantly lamenting how quickly things pass or fall apart will probably not make life feel more meaningful or tolerable.

Worrying all the time about the future can rob you of the meaning and joy of the present because you are not really there to enjoy it when you are mentally and emotionally looking fearfully ahead instead. Being hyper-focused on future goals can be stressful and leave you feeling like you're always running on a treadmill to nowhere since every reached goal is immediately supplanted by a new unreached one if you don't stop for a while to appreciate your accomplishment. Perhaps it will feel better, freer, more unburdened by temporal worries, to stay present, to live in the moment. The Buddha ("Do not dwell in the past, do not dream of the future, concentrate the mind on the present moment"),[92] the Stoics ("Think no longer of life than that which is now present: then shalt thou be truly able to pass the remainder of thy days without troubles and distractions"),[93] psychologists of all stripes and persuasions[94]— they all seem to agree: Live in the moment. Focus on the present. Unfortunately, if you are interested in meaning, this is extremely terrible advice. Luckily, it is also impossible to follow. If we take it less literally, it is only a little bit less terrible advice, and somewhat less impossible to follow.

It is extremely terrible advice because, although obsessing over the past or the future is a temporally distorted attitude that has little to recommend it and will not make life more meaningful or more tolerable, focusing only on the present is a similarly temporally distorted attitude that will not make life more meaningful (though

---

[92] *The Teaching of Buddha*, p. 191 (this exact quote is disputed, but it does present a central tenet or recommendation of Buddhism; see fakebuddhaquotes.com).

[93] See Aurelius, *Meditations of Marcus Aurelius*, Book XII Section 2.

[94] For a classic example, see Rollo May, *Man's Search for Himself*. For contemporary examples, see all manner of pontifications on "mindfulness," e.g., Ekhart Tolle, *The Power of Now*.

it may sometimes make it more tolerable—more on that later). It won't make life more meaningful because the present borrows meaning from the past and the future and, without that meaning, is stripped bare of most meaning.

The past and the future give us reasons for action and help make sense of what we do and how we feel—the explanation aspect of meaning. The fact that you said the umbrella was in the closet yesterday (the past) gives me a reason to go to the closet to get the umbrella now because the cloudy sky and my local newscast give me reason to expect rain on my way home from work (the future).[95]

Value often includes a timeline. The value of love, for example, is most robust when it has a past, a present, and a future: you remember how you met your loved one, how it felt to fall in love, how it feels now to have settled into a quieter but more secure form of love (if you're lucky), and you look forward to playing with your grandchildren together someday. Intimacy is an important aspect of love, and part of knowing another person intimately is knowing their life story, which unfolds over time. The timeline of love enriches the love because it enriches the present love with the value of its past and the hope for its future (as opposed to the shallower "instalove,"[96] so roundly disparaged by romance novel cynics). If your loved one dies, you value the love you had in the past and hold it in your heart to warm you in the present and the future. If you are lonely and looking for love, you look to the future to realize your lovey dreams. You value knowledge, so you seek it in the present, enjoy knowing what you learned in the past, and look forward to continuing to enrich your mind with new knowledge and perhaps to apply or impart some of that knowledge. Justice is rooted in a timeline as well, as we can see by how we express and engage with that value. We try to repair a past miscarriage of justice, we aim for

---

[95] See Cockburn, *Other Times*, pp. 41–49.

[96] Instalove refers to a deep instant love, more than a mere attraction or "love at first sight" (see Katie Bachelder, "Let's Talk Tropes: Instalove," September 4, 2020, https://kat iebachelder.com/2020/09/04/lets-talk-tropes-instalove/).

a society that will be more just in the future. Of course, we value justice in the present as well, just as we value present knowledge and love, but to focus only on the present would leave us with an impoverished account of value. It would make our lives a lot less meaningful.

Impact looks to the past and projects into the future. Not entirely—you have present impact too, and that is meaningful, but a lot of the meaning of your actions and feelings is based on the impact you had in the past and hope to have in the future. The impact you had on the friend you supported through her divorce suffuses your friendship with greater meaning now and in the future. You sit with your nephew while he gets his chemo infusions, grounded in your past love for him leading up to this point, in order to have an impact on his present situation, but also to have an impact on his future. He will remember that he was not abandoned in his illness, even if it eventually kills him.

Significance borrows a great deal from the past and the future as well. Your great-grandmother's wedding ring is significant to you because of its history; the booties you're knitting for the grandchild your daughter is carrying is significant to you because of its future. Momentary significance matters, but ignoring the past and the future deprives you of the depth and multidimensionality of significance over time; it is a prescription for diminishing the significance in your life. It will leave you with less meaning, not more.

Perhaps most obviously, purpose and point borrow a lot of their meaning from the past and the future. You right a wrong, apologize, provide reparations, put flowers on a grave . . . things that have a purpose or point largely because of the past. You build a bridge, change a law, paint a painting, give your children piano lessons, all aimed at or grounded by a purpose that is mostly in the future. You do these things now so that, in the future, things will be a certain way. Even something like taking aspirin for the headache you have now (the painful present), which might seem like the paradigm of doing something for a present purpose—that banging headache!—really relies on the future for its purpose. You're taking the aspirin to stop being in pain for the next few hours, not just for the present moment.[97] In fact, if you're just living in the present, you have no reason to take the aspirin since it takes time to provide relief. Your action would be pointless if it was solely rooted in the present. Admittedly, some things have mostly a present purpose, e.g., smoking a cigarette (delicious and valuably purposeful in the present but the opposite of purposeful in the future, when you will likely suffer its deleterious health effects) or eating a piece of chocolate. These pleasurable activities have mostly a present purpose, which is usually when you most enjoy them. But they may have added value in your pleasant memory of the pleasure and in your looking forward to future pleasures. Purpose and point are almost always more meaningful when put in the context of the past and/or the future.

There is some room here for human variation in temporal focus. Some people are more involved and invested in history, the future, or more long-term projects and commitments (which look to the past and the future for meaning since they are intended to unfold over time) than others, and there is nothing necessarily problematic about that in terms of living a meaningful life because there is meaning to be found in the past, the present, and the future. So long as one does not overly focus on the past, the present, or the future to the point of neglecting one of them or to the point of significantly temporally distorted attitudes, one need not be persnickety about one's temporal focus distribution. And it is true that the longer-term your meaningful endeavors are, the more vulnerable they are to the ravages and erosions of time (because they have all that time to fall apart). It is prudent to balance out past, future, or long-term oriented quests for meaning with meaning in the present, meaning in the current state of what you are doing and of things as they are.

---

[97] Cockburn makes this point in his discussion of concerns for times other than the present (see Cockburn, *Other Times*, p. 184).

Engaging in temporal distortion by being overly focused on the past or the future is usually a meaning mistake (as argued). There is meaning to be found in all the tenses of time, including the present. To be immersed and truly present in the moment with music, a friend, or even the view from your car as you drive by the ocean can imbue your life with present meaning. That is no small thing, and it is no small failure to fail at this, as many of us do. However, being overly focused on the present to the exclusion of the past and the future is also temporally distorted, also a meaning mistake, and probably a worse one.

Being hyper-focused on the present entails a dearth of long-term efforts, projects, and commitments; a deficiency of pursuits that look to the past and/or the future for meaning. If you don't commit and put forth effort toward long-term relationships, plans, ideals, or goals, you have drastically narrowed the ways in which you can achieve meaning and the kinds of meaning available to you. Present-meaning-focused activity such as watching a ballgame, partying, listening to music, appreciating the ocean, or having casual sex will give you some meaning, but the quality, depth, and duration of that sort of meaning is limited. It is limited in its rewards (which tend to match the efforts) in terms of value, significance, impact, explanation, purpose, and point. A life centered on the present falls short of what a person is capable of and what is valuable and meaningful for beings like us.[98] You might have some fun, but you will have less meaning.

If you were truly living in the present, you'd be living like an amnesiac. Consider that. Without a past and a future, your opportunity for meaning would be severely limited, though you might find a form of carefree happiness born of the lightness of memory-free living. (This is where the Buddhists got it right—living in the present can sometimes reduce our suffering.) The novelist Daan Heerma van Voss experienced an episode of Transient Global

---

[98] See Chapter 2.

Amnesia, which he later described as a terrifying profound loss of self, explanation, and causality, yet also with moments of freedom from the stresses of everyday life.[99] In his fiction about time, the physicist Alan Lightman considers a world without memory of the past, noting that without memory, "a person is a snapshot, a two-dimensional image, a ghost."[100]

Living in the moment will result in less coherence and explanation, less significance and value, dubious impact, and a lot less purpose or point. It's a great way to have a meaningless life or, at least, a much less meaningful life. So we should steer clear of this extremely terrible advice for coping with the time-meaning conundrum. Fortunately, this will not be difficult because it is human nature to learn from the past, prepare for the future, and live in tensed time. It is the way our brains are wired and the way we structure our being in the world.[101] It is not even clear what the present, devoid of the past and the future, is[102] (as we can see, in part, from the term "specious," used by James to define "the specious present," as the time duration wherein one's perceptions are considered to be in the present, but still look to the past and the future for coherence):[103]

[99] See Daan Heerma van Voss, "The Day of Forgetting," *New York Times*, May 28, 2014. See also Lewis Hyde, *A Primer for Forgetting: Getting Past the Past*, Farrar, Straus, and Giroux, 2019, Part II. Clair Bennett, who has anterograde amnesia, describes her carefree mood as an upside of her condition of having a three-minute short-term memory such that if she doesn't write something down, she will forget it ever happened. Her father says he hasn't seen her upset since the onset of her condition (https://www.youtube.com/watch?v=ZeiMhUlipTk).

[100] Alan Lightman, *Einstein's Dreams*, Random House, 1993, p. 63.

[101] The brain is a "temporal organ," whose main role is to anticipate the future. That's why it "generates temporal patterns, remembers the past, and endows us with the ability to project ourselves forward in time" (see Buonomano, *Your Brain Is a Time Machine*, p. 232).

[102] Fischer argues against the claim that the present is all there is by noting that the present is informed by the past and looks to the future (see Fischer, "The Problem of Now," *Aeon*, January 8, 2021).

[103] James created the concept of the specious present to describe the unit of our perception of time (see James, *The Principles of Psychology*, pp. 609–650), but he argued that "the specious present . . . is no knife-edge, but a saddleback, with a certain breadth of its own on which we sit perched, and from which we look in two directions into time" (*The Principles of Psychology*, p. 609).

The present, then, is this unfolding zone where something of the past endures and something of the future is foreshadowed, these two directions mingling with and qualifying one another. Unless past and future were already inside the present in this way, no present experience would even be possible; the present would be a mere durationless point too thin to contain any content.[104]

So forget living in the moment as a meaningful lifestyle. It's not at all realistic for us and will reduce meaning. But perhaps we can be less literal about it, and just stop planning for the future or pining for the past and, instead, soak in the pleasures (and pains, let's not forget) of the moment. If we take the extremely terrible advice less literally by trying to train our focus on the present, appreciate the moment, and not think too much about the future or the past, we might succeed in becoming less anxious, having present meaning, and being able to enjoy life a little more (so long as our present is not too painful on its own).[105] We might suffer less, but we will have less meaning, not more. We will have less meaning because, as we have seen, a good deal of meaning comes from considering the past and projecting into the future for impact, significance, value, explanation, purpose, and point. Suffering the erosions of time is the price we pay for meaning. So before deciding to try to live in the present, think about whether this would be a worthwhile trade. Meaning is a heavy price to pay for reduced suffering, and even reduced suffering is not guaranteed by living in the moment because many moments are replete with suffering.

So where should we put our temporal focus? Everywhere. To have a meaningful life, we must live not in the moment but in the fullness of time—the full catastrophe;[106] in the rich, deep, thick,

---

[104] Alison Stone, *Being Born*, Oxford University Press, 2019, p. 211.

[105] Fischer argues that focusing on the present can help even with pain in the present (see Fischer, "We Are All Here Now," *Blog of the APA*, February 11, 2021).

[106] This phrase originates from the film *Zorba the Greek*, 1964, and is said by the lead character, Zorba, in response to being asked if he is married. He replies: "Am I not a man? And is not a man stupid? I'm a man, so I'm married. Wife, children, house—everything.

robust meaning one can only attain by fully appreciating the past, experiencing the present, and anticipating the future. You will likely then suffer the frustrations, worries, angst, longings, pangs, heartbreaks, and sorrows of lost meaning, eroded meaning, ever-transient meaning, as well, but there is no way to have one without the other because they are both dependent on the same phenomenon: time. Sometimes, it will be more meaningful to focus a bit more on the future, perhaps when your present is not very meaningful or when you're young and working your way, paying your dues, toward a more meaningful life. Other times, it will be more meaningful to focus a bit more on the past for meaning, perhaps when you are older and most of your most meaningful opportunities and experiences are in the past.[107] It may sometimes be more meaningful to focus a bit on the present, perhaps when feeling immersed in an experience or interaction can lend depth to it. Yet, even when it seems as if there is nothing like the present for meaning, e.g., as you stare into the mysterious, promising, beautiful depths of your newborn baby's eyes, a lot of that meaningful moment is taking meaning from the past that brought you to that moment, and the future that you hope follows from it. Over the course of a lifetime, it will almost always be most meaningful to remember the past, experience the present, and look forward to the future (including the future of those who will live on after you die)[108] for meaning. A meaningful life is one lived in the fullness of time, and it cannot escape the time-meaning conundrum.

The full catastrophe" (the screenplay, which originates this phrase, was written by Michael Cacoyannis).

[107] de Beauvoir argues that because the elderly are less productive, increasingly powerless, and see themselves "as leftovers from a former age" (p. 435), they look more to the past because that was the time that belonged to them. (This is one way of putting the need to look to the past more for meaning when one's present and future have less of it.) See de Beauvoir, *The Coming of Age* (1970), Patrick O'Brian, trans., W. W. Norton, 1996.

[108] See Scheffler, *Death and the Afterlife*, pp. 15–113.

Forget Time by Living as a Plant

When we think of ourselves as persisting through time, we may be thinking of ourselves as *one* entity living *through* many periods of time until our days are over and we persist no more. We endure for a while and then stop. Alternatively, we may think of ourselves as persisting over time the way objects persist over ranges of space: the *entire* object does not fill every inch of the space it occupies overall. Instead, *each point* of space contains a *part* of the object. Similarly, we may think of *each temporal part* of ourselves— each time period in which we exist—as *filling* the next temporal portion such that there is no "entire" self that passes through time. Just as a tree or a climbing vine fills space by having each part of itself fill a part of space, a person may have each of her temporal parts fill the next part of time, like asphalt is poured to fill the next portion of the road. The term "endure" has been used to express the *entire* you persisting *through* time, and the term "perdure"[109] refers to thinking of *each temporal part* of you *filling* and persisting through each successive temporal duration. Instead of the whole you enduring through time, each successive temporal part of you perdures in each successive time period.[110] To perdure rather than endure over time, you would persist over time the way an object persists through points of space. (The enduring analog for space would be to think of an object as filling all of the space it takes up as one whole entity taking up the entirety of all the space over which it extends as a whole, a view in tension with modern science.)[111] An object perdures by filling the parts of space with the spatial parts of

---

[109] "Perdure" came into this philosophical use with David Lewis, *On the Plurality of Worlds*, Blackwell, 1986, p. 204. Lewis credits Quine with assuming that persistence works this way (Lewis, *On the Plurality of Worlds*, p. 217, refers to W. V. Quine, "Worlds Away," *Journal of Philosophy* 73 [1976]: 859–863).

[110] See Velleman, "So It Goes," *The Amherst Lecture in Philosophy*, Lecture I, 2006, pp. 1–23.

[111] See Yuri Balashov, "Enduring and Perduring Objects in Minkowski Space-Time," *Philosophical Studies* 99 (2000): 120–166.

itself, and you perdure over time by filling successive parts of time with your successive temporal parts rather than by moving your entire self through parts of time.

Velleman suggests that conceiving of living our lives over time as similar to how plants fill space—as perduring rather than enduring—can take the edge off the time-meaning conundrum because we will no longer think of time as passing, as always slipping away from us, or as running out for us. If one exists in time as a tree exists in space, he argues, "growing extensions to occupy it without moving in relation to it,"[112] one can live more in the moment by noting that "I am *of* the moment, which draws my attention away from time's passage,"[113] and thereby draws my attention away from how time erodes meaning: "I would think of myself as filling time rather than passing through it or having it pass me by."[114] Once you think of each temporal part of yourself as filling each successive moment, you might succeed in living in the moment:

> Suppose that I could learn to experience my successive moments of consciousness—*now* and *now* and *now*—as successive notes in a performance with no enduring listener. . . . The result would be that time would no longer seem to pass.[115]

Say this strategy works. What then? If you have successive notes in a performance with no enduring listener, what happens to the symphony? A "now" note followed by another disconnected "now" note, followed by yet another "now" note, adds up to noise. What would tie the experience together and give it meaning and coherence? What would make it music—a symphony rather than

---

[112] Velleman, "So It Goes," p. 14.

[113] Velleman, "So It Goes," p. 20.

[114] Velleman, "So It Goes," p. 14. Velleman doesn't spell out exactly what is problematic about feeling like time is passing you by. I infer from his essay that the time difficulty he is talking about is part of what I have identified as the time-meaning conundrum.

[115] Velleman, "So It Goes," p. 15.

a cacophony? It seems to me that you either succeed in having a succession of nows, of living in the present, with all the loss of meaning that goes with it (as we noted earlier) or you have memory and anticipation connecting the nows, giving you a sense of time and meaning, providing for a beautiful but temporary symphony, and leaving you stuck in the time-meaning conundrum. There is no way to have the meaning that time provides the possibility for without having the erosion that goes with it. Since that is the case, it is more meaningful (and far more realistic) to accept the conundrum. If you're going to hear the sounds, at least let them coalesce into music for a while.

Go Atelic

As we age, the time-meaning conundrum can weigh more heavily on us because we are closer to our own erosion, have less time left to begin or complete our efforts, and may have already experienced or more clearly foresee the erosion of our commitments, relationships, projects, and accomplishments on the horizon. This may contribute to a sense of futility in working so hard and a pressing awareness of ultimate pointlessness. Perhaps this is part of the midlife crisis, especially one of the Schopenhauer variety, wherein the cycle of striving, achieving, boredom, emptiness, and more frustrated striving can strike one as especially fruitless.[116] We may feel time's passage and irreversibility more acutely.[117]

To cope with this difficulty, Kieran Setiya suggests that we focus more on *atelic* pursuits, which, as you may recall,[118] are valuable in their doing rather than in their completion, and less on

---

[116] See Schopenhauer, "On the Sufferings of the World" (1850), *Studies in Pessimism: Arthur Schopenhauer*, T. Baily Saunders, trans., Cosimo Classics, 2007, pp. 5–10.

[117] See Setiya, "The Midlife Crisis," *Philosopher's Imprint* 14 (2014): 1–18, 3.

[118] See Chapter 1, section "Values Are External to Acts and Efforts."

telic pursuits which are aimed at a final end or completion-based. Walking to the store to buy milk is a *telic* activity; walking down the lane for the pleasure of the walk is an *atelic* activity. Setiya argues that many *atelic* pursuits are not only worthwhile but also crucial to maintaining a sense of meaningful purpose throughout the course of a life, particularly as one approaches midlife and beyond.[119] If the purpose or point of your activity is realized while you are engaging in it, it is less vulnerable to the erosion of time, and less subject to the time-meaning conundrum.

As we have noted, transience does not exclude meaning and many transitory pursuits are meaningful without being long lasting or permanent. If we are dismayed by how time erodes meaning, focusing on pursuits not intended to last in the first place seems like a plausible strategy for avoiding the time-meaning conundrum. But this strategy presents problems of its own. If you only walk for pleasure, how will you get milk? Many end-driven pursuits are pursued because we want, need, or value the ends at which they aim. Someone has to build the bridges, the houses, the sewers. Someone has to write the books, grow the food, sew the clothes, clear the path for your fucking walk. Someone has to discover the medicine, conduct clinical trials to see if the medicine works, prescribe the medicine, etc. Even taking the medicine is end-driven, a decidedly *telic* activity, which most middle-aged people engage in with dogged commitment and purpose. Moreover, pursuing ends of value is meaningful, even if some of that value and meaning erodes over time. Spurning end-driven pursuits in order to avoid the ways in which many of our meaningful pursuits are tinged with the poignancy of their eventual erosion seems like cutting off your nose to spite your face. *Telic* activity is too important to us, both practically and meaningfully, to deliberately discount or avoid it.

[119] See Setiya, "The Midlife Crisis," pp. 12–14; and *Midlife: A Philosophical Guide*, Princeton University Press, 2014, pp. 133–134.

This doesn't mean that there is no wisdom to Setiya's advice. For those overly focused on *telic* pursuits, engaging in some *atelic* pursuits may facilitate a more balanced life, and maybe a happier one. But I don't see how it will make life more meaningful beyond correcting an imbalance if one's life is overly focused on the future. Nor do I think it is a prudent or possible way out of the time-meaning conundrum. I don't even think it's the best advice for maintaining a sense of meaningful purpose as you age, even though there seems an obvious prudence to engaging in *atelic* pursuits when you are less likely to live to see your *telic* pursuits through to their ends, because you need not live to see the ends of your purposes achieved in order to meaningfully pursue them (for many pursuits, that is, though not necessarily for all). Others will live on after you, and hopefully continue the work or reap the benefits of your work. To maintain a sense of meaningful purpose as you age, do purposefully meaningful things, even if their purposes will be realized after you die.[120] Choose *telic* pursuits that you enjoy doing or find fulfilling so that their limited *telic* purpose is tempered in your psyche by the fact that they have some simultaneous *atelic* value. If you hate digging and building things, don't become a construction worker. If you love flowers, becoming a florist or working as a landscaper may lend your *telic* pursuit simultaneous *atelic* value. If you are forced by circumstance into *telic* pursuits you cannot find *atelic* value in, then you might console yourself with the *telic* value, the important purposes and point of your work (even if that point is derivative, e.g., to feed your children, an eminently valuable purpose). Of course, there is a limit to the purposefulness we can achieve—an ultimate limit, as we have noted. That's super sad, but it does not exclude Everyday Meaning and the purposes and points therein. And, sure, time will wear away at our purposes, and to the extent that diminishes their meaning, we will have to

---

[120] See Scheffler, *Death and the Afterlife*, pp. 15–113.

accept that if we want to have that meaning in the first place. There is no way to have the meaning time allows for without the erosion it levies.

Live in the Eternal

Several renowned thinkers allude to the ideal of eternity as a way to relieve some of the meaning difficulties posed by time. Spinoza postulates that when we think of things not in relation to time or place but, instead, as contained in god, from the mind of god, or from the perspective of eternal truths not subject to time indexing or constraints (*sub species aeternitatis*),[121] then the mind is eternal as well.[122] Schopenhauer, citing both Spinoza and Buddhism, proposes being released from the misery of life by denying the will and thus becoming one with nature, and timeless.[123] Tolstoy famously advocates for faith as a way to connect with the everlasting infinite god and thereby overcome the brutal facts of time and meaninglessness.[124] Wittgenstein, having been influenced by Tolstoy,[125] considers connecting with the timelessness of the present as a way of living eternally.[126]

[121] Baruch Spinoza, *Ethics* (1677), Edwin Curley, trans., Penguin Classics, 2005, Part V, Proposition XXIII.

[122] Spinoza, *Ethics*.

[123] Schopenhauer, *The World as Will and Representation*, pp. 180–181, 412.

[124] See Tolstoy, *A Confession*.

[125] See Bill Schardt and David Large, "Wittgenstein, Tolstoy, and the Gospel in Brief," *The Philosopher* 89 (2001), among many others.

[126] "If by eternity is understood not as endless temporal duration but timelessness, then he lives eternally who lives in the present," Ludwig Wittgenstein, *Tractatus Logico-Philosophicus* (1921), D. F. Pears and B. F. McGuinness, trans., Humanities Press, 1969, 6.4311. (For more on the connections between Tolstoy and Wittgenstein on eternity and meaning, see John Churchill, "Wittgenstein's Adaptation of Schopenhauer," *The Southern Journal of Philosophy* 21 [1983]: 489–501; and David Joseph Woodruff, "Tolstoy and Wittgenstein: The Life Outside of Time," *The Southern Journal of Philosophy* 60 [2002]: 421–435.)

Transcending time is not easy to fathom, even if we are thinking purely imaginatively and abstractly. If you look at what eternity enthusiasts discuss, you might come away with the sense of a peculiar sort of present. This makes a kind of sense since if there is no time, there is no change, no direction of causation, no past, and no future. So what's left?[127] A kind of a present, but a peculiar kind because the present is normally understood in the context of the flow of time and in contradistinction to the past and the future. The present might vanish into nothingness as we narrow our focus into the nanosecond of the nanosecond of nowness, with no encroachment of past or future. Conversely, we might imagine everything in the present all at once if we think of the specious present continuously widened, as if the lens that captures the one present moment pans further and further out and thus contains more and more in that same one moment.[128]

What these confusingly mystical visions of the eternal have in common is that time does not pass or even exist. Thus, we eliminate the meaning problems posed by time. But, as we know all too well by now, getting rid of time is not good news for meaning. Setting aside how impossible it is for us to live atemporally, or in eternity, it is the opposite of the way to have more meaning because time is needed for meaning.

There is no solution to the time-meaning conundrum. We will have to accept it. Remembering that time not only wears meaning away but is also needed for meaning can serve as a balm to help us live with the time-meaning conundrum. The conundrum is built into the nature of time and the nature of meaning. You take the good with the bad because that's all that's on offer. Alas, that's how meaning comes.

---

[127] St. Augustine seems to reason this way (see Augustine, *Confessions*, Book XI, chapter XI).

[128] See Olla Solomyak, "Above Time: Rabbi Nachman's *Tzaddik* and Enlightened Temporal Experience," *The Monist* 104 (2021): 410–425.

Not Enough Time

We Have Too Little Time

Thirty isn't old if you're a tree.[129] It's not even old if you're a person, but it still means you're probably more than a third of the way through your life. Human life is too short for our reasonable aims and purposes.[130] Having too little time makes achieving meaning— doing significant, valuable things, having an impact, making sense of things, and pursuing or engaging with ends of value—an exhausting, demoralizing race we are not quite built to win because we don't have the time it takes.

Let's start with the basics: love and work[131]—is that too much to ask? Unfortunately, yes it is. By the time you know what kind of work you might do well and find meaningful, it may be too late to do it, and forget about doing a great job of it. Many kinds of fulfilling work take many years of training, leaving you little time to do the work at all, let alone do it well, and forget about doing it as a second or third career attempt. It takes about fourteen years of post-high-school training to become a doctor, about half that to become a lawyer (but then you have to be a lawyer), and you can spend your whole life trying and failing to be a writer or any sort of artist. Many careers that require peak physical conditioning demand a great deal of grueling training and don't last past your years of peak physical condition, leaving you with the rest of your life to do something you have had little time to train for. Jobs that take less time to learn tend to be less rewarding; less meaningful both experientially and financially. So much for work.

---

[129] The origin of this oft-used phrase appears to be unknown.

[130] In fact, human life is so short as to make our lives absurd (see Weinberg, "Why Life Is Absurd").

[131] The primacy of love and work to a meaningful human life is a view usually attributed to Freud, but it is not found in his written work. See Alan C. Elms, "Apocryphal Freud: Sigmund Freud's Most Famous 'Quotations' and Their Actual Sources," *Annual of Psychoanalysis* 29 (2001): 83–104, 9–18.

Love takes time too, both to find and to get good at, if you're fortunate enough to manage either. By the time you have some clue as to who and how you might love without making everyone miserable, your life might be more than halfway done. By the time you develop the patience, wisdom, and understanding that make for a suitable parent, your children will probably be long grown and off doing a bad job raising children of their own.

It doesn't help that by the time we figure anything out, we are already losing our minds. Age-related cognitive decline begins in our *twenties* (!),[132] just as our prefrontal cortex, which is responsible for judgment, is finally completing its lengthy maturation process.[133] The rate of cognitive decline increases as we age, with a steep increase after age sixty.[134] Our learning curve is at cross purposes with meaning (though we may make up for some lost acuity with age-accrued wisdom).[135]

We also waste a lot of time, which is a waste. But who among us manages to avoid that? Lots of wasted time is externally imposed, e.g., sitting in traffic, waiting in line at the DMV, waiting for the plane to board (I can feel myself getting irritated just listing these examples). But we also waste plenty of time all on our own. Wasting time can seem built into the laws of the universe; the Conservation of Wasted Time: waste less time one way and you just end up wasting more time some other way. (Swear off mindless TV and

[132] Timothy A. Salthouse, "When Does Age-Related Cognitive Decline Begin?," *Neurobiology of Aging* 30 (2009): 507–514; and Denise C. Park, Gary Lautenschlager, Trey Hedden, Natalie S. Davidson, Anderson D. Smith, and Pamela K. Smith, "Models of Visuospatial and Verbal Memory Across the Adult Life Span," *Psychology and Aging* 17 (2002): 299–320.

[133] Mariam Arain, Maliha Haque, Lina Johal, Puja Mathur, Wynand Nel, Afsha Rais, Ranbir Sandhu, and Sushil Sharms, "Maturation of the Adolescent Brain," *Neuropsychiatric Disease and Treatment* 9 (2013): 449–461.

[134] See Salthouse, *Major Issues in Cognitive Aging*, Oxford University Press, 2010, chapter 1, and Salthouse, "Consequences of Age-Related Cognitive Declines," *Annual Review of Psychology* 63 (2012): 201–226; among many others.

[135] See Monika Ardelt, Stephen Pridgen, and Kathryn L. Nutter-Pridgen, "The Relation Between Age and Three-Dimensional Wisdom: Variations by Wisdom Dimensions and Education," *The Journal of Gerontology Series B* 73 (2018): 1339–1349.

you might find yourself playing mindless video games; swear off mindless video games and you might find yourself gazing at all the odd spots in the ceiling or mindlessly scrubbing the bathroom tile grout to pointless whiteness, etc.) The struggle and self-flagellation devoted to the doomed attempt to stop wasting time is likely merely another way to waste your time. However, perhaps by making sure to devote a significant amount of time to meaningful pursuits, we can forgive ourselves for not being efficiency machines. That might be a more productive approach to being meaningfully productive than aiming outright at eliminating time waste. Regardless, the fact remains that we have too little time and, with some spectacular exceptions of immense achievement in a short time (e.g., Mozart who died at thirty-five, Lord Byron who died at thirty-six, or Keats who died at twenty-five), we seem condemned to waste a considerable part of that paltry, sad allotment.[136]

Even worse, because we have so little time to begin with, we have to do everything at once during our short period of pseudo-competent adulthood. We have to work, raise children, rustle up some food and try to render it palatable, make sure we aren't breeding mold or attracting rats, pay the bills, get the teeth cleaned, the gutters cleaned, the snow shoveled, the toilet unclogged. Oh, and spend many hours of every single day sleeping. No wonder we don't do things very well. We don't have the time to become skilled, and we have to do too much at once.[137] Meaning will not come easy.

Nor will it come cheap, considering that getting the most meaning out of our short lives requires paying attention, changing things, and suffering (more on that in a bit). We have not managed

---

[136] See John Anderer, "Stuck on Hold? Average Person Loses 26 Days Each Year to Wasted Time," *Study Finds*, January 22, 2022. Anderer details a widely reported survey conducted by OnePoll in January 2022.

[137] It's common sense and common experience that when we do too much at once, we tend to make more mistakes. For scientific evidence, see Etienne Koechlin and Sylvain Charron, "Divided Representation of Concurrent Goals in the Human Frontal Lobes," *Science* 328 (2010): 360–363; Eyal Ophir, Clifford Nass, and Anthony D. Wagner, "Cognitive Control in Media Multitaskers," *PNAS (Proceedings of the National Academy of Sciences)* 106 (2009): 15583–15587; among many others.

to make human life actually last much longer over the course of human history, though we have managed to give many more people a shot at a full human lifespan,[138] which is a phenomenal accomplishment that puts meaning more within reach for many more people. There are some things we can do to make life feel longer, which might also serve to make life feel more significant, valuable, impactful, and purposeful. That might translate into life actually being more significant, impactful, valuable, and purposeful to the degree to which subjectively slowing time down allows for deeper or more significant engagement with meaningful pursuits, and/or enables us to more accurately perceive and remember the meaning we have attained over the years. To slow down the subjective experience of time over the course of our lives so that, to the extent possible, we can more fully engage in and appreciate the meaning in our lives and not feel like it passes us by in a flash, we will have to pay attention, change, and suffer.

Because our brains are wired to learn from the past, predict the future, and attend to danger, when nothing particularly novel is going on, the brain registers the situation as "same-old, same-old," and does not waste energy paying attention.[139] Thus we hardly notice or remember what becomes usual to us, and the passing

[138] Human life expectancy has increased significantly over time, but the human lifespan has not increased much, if at all. Some argue that will change. See Christine L. Himes, "Elderly Americans Are Living Longer and Healthier Lives," *Population Bulletin* 56 (2002): 4–40; Julia Hynes, "The Oldest-Old in Pre-Industrial Britain: Centenarians before 1800—Fact or Fiction?," Bernard Jeune and James W. Vaupel, Eds., *Exceptional Longevity: From Prehistory to the Present*, Odense Monographs on Population Aging, Volume 2, Odense University Press, 1995; and Michael Pearce and Adrian Raftery, "Probabilistic Forecasting of Maximum Human Lifespan by 2100 Using Bayesian Population Projections," *Demographic Research* 44 (2021): 1271–1294.

[139] See Peter Ulric Tse, James Intriligator, José Rivest, and Patrick Cavanagh, "Attention and the Subjective Expansion of Time," *Perception & Psychophysics* 66 (2004): 1171–1189; Rolf Ulrich, Judith Nitschke, and Thomas Rammsayer, "Perceived Duration of Expected and Unexpected Stimuli," *Psychological Research* 70 (2006): 77–87; and Vani Pariyadath and David M. Eagleman, "Subjective Duration Distortions Mirror Neural Repetition Suppression," *PLOS ONE*, 7, December 12, 2012; among many others.

of familiar time hardly registers.[140] That's one reason why time seems to pass more quickly as we get older. To avoid feeling like your life has passed you by, it pays to pay attention and to give yourself something to pay attention to. Change demands attention, so changing things up might make your life feel longer, though whether that is a meaning enhancer depends on the nature of the change. Moving residences, for example, is a change that usually demands attention. It can delineate one time of life from another, as in, "that happened in our old house," or "that was before we moved to this country," etc., and, in that way, pause the blur of your life into a more attended-to clearer picture. But it's very stressful, reportedly on-par with traumatic events such as the death of a spouse or divorce,[141] and, in itself, not necessarily meaningful. However, happily, most meaningful efforts, engagements, and pursuits involve profoundly more fulfilling and less harrowing change than moving. Learning, creating, loving, growing things, taking care of living things or beautiful things, working toward valuable ends—all of these pursuits involve change, and all involve regular, everyday life and engagements with Everyday Meaning. There is no need to change things in your life merely to slow time down; no need to move to the next town just to mix it up. Change is built into Everyday Meaning, and the more you engage with it, the more meaning you pursue, the less your life will seem to fly by without your noticing, and the more meaningful it will be, both objectively and subjectively. To make the most meaning of your time, you have

---

[140] See Thomas A. Stokes, Allaire K. Welk, Olga A. Zielinska, and Douglas J. Gilla, "The Oddball Effect and Inattention Blindness: How Unexpected Events Influence Our Perceptions of Time," *Proceedings of the Human Factors and Ergonomics Society* 61 (2017): 1753–1757; and Bilger, "The Possibilian"; among many others.

[141] A widely reported 2020 poll conducted by OnePoll for an American moving company found that moving tops the list of stressful life events. See SWNS, "Many Claim This Event Is More Stressful Than Divorce or Having Kids," *New York Post*, September 30, 2020; and Anderer, "Moving Is More Stressful Than Getting Divorce, Becoming a Parent, Survey Finds," *StudyFinds*, October 1, 2020; among many others. For a challenge to this view, see Claudia Hammond, "Is Moving Home One of Life's Most Stressful Events?" *BBC, Future*, July 8, 2014.

to live full out: engage with meaningful pursuits and accept the suffering of time's wounds that is inevitably part of living a full, meaningful life.

Who needs suffering? Anyone who wants meaning. We have already established that the suffering caused by the time-meaning conundrum is inescapable. Time is needed for meaning, and the erosion of time is hard for us to bear; it imposes tragic losses. We can try to make the suffering caused by time's erosions less salient to us by doing our best to ignore the reality of time: its limits (live in the eternal); its passage (live in the present); its erosive and entropic effects (go *atelic*); but we will then lose the opportunities for deeper meaning that engaging in meaningful pursuits over time allows us. So we will have to suffer for meaning. We can take this to comical ends if we are hell-bent on making life seem longer just to seem longer, as Joseph Heller explained in this exchange between two soldiers, Dunbar and Clevinger, in *Catch-22*:

Dunbar loved shooting skeet because he hated every minute of it and time passed so slowly....

"I think you're crazy," was the way Clevinger had responded to Dunbar's discovery...

"I really do. I'll even go so far as to concede that life seems longer if –

" – *is* longer i – "

" – *is* longer? – *Is* longer? All right *is* longer if it's filled with periods of boredom and discomfort, b –" ...

"Do you know how long a year takes when it's going away?" Dunbar repeated to Clevinger. "This long." He snapped his fingers. "A second ago you were stepping into college with your lungs full of fresh air.... A half minute before that you were stepping into high school, and an unhooked brassiere was as close as you ever hoped to get to Paradise. Only a fifth of a second before that you were a small kid with a ten-week summer vacation that lasted a hundred thousand years and still ended too soon.

Zip! They go rocketing by so fast. How the hell else are you ever going to slow time down?" Dunbar was almost angry when he finished.

"Well, maybe it's true," Clevinger conceded unwillingly in a subdued tone. "Maybe a long life does have to be filled with many unpleasant conditions if it's to seem long. But in that event, who wants one?"

"I do," Dunbar told him.

"Why?" Clevinger asked.

"What else is there?"[142]

Dunbar's absurd logic has its kernel of truth. Life is too short, and it will indeed feel longer if you suffer. We can learn from Clevinger's reasoning as well. Suffering is a time win-win because it makes you feel like life is longer while also making you care less if it is shorter because it's so painful. What is silly about Dunbar is his deliberate cultivation of suffering. Although it is true that you cannot have meaning without suffering and suffering helps us notice time rather than have it zip by, there is no need to seek it out because time's erosion hits us all. It will find you. Don't worry, you'll suffer.

We Have No Guaranteed Time

Other than paying attention, engaging in meaningful change, and accepting suffering, extending the human lifespan (how long we are biologically able to live) and life expectancy (how long we can expect to live, given our current conditions) via medical and societal advances are promising ways to mitigate how short our lives are for the meaningful things we want to do with them. Speed limits,

[142] Joseph Heller, *Catch-22*, Dell Publishing, 1955/1961, pp. 39–40.

cancer treatments, statins, peace, and immunizations against potentially lethal diseases, etc., are all good steps toward making it possible for us to have longer and thereby more meaningful lives. Longevity alone will not give us meaning, but a longer life gives us more opportunities for meaningful engagement and more time to become skilled at that. I am not arguing for trying to live forever— as we saw, that is no meaning panacea.[143] But living for, say, a healthy one hundred and fifty or two hundred years would likely increase our chances for achieving and appreciating meaning.

The specter of death—the fragility and precarity of life—is one of the worst aspects of the human condition, and it threatens the meaning in our lives because we cannot count on being able to finish our projects, have a chance to start them, complete our efforts, follow through on our commitments, or enjoy what we have. Every moment is fraught with peril. There is nothing you can count on.[144] We can't really fix this horrible horribility. All we can do is try to alleviate it by making things safer and doing our best to ignore how wretchedly vulnerable it all remains nonetheless.[145]

[143] See Chapter 4.

[144] The specter of death is captured by John Iriving in his classic, *The World According to Garp* (1976): "If Garp could have been granted one vast and naïve wish, it would have been that he could make the world *safe*. For children and for grownups. The world struck Garp as unnecessarily perilous for both" (Modern Library, 1998, p. 397). Irving expanded on this theme in "An Afterword," written in 1998: "Garp lives 'in a safe suburb of a small, safe city,' but neither he nor his children are safe. The Under Toad will get him in the end—as it gets his mother, as it gets his younger son. 'Just be careful!' Garp is always telling his children, as I am still telling mine.... When Garp was published, people who'd lost children wrote to me. 'I lost one too,' they told me. I confessed to them that I hadn't lost any children. I'm just a father with a good imagination. In my imagination, I lose my children every day" (p. 521).

[145] For a poetic take on this, see Edna St. Vincent Millay: "Read history, thus learn how small a space / You many inhabit, nor inhabit long / In crowding Cosmos – in that confined place / Work boldly; build your flimsy barriers strong; / Turn round and round, make warm your nest; among / The other hunting beasts, keep heart and face, – / Not to betray the doomed and splendid race / You are so proud of, to which you belong. / For trouble comes to all of us: the rat / Has courage, in adversity, to fight; / But what a shining animal is man, / Who knows, when pain subsides, that is not that, / For worse than that must follow – yet can write / Music; can laugh; play tennis; even plan" (Edna St. Vincent Millay, *Mine the Harvest*, Harper & Brothers, 1954, Sonnet CLXXI, p. 132).

Conclusion

There is no way out of the time-meaning conundrum. We will have to take our lumps and find our meaning as time allows; in the coming and going of the tides, in the rhythms of life and its attritions. Time will allow us our meaning opportunities and then slowly wear some meaning—but not all—away. To make the most meaning out of your time, try to notice things, change things by engaging with meaning and its pursuit, and be prepared to suffer. Be careful. Wash your hands, do your damnedest to avoid war, and, whatever you do, don't die young. Remember that you're a temporary thing with no ultimate purpose that is not expected to last so it is no meaning tragedy that you don't. Remember that transience does not exclude meaning. And, finally: If you're doomed and privileged to be a pathetic, dazzling, insignificant, magnificent, awesome, ultimately pointless yet intrinsically valuable temporary thing, like a firefly on a summer's eve . . . well, then mourn your losses, take your instant, and flash your light, baby.

Bibliography

Abe, Masao. "The Meaning of Life in Buddhism." In Joseph Runzo, and Nancy M. Martin, Eds., *The Meaning of Life in World Religions*. Oneworld Publications, 2000.

Adams, Robert M. "Comment." In Susan Wolf, Eds., *Meaning in Life and Why It Matters*. Princeton University Press, 2010.

Adorno, Theodor. *Metaphysics: Concepts and Problems*. Trans. Edmund Jephcott. Ed. Rolf Tiedemann. Stanford University Press, 2000.

Agarwal, Ritu, and Elena Karahanna. "Time Flies When You're Having Fun: Cognitive Absorption and Beliefs About Information Technology Usage." *MIS Quarterly* 24 (2000): 665–694.

Alweiss, Lilian. "Heidegger and 'the Concept of Time.'" *History of the Human Sciences* 15 (2002): 117–132.

American Psychiatric Association. *Diagnostic and Statistical Manual of Mental Disorders, Fifth Edition, Text Revision (DSM-5-TR)*. APA, 2022.

American Psychological Association Dictionary of Psychology. 2020. https://diction ary.apa.org/flow.

Anderer, John. "Moving Is More Stressful Than Getting Divorced, Becoming a Parent, Survey Finds." *StudyFinds*, October 1, 2020. https://studyfinds.org/mov ing-more-stressful-than-divorce-having-kids/.

Anderer, John. "Stuck on Hold? Average Person Loses 26 Days Each Year to Wasted Time." *Study Finds*, January 22, 2022. https://studyfinds.org/loses-26-days-was ted-time/.

Anderson, Elizabeth. *Value in Ethics and Economics*. Harvard University Press, 1993.

Aquinas, Thomas. *Summa Theologiae* [1265–1274]. Trans. Benziger Bros. Fathers of the English Dominican Province, 1947.

Arain, Mariam, Maliha Haque, Lina Johal, et al. "Maturation of the Adolescent Brain." *Neuropsychiatric Disease and Treatment* 9 (2013): 449–461.

Ardelt, Monika, Stephen Pridgen, and Kathryn L. Nutter-Pridgen. "The Relation Between Age and Three-Dimensional Wisdom: Variations by Wisdom Dimensions and Education." *The Journal of Gerontology Series B* 73 (2018): 1339–1349.

Aristotle. *Nicomachean Ethics* [c. 350 BC]. Trans. Terence Irwin. Hackett Publishing Company, 1999.

Aristotle. *Physics* [c. 384–322 BC]. Trans. C. D. C. Reeve. Hackett Publishing Company, 2018.

Arpaly, Nomy. "Desire and Meaning in Life." In Iddo Landau, Ed., *The Oxford Handbook of Meaning in Life*. Oxford University Press, 2022.

St. Augustine. *Confessions* [c. 400]. Trans. E. B. Pusey. Project Gutenberg, 2023.

Aurelius, Marcus. *Meditations of Marcus Aurelius* [c. 171–175]. Trans. Meric Casaubon. Philaletheians, 2013.

Bachelder, Katie. "Let's Talk Tropes: Instalove." September 4, 2020. https://katieba chelder.com/2020/09/04/lets-talk-tropes-instalove/.

Baggett, David, and Jerry L. Walls. *Good God: The Theistic Foundations of Morality*. Oxford University Press, 2011.

Baggini, Julian. *What's It All About?: Philosophy and the Meaning of Life*. Oxford University Press, 2007.

Baier, Kurt. "The Meaning of Life." Lecture delivered at Canberra University College, 1957. Reprinted in E. D. Klemke and Steven M. Cahn, Eds., *The Meaning of Life: A Reader*. Oxford University Press, 2008.

Baird, Christopher S. "Does Time Go Faster at the Top of a Building Compared to the Bottom?" *Science Questions with Surprising Answers*, June 4, 2013. https://www.wtamu.edu/~cbaird/sq/2013/06/24/does-time-go-faster-at-the-top-of-a-building-compared-to-the-bottom/#:~:text=Gravitational%20time%20dilat ion%20occurs%20because,the%20slower%20time%20itself%20proceeds.

Balashov, Yuri. "Enduring and Perduring Objects in Minkowski Space-Time." *Philosophical Studies* 99 (2000): 120–166.

Barnes, Julian. *Nothing to Be Frightened Of*. Knopf, 2008.

de Beauvoir, Simone. *All Men Are Mortal* [1946]. Trans. Leonard M. Friedman, Norton, 1992.

de Beauvoir, Simone. *The Coming of Age* [1970]. Trans. Patrick O'Brian, Norton 1996.

Becker, Ernest. *The Denial of Death*. Free Press; Simon & Schuster, 1973.

Benatar, David. *Better Never to Have Been: The Harm of Coming into Existence*. Oxford University Press, 2006.

Benatar, David. *The Human Predicament*. Oxford University Press, 2017.

Bennett, Clair. "The Girl with the Three-Minute Memory." July 11, 2017. https://www.youtube.com/watch?v=ZeiMhUlipTk.

Berk, Kiki, and Joshua Teply. "Sartre and Heidegger on Death and Meaning in Life." *Second International Conference on Philosophy and Meaning in Life*, 2019, Waseda University (unpublished manuscript).

Bilger, Burkhard. "The Possibilian: What a Brush with Death Taught David Eagleman About the Mysteries of Time and the Brain." *The New Yorker*, April 18, 2011, 54–65.

Block, Richard A., Peter A. Hancock, and Dan Zakay. "How Cognitive Load Affects Duration Judgments: A Meta-analytic Review." *Acta Psychologica* 134 (2010): 330–343.

Boltzmann, Ludwig. "The Second Law of Thermodynamics" [1886]. In Brian McGuinness, Ed., *Theoretical Physics and Philosophical Problems*. Reidel Publishing Company, 1975.

Bongino, Dan. *The Gift of Failure*. Liberatio Protocol, 2023.

The Book of Common Prayer [1549]. Anglican Liturgy Press, 2019.

Borges, Jorge Luis. "The Immortal." *Labyrinths*. New Directions Press, 1962.

Bradatan, Costica. *In Praise of Failure: Four Lessons in Humility*. Harvard University Press, 2023.

Bramble, Ben. "Consequentialism About Meaning in Life." *Utilitas* 27 (2015): 445–459.

Brann, Eva. *What, Then, Is Time?* Rowman & Littlefield, 1999.

Brännmark, Johan. "Leading Lives: On Happiness and Narrative Meaning." *Philosophical Papers* 32 (2003): 321–343.

de Bres, Helena. "Narrative and Meaning in Life." *Journal of Moral Philosophy* 15 (2018): 545–571.

Brown, Waka Takahashi. "Introduction to Buddhism." *Stanford Program on International and Cross-Cultural Education*, December 2002. https://spice.fsi. stanford.edu/docs/introduction_to_buddhism.

Buben, Adam. "Heidegger and the Supposed Meaninglessness of Personal Immortality." *Journal of the American Philosophical Association* 2 (2016): 384–399.

The Buddha. *The Middle Length Discourses of the Buddha.* Trans. Bhikkhu Bodhi, and Bhikkhu Nanamoli. Wisdom Publications, 1995.

The Buddha. *The Teaching of Buddha: The Buddhist Bible: A Compendium of Many Scriptures Translated from the Japanese.* The Federation of All Young Buddhist Associations of Japan, 1934.

Bug, Burgundy. "How Animals Perceive Time." *The Burgundy Zine*, April 16, 2020. https://burgundyzine.com/how-animals-perceive-time/.

Buonomano, Dean. *Your Brain Is a Time Machine: The Neuroscience and Physics of Time.* W. W. Norton & Company, 2017.

Burkeman, Oliver. *Four Thousand Weeks: Time Management for Mortals.* Farrar, Straus, and Giroux, 2021.

Cacoyannis, Michael. *Zorba the Greek.* 1964.

Calhoun, Chesire. *Doing Valuable Time: The Present, the Future, and Meaningful Living.* Oxford University Press, 2018.

Campbell, Leah, and Richard Bryant. "How Time Flies: A Study of Novice Skydivers." *Behavior Research and Therapy* 45 (2007): 1389–1392.

Campbell, Stephen A., and Sven Nyholm. "Anti-Meaning and Why It Matters." *Journal of the American Philosophical Association* 1 (2015): 694–711.

Camus, Albert. *The Myth of Sisyphus* [1942]. Trans. Justin O'Brien. Vintage/ Penguin Random House, 2018.

Chappell, Richard Yetter. "Deontic Pluralism and the Right Amount of Good." In Douglas W. Portmore, Ed., *The Oxford Handbook of Consequentialism.* Oxford University Press, 2020.

Churchill, John. "Wittgenstein's Adaptation of Schopenhauer." *The Southern Journal of Philosophy* 21 (1983): 489–501.

Cicero, Marcus Tullius. *De finibus* [45 BC]. Trans. Walter Miller. Harvard University Press, 1913.

Cicero, Marcus Tullius. *The Political Works of Marcus Tullius Cicero: Comprising his Treatise on the Commonwealth; and his Treatise on the Laws* [c. 58–43 BC]. Trans. Francis Foster Barham. Edmund Spettigue, 1841–1842.

Cockburn, David. *Other Times: Philosophical Perspectives on Past, Present, and Future.* Cambridge University Press, 1997.

Collins, Steven. *Nirvana: Concept, Imagery, Narrative.* Cambridge University Press, 2010.

Cooper, David E. "Life and Meaning." *Ratio* 18 (2005): 125–137.

Corish, Denis. "Could Time Be Change?" *Philosophy* 66 (1969): 363–381.

Cottingham, John. "Meaningfulness, Eternity, and Theism." In Joshua Seachris and Stewart Goetz, Eds., *God and Meaning: New Essays*. Bloomsbury, 2016.

Cottingham, John. "Theism and Meaning in Life." *European Journal for Philosophy of Religion* 8 (2016): 47–58.

Cowan, Nelson. "Life Is Pointless—Good Point . . . and How Do You Feel about That?" *Journal of Controversial Ideas* 2 (2022): 13.

Cowan, Tyler. *What Price Fame*. Harvard University Press, 2000.

Dahl, Norman. "Morality and the Meaning of Life: Some First Thoughts." *Canadian Journal of Philosophy* 17 (1987): 1–22.

Danckert, James, and John D. Eastwood. *Out of My Skull: The Psychology of Boredom*. Harvard University Press, 2020.

Davison, Scott. "God and Intrinsic Value." In Klass J. Kraay, Ed., *Does God Matter? Essays on the Axiological Consequences of Theism*. Routledge, 2018.

Descartes, René. *Meditations on First Philosophy* [1641]. Trans. Donald A. Cress. Hackett Publishing Company, 1993.

Dworkin, Ronald. *Justice for Hedgehogs*. Harvard University Press, 2011.

Dyer, Frank Lewis, and Thomas Commerford. *Edison: His Life and Inventions*, Vol. 2. Harper & Brothers, 1919.

Ellis, George. "On the Flow of Time." *FXQi*, 2008. https://arxiv.org/pdf/0812.0240.pdf.

Elms, Alan C. "Apocryphal Freud: Sigmund Freud's Most Famous 'Quotations' and Their Actual Sources." *Annual of Psychoanalysis* 29 (2001): 83–104.

Epstein, Mark. *The Trauma of Everyday Life*. Penguin Books, 2014.

Ertz, Susan. *Anger in the Sky*. Hodder & Stoughton, 1943.

Evers, Daan, and Gerlinde Emma van Smeden. "Meaning in Life: A Defense of the Hybrid View." *Southern Journal of Philosophy* 54 (2016): 355–371.

Farina, Dave. *Professor Dave Explains*. "General Relativity: The Curvature of Spacetime." 2017. https://www.youtube.com/watch?v=R7V3koyL7Mc.

Feinberg, Joel. "Absurd Self-Fulfillment." In Peter Van Inwagen, Ed., *Time and Cause*. Reidel Publishing Company, 1980.

Feynman, Richard. *Physics Lectures*, 42 "Curved Space." CalTech, 2013. https://www.feynmanlectures.caltech.edu/II_42.html#Ch42-SUM.

Fischer, John Martin. *Death, Immortality, and Meaning in Life*. Oxford University Press, 2020.

Fischer, John Martin. "The Problem of Now." *Aeon*, January 8, 2021.

Fischer, John Martin. "We Are All Here Now." *Blog of the APA*, February 11, 2021. https://blog.apaonline.org/2021/02/11/we-are-all-here-now/.

Fischer, John Martin. "Why Immortality Is Not So Bad." *International Journal of Philosophical Studies* 2 (1994): 257–270.

Fletcher, Guy. "The Locative Analysis of *Good For* Formulated and Defended." *Journal of Ethics and Social Philosophy* 6 (2012): 1–27.

Ford, Henry, in collaboration with Samuel Crowther. *My Life and Work*. Garden City Publishing Company, 1922.

Frankfurt, Harry. "The Importance of What We Care About." *Synthese* 53 (1982): 257–272.

"Franz Kafka." 2007–2025. https://www.kafka-online.info/.

Gable, Philip A., and Bryan D. Poole. "Time Flies When You're Having Approach-Motivated Fun: Effects of Motivational Intensity on Time Perception." *Psychological Science* 23 (2012): 879–886.

Georgia State University. Hyperphysics. "Time Dilation." 2024. http://hyperphys ics.phy-astr.gsu.edu/hbase/Relativ/tdil.html.

Glasgow, Joshua. *The Significance Impulse.* Oxford University Press, 2024.

Goetz, Stewart. "Hedonistic Happiness and Life's Meaning." In Joshua Seachris and Stewart Goetz, Eds., *God and Meaning: New Essays.* Bloomsbury, 2016.

Goetz, Stewart. *The Purpose of Life: A Theistic Perspective.* Continuum; Bloomsbury, 2012.

Goff, Philip. *Why: The Purpose of the Universe.* Oxford University Press, 2023.

Goodreads. "Goodreads." 2025. https://www.goodreads.com/quotes/49827-the-meaning-of-life-is-that-it-stops.

Gray, John. *Feline Philosophy: Cats and the Meaning of Life.* Picador/Farrar, Strauss, and Giroux, 2020.

Hägglund, Martin. *This Life: Why Mortality Makes Us Free.* Profile Books, 2019.

Hamilton, John. "When Cute Is Too Much, the Brain Can Get Aggressive." *National Public Radio, Morning Edition*, December 31, 2018. https://www.keranews.org/ 2018-12-31/when-too-cute-is-too-much-the-brain-can-get-aggressive.

Hammond, Claudia. "Is Moving Home One of Life's Most Stressful Events?" *BBC, Future*, July 8, 2014. https://www.bbc.com/future/article/20140709-is-moving-home-that-stressful.

Harman, Gilbert. *The Nature of Morality: An Introduction to Ethics.* Oxford University Press, 1977.

Harris, Harriet A. *God, Goodness, and Philosophy.* Routledge, 2011.

Harris, Matthew A., Caroline E. Brett, Wendy Johnson, and Ian J. Deary. "Personality Stability from Age 14 to Age 77 Years." *American Psychology and Aging* 31 (2016): 862–874.

Harvey, Samantha. *The Shapeless Unease: A Year of Not Sleeping.* Grove Press, 2020.

Healy, Kevin, Luke McNally, Graeme D. Ruxton, et al. "Metabolic Rate and Body Size Are Linked with Perception of Temporal Information." *Animal Behavior* 86 (2013): 685–696.

Hegel, Wilhelm Friedrich. *Encyclopedia of the Philosophical Sciences*, Part II: *Philosophy of Nature* [1830]. Trans. A. V. Miller. Oxford University Press, 1970.

Heidegger, Martin. *Being and Time* [1927]. Trans. John Macquarrie and Edward Robinson. Martino Fine Books, 2019.

Heim, Albert von St. Gallen. "Remarks on Fatal Falls." [1892]. Trans. Russell Noyes, Jr., and Roy Kletti. *Omega: Journal of Death and Dying* 3 (1972): 45–52.

Heisenberg, Werner. "On the Perceptual Content of Quantum Theoretical Kinematics and Mechanics." *Z. Physics* 33 (1925): 879–893.

Heller, Joseph. *Catch-22.* Dell Publishing, [1955] 1961.

Heys, James G., and Daniel A. Dombeck. "Evidence for a Subcircuit in Medial Entorhinal Cortex Representing Elapsed Time During Immobility." *Nature Neuroscience* 21 (2018): 1574–1582.

Hick, John. "The Religious Meaning of Life." In Joseph Runzo and Nancy M. Martin, Eds., *The Meaning of Life in World Religions.* Oneworld Publications, 2000.

Hicks, Robert E., George W. Miller, and Marcel Kinsbourne. "Prospective and Retrospective Judgments of Time as a Function of Amount of Information Processed." *The American Journal of Psychology* 89 (1976): 719–730.

Himes, Christine L. "Elderly Americans Are Living Longer and Healthier Lives." *Population Bulletin* 56 (2002): 4–40.

Holt, Jim. *Why Does the World Exist?* Liveright, 2012.

Huffington, Arianna. May 19, 2019. https://twitter.com/ariannahuff/status/1130 172552352063489?lang=en.

Hume, David. *Dialogues Concerning Natural Religion.* 1779. https://www.gutenb erg.org/ebooks/4583.

Hume, David. *A Treatise of Human Nature.* 1739. https://www.gutenberg.org/ebo oks/4705.

Hurka, Thomas. "Against Good For." *Philosophical Quarterly* 71 (2021): 803–822.

Husserl, Edmund. *Phenomenology of Internal Time Consciousness* [1904–1905]. Trans. James S. Churchill. Indiana University Press, 1964.

Hyde, Lewis. *A Primer for Forgetting: Getting Past the Past.* Farrar, Straus, and Giroux, 2019.

Hynes, Julia. "The Oldest-Old in Pre-Industrial Britain: Centenarians Before 1800—Fact or Fiction?" In Bernard Jeune and James W. Vaupel, Eds., *Exceptional Longevity: From Prehistory to the Present.* Odense Monographs on Population Aging, Vol. 2. Odense University Press, 1995.

Ilievski, Viktor. "Eternity and Time in Plato's Timeus." *Živa Antika* 65 (2015): 5–22.

van Inwagen, Peter. *Metaphysics,* 2nd edition. Westview Press, 2002.

Irving, John. "An Afterword." In *The World According to Garp.* Modern Library, 1998.

Irving, John. *The World According to Garp* [1976]. Modern Library,1998.

James, William. *The Principles of Psychology.* Henry Holt, 1890.

Jewish Virtual Library, "ein-sof," American-Israeli Cooperative Enterprise, 1998–2024.

Johansson, Jens, and Frans Svensson. "Subjectivism and Objectivism About Meaning in Life." In Iddo Landau, Ed., *The Oxford Handbook of Meaning in Life.* Oxford University Press, 2022.

Joiner, Thomas. *Lonely at the Top: The High Cost of Men's Success.* St. Martin's Press, 2011.

Joske, W. D. "Philosophy and the Meaning of Life." *Australasian Journal of Philosophy* 52 (1974): 93–104.

Kagan, Shelly. *Death.* Yale University Press, 2012.

Kahane, Guy. "If There Is a Hole, It Is Not God Shaped." In Klass J. Kraay, Ed., *Does God Matter? Essays on the Axiological Consequences of Theism.* Routledge, 2018.

Kahane, Guy. "Our Cosmic Insignificance." *Nous* 48 (2014): 745–772.

Kamm, Frances. "Rescuing Ivan Ilych: How We Live and How We Die." *Ethics* 113 (2003): 202–233.

Kant, Immanuel. *Critique of Pure Reason* [1781]. Trans. Norman Kemp Smith. St. Martin's Press, 1965.

Kant, Immanuel. *Critique of Practical Reason* [1788]. Trans. Werner S. Pluhar. Hackett Publishing Company, 2002.

Kant, Immanuel. *Groundwork for the Metaphysics of Morals* [1785]. Ed. and Trans. Allen Wood. Yale University Press, 2002.

Kauppinen, Antti. "Meaningfulness and Time." *Philosophy and Phenomenological Research* 84 (2012): 345–377.

Kierkegaard, Søren. *Fear and Trembling* [1843]. Trans. Alastair Hannay. Penguin Classics, 1986.

Koechlin, Etienne, and Sylvain Charron. "Divided Representation of Concurrent Goals in the Human Frontal Lobes." *Science* 328 (2010): 360–363.

Kolodny, Niko. "That I Should Die and Others Live." In Samuel Scheffler, Ed., *Death and the Afterlife*. Oxford University Press, 2013.

Korsgaard, Christine. *Fellow Creatures: Our Obligations to Other Animals*. Oxford University Press, 2018.

Korsgaard, Christine. "On Having a Good." *Philosophy* 89 (2014): 405–429.

Landau, Iddo. *Finding Meaning in an Imperfect World*. Oxford University Press, 2017.

Langworth, Richard M., Ed. *Churchill by Himself: In His Own Words*. Rosetta Books, 2008.

Leak, Ryan. *Chasing Failure: How Falling Short Sets You Up for Success*. Thomas Nelson, 2022.

Lee, Geoffrey. "Temporal Experience and the Temporal Structure of Experience." *Philosopher's Imprint* 14 (2014): 1–22.

Leibniz, Gottfried Wilhelm. *Metaphysical Foundations of Mathematics* [1714]. Trans. Leroy E. Loemker. University of Chicago Press, 1956.

Leibniz, Gottfried Wilhelm. *The Monadology* [1714]. Trans. Robert Latta [1898]. Independently published, 2024.

Levy, Neil. "Downshifting and Meaning in Life." *Ratio* 18 (2005): 176–189.

Lewis, David. *On the Plurality of Worlds*. Blackwell, 1986.

Libretexts/Chemistry. "2nd Law of Thermodynamics." August 15, 2020. https://chem.libretexts.org/Bookshelves/Physical_and_Theoretical_Chemistry_Textbook_Maps/Supplemental_Modules_(Physical_and_Theoretical_Chemistry)/Thermodynamics/The_Four_Laws_of_Thermodynamics/Second_Law_of_Thermodynamics.

Lightman, Alan. *Einstein's Dreams*. Random House, 1993.

Longman, Tremper, III. "'Meaningless, Meaningless, Says Qohelot': Finding the Meaning of Life in the Book of Ecclesiastes." In Joshua Seachris and Stewart Goetz, Eds., *God and Meaning: New Essays*. Bloomsbury, 2016.

Lovejoy, Arthur. *The Great Chain of Being: A Study of the History of an Idea*. Harvard University Press, 1936.

Lucas, Jim. "What Is the Second Law of Thermodynamics?" *Live Science*, February 7, 2022. https://www.livescience.com/50941-second-law-thermodynamics.html.

Mackie, J. L. *Ethics: Inventing Right and Wrong*. Penguin Books, 1977.

Mackie, J. L. *The Miracle of Theism: Arguments for and Against the Existence of God*. Oxford University Press, 1983.

Maitzen, Stephen. "The Problem of Magic." In Klass J. Kraay, Ed., *Does God Matter? Essays on the Axiological Consequences of Theism*. Routledge, 2018.

Markosian, Ned. "Meaning in Life and the Nature of Time." In Iddo Landau, Ed., *The Oxford Handbook of Meaning in Life*. Oxford University Press, 2022.

Matt, Daniel Chanan. *The Essential Kabbalah: The Heart of Jewish Mysticism*. Castle Books, 1997.

Mawson, Timothy. *Monotheism and the Meaning of Life*. Cambridge 2019.

Mawson, Timothy. "Theism and Meaning in Life." In Iddo Landau, Ed., *The Oxford Handbook of Meaning in Life*. Oxford University Press, 2022.

Mawson, Timothy. "What God Could (and Couldn't) Do to Make Life Meaningful." In Joshua Seachris and Stewart Goetz, Eds., *God and Meaning: New Essays*. Bloomsbury, 2016.

May, Rollo. *Man's Search for Himself*. W. W. Norton & Company, 1953.

May, Todd. *Death.* Acumen, 2009; Routledge, 2014.

May, Todd. "Death, Mortality, and Meaning." In Michael Cholbi and Travis Timmerman, Eds., *Exploring the Philosophy of Death and Dying.* Routledge, 2021.

McDowell, John. "Might There Be External Reasons?" In J. E. J. Altham, Ed., *World, Mind, and Ethics.* Cambridge University Press, 1995.

McTaggart, J. M. E. "The Unreality of Time." *Mind* 17 (1908): 457–473.

Metz, Thaddeus. "Comparing the Meaningfulness of Finite and Infinite Lives: Can We Reap What We Sow If We Are Immortal?" *Royal Institute of Philosophy Supplement* 90 (2021): 105–123.

Metz, Thaddeus. *Meaning in Life.* Oxford University Press, 2014.

Metz, Thaddeus. "Recent Work on the Meaning of Life." *Ethics* 112 (2002): 781–814.

Metz, Thaddeus, and Joshua Seachris. *What Makes Life Meaningful? A Debate.* Routledge, 2024.

Milgram, Elijah. *Mill and the Meaning of Life.* Oxford University Press, 2019.

Mill, John Stuart. *On Liberty.* J. W. Parker & Son, 1859.

Mill, John Stuart. *Utilitarianism.* 1861.

Millay, Edna St. Vincent. *Mine the Harvest.* Harper & Brothers, 1954.

Mishna. *Sanhedrin* [c. 100–300]. Trans. Sefaria. Koren-Steinsaltz.

Mitchell-Yellin, Benjamin. "How to Live a Never-Ending Novella (Or, Why Immortality Needn't Undermine Identity)." In Michael Cholbi and Travis Timmerman, Eds., *Exploring the Philosophy of Death and Dying.* Routledge, 2021.

Mousseau, Jessica. "Taoism Beliefs and Holidays." *Diversity Resources,* 2024. https://www.diversityresources.com/taoism-beliefs-and-holidays/.

Mufti, Imam Kamil. "Meaning of Life in Islam." *Arab News,* June 4, 2024. https://www.arabnews.com/islam-perspective/news/868496.

Mulgan, Tim. *Purpose in the Universe: The Moral and Metaphysical Case for Ananthropocentric Purposivism.* Oxford University Press, 2015.

Nagel, Thomas. "The Absurd." *The Journal of Philosophy* 68 (1971): 716–727.

Nagel, Thomas. *The Last Word.* Oxford University Press, 2001.

Nagel, Thomas. *Mortal Questions.* Cambridge University Press, 1979.

Nagel, Thomas. *The Possibility of Altruism.* Princeton University Press, 1970.

Nagel, Thomas. *What Does It All Mean? A Very Short Introduction to Philosophy.* Oxford University Press, 1987.

National Geographic. "Education: Taoism." 1996–2025. https://education.nationalgeographic.org/resource/taoism/.

The New Testament, King James version, 2 Corinthians [c. 53–55].

The New Testament, King James version, Acts [c. 60–90].

The New Testament, King James version, James [c. 44–48].

The New Testament, King James version, Peter [c. 62–64].

The New Testament, King James version, Revelations [c. 95–96].

The New Testament, King James version, Romans [c. 55–58].

Newton, Sir Isaac. *Principia Mathematica* [1686]. Trans. Andrew Motte. Daniel Adee, 1846.

Nichols, Shaun, and Michael Bruno. "Intuitions About Personal Identity: An Empirical Study." *Philosophical Psychology* 23 (2010): 293–312.

Nietzsche, Friedrich. *Beyond Good and Evil* [1886]. Trans. R. J. Hollingdale. Penguin, 2003.

Nozick, Robert. *Philosophical Explanations.* Harvard University Press, 1981.

Nussbaum, Martha. "Human Capabilities, Female Human Beings." In Jonathan Glover and Martha Nussbaum, Eds., *Women, Culture, and Development.* Oxford University Press, 1985.

Nussbaum, Martha. *The Therapy of Desire.* Princeton University Press, 1994.

Obayashi, Hiroshi, Ed. *Death and the Afterlife: Perspectives of World Religions.* Praeger, 1991.

Ólafsson, Björn. "New Research on Animal Communication Shows Their Cultures Are Often Complex and Cumulative." *Sentient Science,* May 1, 2024. https://sentientmedia.org/new-research-animal-communication/.

The Old Testament, Genesis. [c. 1400 BC/disputed], The Contemporary Torah, Trans. Sefaria. Jewish Publication Society.

Ophir, Eyal, Clifford Nass, and Anthony D. Wagner. "Cognitive Control in Media Multitaskers." *PNAS (Proceedings of the National Academy of Sciences)* 106 (2009): 15583–15587.

Owen, John. *Communion with God: Fellowship with the Father, Son, and Holy Spirit.* Christian Classics Ethereal Library, 1657. https://ccel.org/ccel/owen/communion/communion.

Palmer, Jared W. "Meaning in Life and Becoming More Fulfilled." *Journal of Ethics and Social Philosophy* 20 (2021): 1–29.

Pariyadath, Vani, and David M. Eagleman. "Subjective Duration Distortions Mirror Neural Repetition Suppression." *PLOS One* (December 12, 2012). https://journals.plos.org/plosone/article?id=10.1371/journal.pone.0049362.

Park, Denise C., Gary Lautenschlager, Trey Hedden, et al. "Models of Visuospatial and Verbal Memory Across the Adult Life Span." *Psychology and Aging* 17 (2002): 299–320.

Paul, L. A. "Experience and the Arrow." In A. Wilson, Ed., *Chance and Temporal Asymmetry.* Oxford University Press, 2015.

Pearce, Michael, and Adrian Raftery. "Probabilistic Forecasting of Maximum Human Lifespan by 2100 Using Bayesian Population Projections." *Demographic Research* 44 (2021): 1271–1294.

The Physics Classroom. "Newton's Law of Gravitation." 1996–2024. https://www.physicsclassroom.com/class/circles/Lesson-3/Newton-s-Law-of-Universal-Gravitation.

Plato. *Euthyphro* [c. 380 BC], *Plato: Five Dialogues: Euthyphro, Apology, Crito, Meno, Phaedo,* [c. 387–400 BC]. Trans. G. M. A. Grube. Hackett Publishing Company, 2002.

Plato. *Timeus* [360 BC]. Trans. Donald J. Zeyl. Hackett Publishing Company, 2000.

Plucker, A. J., and J. J. Levy. "The Downside of Being Talented." *American Psychologist* 56 (2001): 75–76.

Pope John Paul II. "Catechesis at the General Audience." July 21, 1999. https://www.vatican.va/content/john-paul-ii/en/audiences/1999/documents/hf_jp-ii_aud_21071999.html (Website of The Vatican: https://www.vatican.va/content/vatican/en.html).

Prior, A. N. "Thank Goodness That's Over." *Philosophy* 34 (1959): 12–17.

Prosser, Simon. *Experiencing Time*. Oxford University Press, 2016.

Proust, Marcel. *Remembrance of Things Past*, Vol. 1 [1913]. Trans. C. K. Scott Moncrieff and Terence Kilmartin. Vintage Books; Random House,1981.

Quine, W. V. "Worlds Away." *Journal of Philosophy* 73 (1976): 859–863.

Quinn, Philip L. "How Christianity Secures Life's Meaning." In Joseph Runzo and Nancy M. Martin, Eds., *The Meaning of Life in World Religions*. Oneworld Publications, 2000.

Qur'an. c. 610–632. "The Notable Qur'an." *Qur'an.com*, 1995. https://legacy.quran.com/.

Railton, Peter. "Moral Realism." *The Philosophical Review* 95 (1986): 163–207.

Raphael, Simcha Paull. *Jewish Views of the Afterlife*, 2nd edition. Rowman & Littlefield, 2009.

Ray, Amadine E., George A. Michael, Corina Dondas, et al. "Pain Dilates Time Perception." *Scientific Reports* 7 (2017): 15862.

Robinson, Bryan. "How Arianna Huffington Is Transforming America's Workplace to Benefit You." *Forbes*, January 15, 2020. https://www.forbes.com/sites/bryanr obinson/2020/01/15/how-arianna-huffington-the-meryl-streep-of-busine sswomen-is-transforming-americas-workplace/.

Rooney, David. *About Time: A History of Civilization in Twelve Clocks*. W. W. Norton & Company, 2021.

Rosati, Connie. "The Makropolous Case Revisited: Reflections on Immortality and Agency." In Ben Bradley, Fred Feldman, and Jens Johansson, Eds., *The Oxford Handbook of the Philosophy of Death*. Oxford University Press, 2013.

Roth, Philip. *The Dying Animal*. Vintage Books/Random House, 2001.

Rovelli, Carlo. *The Order of Time*. Riverhead Books, 2018.

Runzo, Joseph. "Meaning and Asian Religions." In Joseph Runzo and Nancy M. Martin, Eds., *The Meaning of Life in World Religions*. Oneworld Publications, 2000.

Runzo, Joseph, and Nancy M. Martin. "Love, Relationships, and Religion." In Joseph Runzo, and Nancy M. Martin, Eds., *The Meaning of Life in World Religions*. Oneworld Publications, 2000.

Ruse, Michael. *On Purpose*. Princeton University Press, 2018.

Russell, Bertrand. "A Free Man's Worship" [1903]. In Robert E. Egner and Lester E. Denonn, Eds., *The Basic Writings of Bertrand Russell 1903–1959*. Simon and Schuster, 1961.

Rustomji, Nerina. *The Garden and the Fire: Heaven and Hell in Islamic Culture*. Columbia University Press, 2009.

Salthouse, Timothy A. "Consequences of Age-Related Cognitive Declines." *Annual Review of Psychology* 63 (2012): 201–226.

Salthouse, Timothy A. *Major Issues in Cognitive Aging*. Oxford University Press, 2010.

Salthouse, Timothy A. "When Does Age-Related Cognitive Decline Begin?" *Neurobiology of Aging* 30 (2009): 507–514.

Sartre, Jean-Paul. *Being and Nothingness* [1943]. Trans. Sarah Richmond. Washington Square Press, 2018.

Sartre, Jean-Paul. *Existentialism Is a Humanism* [1946]. Trans. Carol Macomber. Yale University Press, 2007.

Schardt, Bill, and David Large. "Wittgenstein, Tolstoy, and the Gospel in Brief." *The Philosopher* 89 (2001). https://www.the-philosopher.co.uk/2001/04/wittgenstein-tolstoy-and-the-gospel-in.html.

Scheffler, Samuel. *Death and the Afterlife*. Oxford University Press, 2013.

Schopenhauer, Arthur. "On the Sufferings of the World" [1850]. In *Studies in Pessimism: Arthur Schopenhauer*. Trans. T. Baily Saunders. Cosimo Classics, 2007.

Schopenhauer, Arthur. "On the Vanity of Existence" [1818]. In *Essays and Aphorisms*. Trans. R. J. Hollingdale. Penguin Books, 1970.

Schopenhauer, Arthur. *The World As Will and Representation* [1818], Vol. 2. Trans. E. F. J. Payne. Dover,1958.

Scott-Phillips, Thom, and Christophe Heintz. "Animal Communication in Linguistic and Cognitive Perspective." *Annual Review of Linguistics* 9 (2023): 93–111.

Seachris, Joshua. "The Meaning of Life and Scripture's Redemptive-Historical Narrative: Illuminating Convergences." In Joshua Seachris and Stewart Goetz, Eds., *God and Meaning: New Essays*. Bloomsbury, 2016.

Seinfeld. "The Apartment." Season 2, Episode 10, first aired April 4, 1991, written by Peter Mehlman.

Sen, Amartya. *Commodities and Capabilities*. Oxford University Press, 1985.

Setiya, Kieran. *Midlife: A Philosophical Guide*. Princeton University Press, 2014.

Setiya, Kieran. "The Midlife Crisis." *Philosopher's Imprint* 14 (2014):1–18.

Dr. Seuss. *The Cat in the Hat*. Random House, 1957.

Shakespeare, William. *As You Like It* [c. 1600]. Project Gutenberg, 1998.

Shakespeare, William. *Hamlet* [1603]. Early American Imprints, Series 1, no. 27692, 1794.

Shand, John. "How to Live." *The Journal of the Royal Institute of Philosophy* 82 (2007): 347–348.

Shoemaker, Sydney. "Identity, Properties, and Causality." *Midwest Studies in Philosophy* 4 (1979): 321–342.

Shoemaker, Sydney. "Personal Identity: A Materialist's Account." In Sydney Shoemaker and Richard Swinburne, Eds., *Personal Identity*. Wiley-Blackwell, 1991.

Shoemaker, Sydney. "Time Without Change." *The Journal of Philosophy* 66 (1969): 363–381.

Silk, Joseph. *The Big Bang*, 3rd edition. W. H. Freeman and Co., 2000.

Small, Helen. *The Long Life*. Oxford University Press, 2007.

Smuts, Aaron. "The Good Cause Account of the Meaning of Life." *Southern Journal of Philosophy* 51 (2013): 536–562.

Solomon, Sheldon, Jeff Greenberg, and Tom Pyszczynski. *The Worm at the Core: On the Role of Death in Life*. Random House, 2015.

Solomyak, Olla. "Above Time: Rabbi Nachman's *Tzaddik* and Enlightened Temporal Experience." *The Monist* 104 (2021): 410–425.

Spinoza, Baruch. *Ethics* [1677]. Trans. Edwin Curley. Penguin Classics, 2005.

Stokes, Thomas A., Allaire K. Welk, Olga A. Zielinska, and Douglas J. Gilla. "The Oddball Effect and Inattention Blindness: How Unexpected Events Influence Our Perceptions of Time." *Proceedings of the Human Factors and Ergonomics Society* 61 (2017): 1753–1757.

Stone, Alison. *Being Born*. Oxford University Press, 2019.

Strawson, Galen. *Things That Bother Me: Death, Freedom, the Self, Etc.* New York Review of Books, 2018.

Street, Sharon. "Nothing 'Really' Matters, but That's Not What Matters." In Peter Singer, Ed., *Does Anything Really Matter? Essays on Parfit and Objectivity.* Oxford University Press, 2017.

Sturgeon, Nicholas. "Moral Explanations." In David Copp and David Zimmerman, Eds., *Morality, Reason, and Truth: New Essays on the Foundations of Ethics.* Roman and Allenheld, 1985.

Swift, Jonathan. "The Ladies Dressing Room" [1732]. In Herbert Davis, Ed., *Swift: Poetical Works.* Oxford University Press, 1967.

Swinburne, Richard. "How God Makes Life a Lot More Meaningful." In Joshua Seachris and Stewart Goetz, Eds., *God and Meaning: New Essays.* Bloomsbury, 2016.

SWNS. "Many Claim This Event Is More Stressful Than Divorce or Having Kids." *New York Post*, September 30, 2020. https://nypost.com/2020/09/30/some-peo ple-claim-this-is-more-stressful-than-marriage-divorce-and-even-having-kids/.

Taliaferro, Charles. "The Expansion and Contraction of the Meaning of Life." In Joshua Seachris and Stewart Goetz, Eds., *God and Meaning: New Essays.* Bloomsbury, 2016.

Talmud. *Brachot* [c. 500] The William Davidson Talmud. Trans. Sefaria. Koren-Steinsaltz, 2017. https://www.sefaria.org/Berakhot.17a.12?lang=bi&with= Share&lang2=en.

Talmud, *Sanhedrin* [c. 450–550] The William Davidson Talmud. Trans. Sefaria. Koren-Steinsaltz, 2017. https://www.sefaria.org/Sanhedrin.37a?lang=bi.

Tartaglia, James. *Philosophy in a Meaningless Life*. Bloomsbury, 2016.

Taylor, Richard. *Good and Evil*. Prometheus, 1970.

Taylor, Richard. "Time and Life's Meaning." *The Review of Metaphysics* 40 (1987): 675–686.

Thomson, Judith Jarvis. "The Right and the Good." *Journal of Philosophy* 94 (1997): 273–298.

Thomson, William, and Rudolph Clausius. "The Second Law of Thermodynamics." 2025. https://www.britannica.com/science/second-law-of-thermodynamics.

Thoreau, Henry David. *Walden* [1854]. In *The Writings of Henry David Thoreau,* vol. 2. Houghton Mifflin, 1906.

Tolle, Ekhart. *The Power of Now: A Guide to Spiritual Enlightenment.* New World Library, 2004.

Tolstoy, Leo. *A Confession* [1882]. Trans. Alymer Maude and Louise Maude. Dover Publications, 2005.

Toohey, Peter. *Hold On: The Life, Science, and Art of Waiting.* Oxford University Press, 2020.

Tooley, Michael. "Axiology: Theism Versus Widely Accepted Monotheisms." In Klass J. Kraay, Ed., *Does God Matter? Essays on the Axiological Consequences of Theism.* Routledge 2018.

Trisel, Brooke Alan. "How Human Life Matters in the Universe." *Journal of Philosophy of Life* 9 (2019): 1–15.

Tse, Peter Ulric, James Intriligator, José Rivest, and Patrick Cavanagh. "Attention and the Subjective Expansion of Time." *Perception & Psychophysics* 66 (2004): 1171–1189.

Turp, Michael-John, Brylea Hollinshead, and Stephen Rowe. "Don't Worry, Be Happy: The Gettability of Ultimate Meaning." *Journal of Controversial Ideas* 2 (2022): 9–37.

Ulrich, Rolf, Judith Nitschke, and Thomas Rammsayer. "Perceived Duration of Expected and Unexpected Stimuli." *Psychological Research* 70 (2006): 77–87.

Uzan, Pierre. "The Arrow of Time and Meaning." *Foundations of Science* 12 (2007): 109–137.

Velleman, David. "Dying." *Think* 11 (2012): 29–32.

Velleman, David. "The Self as Narrator." In John Christman and Joel Anderson, Eds., *Autonomy and the Challenges to Liberalism*, 56–73. Cambridge University Press, 2005.

Velleman, David. "So It Goes." *The Amherst Lectures in Philosophy*, Lecture I, 2006, 1–23.

Velleman, David. "Well-Being and Time." *Pacific Philosophical Quarterly* 72 (1991): 48–77.

The Vienna Review. "Franz Kafka: 'The Meaning of Life Is That It Stops.'" 2012. https://www.theviennareview.at/archives/2012/franz-kafka-the-meaning-of-life-is-that-it-stops.

Vohs, Kathleen, and Brandon J. Schmeichel. "Self-Regulation and the Extended Now: Controlling the Self Alters the Subjective Experience of Time." *Journal of Personality and Social Psychology* 85 (2003): 217–230.

Vonnegut, Kurt. *Slaughterhouse-Five* [1969]. Dial Press, 2009.

van Voss, Daan Heerma. "The Day of Forgetting." *New York Times*, May 28, 2014. https://archive.nytimes.com/opinionator.blogs.nytimes.com/2014/05/28/the-day-of-forgetting/.

Wadia, A. R. "The Philosophical Implications of the Doctrine of Karma." *Philosophy East and West* 15 (1965): 145–152.

Ward, Keith. "Religion and the Question of Meaning." In Joseph Runzo and Nancy M. Martin, Eds., *The Meaning of Life in World Religions*. Oneworld Publications, 2000.

Weinberg, Rivka. "Between Sisyphus's Rock and a Warm and Fuzzy Place: Procreative Ethics and the Meaning of Life." In Iddo Landua, Ed., *The Oxford Handbook of Meaning in Life*. Oxford University Press, 2022.

Weinberg, Rivka. "Replies to Critics." *Journal of Controversial Ideas* 2 (2022). https://journalofcontroversialideas.org/article/2/1/186/htm.

Weinberg, Rivka. "Ultimate Meaning: We Don't Have It, We Can't Get It, and We Should Be Very, Very Sad." *Journal of Controversial Ideas* 1 (2021): 4–24.

Weinberg, Rivka. "Why Life Is Absurd: A Consideration of Time, Space, Relativity, Meaning and Absurdity (Yep, All of It)." *New York Times*, January 11, 2015. https://archive.nytimes.com/opinionator.blogs.nytimes.com/2015/01/11/why-life-is-absurd/.

Whiten, Andrew. "The Burgeoning Reach of Animal Culture." *Science* 372 (2021): 6537.

Whitman, Walt. *Leaves of Grass*. Rome Brothers, 1855.

Wielenberg, Erik. *Value and Virtue in a Godless Universe*. Cambridge University Press, 2005.

Wiggins, David. "Truth, Invention, and the Meaning of Life." *Proceedings of the British Academy* 62 (1976): 331–378.

Wikipedia. "Special Relativity." 2025. https://en.wikipedia.org/wiki/Special_relativity.

Wikipedia. "Taoism." subheading "Soteriology and Religious Goals." 2025. https://en.wikipedia.org/wiki/Taoism#cite_ref-FOOTNOTERobinet199750_62-0.

Williams, Bernard. "Internal and External Reasons." In Ross Harrison, Ed., *Rational Action: Studies in Philosophy and Social Science*. Cambridge University Press, 1979.

Williams, Bernard. *Philosophy as a Humanistic Discipline*. Princeton University Press, 2006.

Williams, Bernard. *Problems of the Self*. Cambridge University Press, 1973.

Wittgenstein, Ludwig. *Tractatus Logico-Philosophicus* [1921]. Trans. D. F. Pears, and B F. McGuinness. Humanities Press, 1969.

Wolf, Susan. *Meaning in Life and Why It Matters*. Princeton University Press, 2010.

Woodruff, David Joseph. "Tolstoy and Wittgenstein: The Life Outside of Time." *The Southern Journal of Philosophy* 60 (2002): 421–435.

Yalom, Irvin. *Existential Psychotherapy*. Basic Books, 1980.

Yalom, Irvin. *Staring at the Sun: Overcoming the Terror of Death*. Jossey-Bass/Wiley, 2009.

Zohar [c. 1250–1305]. Trans. David Solomon. Margalya Press, 2024.

Index

For the benefit of digital users, indexed terms that span two pages (e.g., 52–53) may, on occasion, appear on only one of those pages.